Reflections on Oceans and Puddles

One Hundred Reasons to be Enthusiastic, Grateful and Hopeful

Larry Bell

Reflections on Oceans and Puddles: One Hundred Reasons to be Enthusiastic, Grateful and Hopeful

Other books by Larry Bell:

Scared Witless: Prophets and Profits of Climate Doom
Climate of Corruption: Politics and Power behind the Global Warming Hoax
Cosmic Musings: Contemplating Life beyond Self

STAIRWAY PRESS—Apache Junction

Cover Design by Chris Benson
www.BensonCreative.com

STAIRWAY≡PRESS

www.StairwayPress.com
1000 West Apache Trail—Suite 126
Apache Junction, AZ 88120 USA

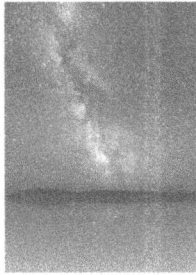

Preface: Beyond Regrets

THIS BOOK DRAWS upon an unpublished series of short essays that I wrote over twenty years ago for my two sons when they were young. It serves to share a variety of personal thoughts and advice to help guide them as a father in pursuing fully constructive and satisfying lives.

One of my own few lingering regrets in life is that I really never got to know my father as well as I have wished. As a child and young adult I looked up to him, but we didn't have what might be characterized as a close and active relationship. I moved away from my home town on the day following high school graduation and returned only for somewhat infrequent and short visits thereafter. Later, as two adults, we developed a strong bond of mutual respect and friendship, but seldom discussed personal experiences, perceptions and ideas. Since his death, I have come to regard that lost opportunity with increasing sadness.

The principal motivation that led me to write the original essays was to share reflections gained through my own life experiences and lessons so that my children will never know similar regrets. Recognizing that these monologues are no substitute for togetherness and two-way conversations, written narrative does afford some special advantages. One is the discipline it imposes to decide what might be most relevant to discuss, to organize thoughts which are sometimes complex and confusing, and to express them as carefully and clearly as possible.

Another priority was to provide a record of possible usefulness when I am no longer around to participate more directly as the father in their lives…or as the future grandfather in their children's. My decision to now update and publish these thoughts lies in hope that my life experiences and insights may have broader value to others of all ages as well. In doing so, I will also hope that some who read this will be prompted to record their own personal reflections to share with loved ones.

While, as the title suggests, these reflections address topics which may generally be regarded as ranging from large to small, this is not intended to imply that *bigger* subjects are most important in any fundamental aspect. Marvels revealed by inner workings of a cell or atom are not necessarily of any less significance than those associated with the outer workings of the Universe. Nor do I hold that a concept of *God* that is contemplated through elaborate philosophical and religious discourses more profound than one recognized in the elegant beauty of a flower or a kind and unselfish act.

Having written literally hundreds of column articles for *Forbes* and *Newsmax* as well as four rather recent books, (the latest, *Beyond Flagpoles and Footsteps*, coauthored with Apollo XI Astronaut Buzz Aldrin), this work is quite different. Rather than offering a stylistically consistent treatment of discussion topics, it is intentionally conceived as scrapbook collection of impressions and ideas that are freely conveyed in any form and spirit which seems most natural for each. This condition mirrors real life as I have known it, with different situations evoking different sentiments and moods.

Some noted elements of this update incorporate parts and passages which appear in my book *Cosmic Musings: Contemplating Life beyond Self* (Stairway Press, 2016). This has been done selectively and sparingly to convey special relevance that I attach to those offerings.

Some of the text also violates an editorial rule that I usually honor by using first-person references quite extensively in some parts. This liberty has been taken for two main reasons.

First, I wish to remind the reader that my observations are personal, and as such, are intended to stimulate mental dialog rather than attempt to persuade others to agree with me.

Second, since they reflect my own mind and experiences, it is only forthright and fair that I accept full blame for them.

Why are 100 topics all neatly divided into subdivisions of five major headings, each containing four subheadings which, in turn, relate to five subjects? One reason is because those are nice tidy numbers which seem to be as good as any others. Another reason is because I am compulsive about order, even though I may deny this tomorrow.

Perhaps in doing so, this will challenge and motivate some of you to surpass this effort by presenting one hundred and one of your own reasons to be enthusiastic and hopeful.

I hope so.

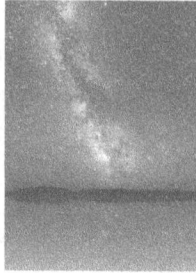

About Larry...

LARRY BELL IS AN endowed professor at the University of Houston where he founded the Sasakawa International Center for Space Architecture (SICSA) and the graduate program in space architecture. He is the author of *Climate of Corruption: Politics and Power behind the Global Warming Hoax*, *Scared Witless: Prophets and Profits of Climate Doom*, *Cosmic Musings: Contemplating Life Beyond Self*, and more than 500 online on a wide variety of topics as a *Forbes* and *Newsmax* contributor, some of which have also been featured in their hard-copy magazine publications.

Larry's professional aerospace work and interviews have appeared in numerous TV and print media productions which include the History Channel, Discovery Channel-Canada, NASA Select and leading national and international newspapers, popular magazines and professional journals. His many awards include certificates of appreciation from NASA Headquarters and two highest honors for his contributions to international space development awarded by Russia's leading aerospace society.

Dedication

To my sons Aaron and Ian, my best reasons for being enthusiastic and hopeful.

Table of Contents

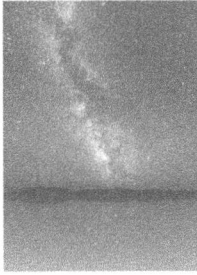

Embracing Life's Potentials— Your Real and Eternal Nature

A universe of possibilities has been extended to you. Understand them through gifts of awareness and intellect that God has provided. Life is the realization of heaven. Recognize that you are already there, value its treasures, and use them wisely.

Being a Born Winner

IF YOU TEND to be somewhat complacent about life, then you might consider that you were born against incredible odds. Let's just take just a few moments to think about some statistics.

Your mother came into this world with about one million ova and only about 400 of these could be expected to ever mature into eggs. Of those eggs, most waited decades for an opportunity to experience fertile fulfillment, only to be swept away in *red floods*.

Your father's contenders for self-actualization had chances which were far worse. Assuming that your dad was typical, he produced about 200 million sperm cells every day, until numbers began to taper off at around the age of 45. If you were conceived when he was about 30 years old, we might imagine that more than 1.7 million of those unfortunate little tadpoles fell by the wayside before they could enter anyone's gene pool.

When your opportunity as a sperm came along you faced awesome competition. There you were, one among 3 billion so would-be half brothers and sisters, waiting to participate in the win-or-die *Ovarian Marathon*. Timing for all contestants was critical. What if the egg wasn't waiting? What if your father was away on a business trip...or maybe fishing? What if your mother had a headache?

Of course the results are now history. The race wasn't cancelled after all. Released with a mighty surge, you swam with heroic determination and were the first to reach the finish line, which hardened around you as a barrier to all others. You then shared your genetic treasures to begin a whole new life.

As remarkable as that victory was, it reveals only one episode among countless events of unbelievably good fortune that supported your success.

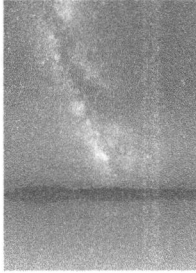

The Great Ovarian Marathon

WHAT IF YOUR father and mother had never met? Recognizing that the United States population alone is more than 300 million people, they both had many other mates to choose from. Not only did their lives have to intersect at the same place and time, all conditions in their personal circumstances had to be compatible for that relationship to occur. Similar coincidences (or divinely orchestrated plans) had also to occur in the lives of your grandparents. Your birth, in fact, depended upon a unique and unbroken chain of events involving ancestors over a period of many millions, perhaps billions, of years.

These improbable events leading up to you becoming you may have limited meaning to those whose lives are not directly connected to your own. Beyond your spouse, your children and their children, ad-infinitum, most everyone else's life would probably go on in pretty much the same fashion if you hadn't arrived on the scene.

On the other hand, being born is the opportunity of your lifetime! It is an opportunity to let people appreciate what they would be missing without you. It is an opportunity to make good use of that genetic potential that you have won to experience life as fully as possible.

It is easy to forget that you are a winner when you are surrounded by people who take both their own lives—and yours, for granted. You might remind yourself that being only one person in a general population of billions does not make you, or them, less special. This is easiest to remember when you put yourself in the company of people who recognize that they are winners too. In accepting their own importance, they are likely to respect your value as well.

People who view themselves as losers have little to celebrate—and even less to share. They miss the fact that good relationships are win-win situations that begin with self.

Being Part of Something Really Big

MY EARLIEST MEMORY of self-revelation is when I was a child, probably about seven or eight years old, sitting quietly alone outside my house. The long Wisconsin winter had retreated, and grass had begun to appear amidst remaining patches of melting snow. The Sun was warm on my back, and the musky fragrance of wet earth was strong.

It suddenly dawned on me that I was directly connected to that magical world of my backyard. The materials that comprised the earth, grass, trees and even stones were the same stuff that I was made of. I wasn't just a spectator experiencing Nature. I was actually part of Nature, and somehow always would be, long after the trees were gone.

That awareness was very exciting to me then, and it continues to be now.

We are truly creatures of the natural Universe. The elements constituting every part of us and our beautiful blue planet have passed through other fiery stars, now gone, long before our mother Sun was born. Each of those elements, in turn, are comprised of atoms which are like tiny solar systems containing tremendous energy, each with a proton and neutron nucleus orbited by electrons that together direct the complex chemistry of life.

The Universe that spawned us is unimaginably vast and marvelous. Consider, if you will, that there are estimated to be more than 100 billion stars in our Milky Way Galaxy, most of which are larger than our *yellow dwarf* Sun.

This spiral wheel is about 100,000 light years in diameter. If we were somehow able to travel to a different star in our galaxy every hour of the day and night, it would take about six million years—much longer than humans have existed—to visit only about half of them.

Now, also consider that there are estimated to be more than 100 billion galaxies in our known Universe. The Universe has existed for about 18 billion years, and is constantly changing, like a garden where new plants bud as others wither on a cosmic time schedule.

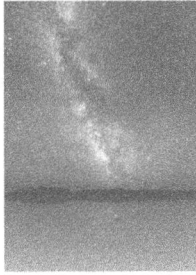

Life in a Cosmic Suburb

FROM OUR VANTAGE point on a spiral arm of our galaxy, it is difficult to grasp the reality that those distant stars, and the planets and ghostly clouds which surround them, are part of our personal world.

Humankind has a history of resisting observations which have placed us outside the center of the Universe. In reality, the Universe probably has no center, except for maybe a theoretical point where a *Big Bang* first set everything in motion.

However, there is nothing to be upset about. The real estate we occupy has a wonderful location with a spectacular view.

Another difficulty that many people seem to have with a cosmic perspective is that they feel it diminishes their significance. While it is true that our home planet and human bodies are small relative to the Universe, we should remember that everything is small relative to the Universe.

Does size really have anything at all to do with importance?

Are boulders more important than hamsters?

Is Saturn more important than the Earth?

It seems to me that either everything is important, or nothing is. And that is purely a matter of personal decision.

The idea of a changing Universe can also be discomforting

for some. If planets, stars and maybe even galaxies are constantly being born and changing, ultimately only to die, then where does our human destiny lie? On what permanent ground can we build our spiritual refuge?

One answer is that change is the essential nature of life and spirit. Everything that we have the good judgment to enjoy is dynamic, revealing new dimensions of possibility with each transformation and discovery.

The exciting news, if we can accept it, is that Nature is eternal and as manifestations of that wondrous force, then we are too.

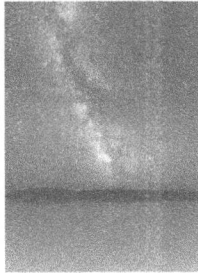

Contemplating God

WHEN ASKED BY a rabbi if he believed in God, Albert Einstein responded:

> I believe in Spinoza's God who reveals himself in the orderly harmony of what exists, not in a God who concerns himself with the fares and actions of human beings.

Dutch philosopher, Baruch Spinoza (1632-1677), perceived God and Nature as one. He wrote:

> Whether we say therefore...that all things happen according to the laws of nature, or are ordered by the decree and direction of God, we say the same thing.

Spinoza regarded the intellectual love of reality to be the highest end for humans. Since God could not possibly stand apart from Nature, it followed that the Universe is divine: eternal, infinite and the cause of its own existence...hence worthy of our awe and reverence.

As with many others, I too have been asked if I believe in

God. The easiest response would be to say *yes* and simply let it go at that. Not wanting to offend those whose concepts of a *Supreme Deity* are based upon very specific definitions, that answer would be partially true. We would probably agree that God is love, God is good, and God is Nature.

We could likely also agree that God created Man in his own image. By this, I would personally mean that if God is Nature, then Man, like all things, is a representative incarnation of Nature. By accepting the fact that God is love and God is good, then it follows that Nature is also love and good. I wouldn't want it any other way!

My doubts arise when people apply the God-Man relationship very literally. Homo-centric views of creation which envision a world made exclusively for people are not appealing to me. If God truly had that in mind, it seems unlikely that he would have bothered to make the Universe so large and marvelous. It would be like building a whole nation of cities to accommodate residents of a single planetary household.

If God created the Earth only for human purposes, then I am also perplexed by the fact that He invested so much creativity making such an incredible variety of other creatures, large and small, which seem to have little or no connection to us. These include countless types of dinosaurs that roamed our planet for millions of years...long before the first Homo sapiens child clutched an acorn toy. They also include microorganisms, insects, reptiles, birds and animals of endless descriptions that would probably be more content if we had never arrived on the scene.

A Natural Perspective

IF PEOPLE TRULY recognize themselves to be reflections of God's love and goodness, it is difficult to comprehend cruel travesties that have been justified in His name. How many senseless wars and acts of fiendish brutality have been perpetrated under the guise of divine guidance?

History has taught us that when neighbors claim to have God on their side, it's probably a good idea to get the children inside the house and lock livestock in the barn. And when they tell us that God has given them a message which we must believe or suffer eternal damnation, we might question the authenticity of their direct spiritual channels. They are either quite misguided in failing to recognize God's loving Nature, or are attempting to manipulate us through fear...maybe even both. In any event, it isn't nice.

It is much easier from my own point of view to be clear about what God isn't, than to explicitly define what God is or wants. Generally speaking, however, a loving God would expect us to be compassionate, respecting the importance of life. A wise God would expect us to use our naturally gifted curiosity, and to value intelligence over fixed dictates of faith.

During my childhood and youth, people around me seldom,

if ever, talked about religion. Most of us attended one church or another. Almost everyone I knew was Christian, and being cursed with more than an ordinary share of curiosity, I found it impossible to escape questions concerning many aspects of theology.

Since I was unaware that anyone else, except for maybe some evil people, had similar uncertainties, I arranged a meeting to discuss this dilemma with my minister. In particular, I wondered why a God who was so great as to be able to create a Universe would really care if humans worshiped Him. And why would a loving God create a hell for those who didn't? Instead, wouldn't the God who blessed us with natural curiosity and intelligence intend us to guiltlessly use these gifts?

My minister, a kind and thoughtful man, admitted that he also had similar questions—but asked me to please not mention this to anyone else.

I regretted having lived with that private guilt for so long after he suggested that I consider a life in the ministry.

Celebrating Religious Principles

WHILE THERE IS no single religious orthodoxy I subscribe to, I respect fundamental societal principles attached to many.

It may be useful to remember that the most ancient Jewish scriptures are steeped in democratic ideals and incorporate concern for moral aid and tolerance among all people. These concepts have had powerful influences upon other religions, including Christianity and Islam.

Mohammad and Buddha preached that there is no separation between the physical and spiritual world. The *Quran* instructs us to observe God's creation, work to understand those natural systems, and constantly endeavor to seek knowledge.

Secular lessons have also advanced our understanding of natural and moral principles. Aristotle, Plato and Socrates are credited with establishing the foundations of modern philosophy and ethical reasoning in ancient Greece that later influenced the thinking of Saint Thomas Aquinas in the 13th century, and Charles Darwin in the 20th.

It's also only reasonable to mention that religious orthodoxies have not always embraced scientific discoveries.

Galileo defended his belief that our Earth revolves around the Sun in the face of 17th century charges of heresy by leaders of the Roman Catholic Church. That concept displaced Man from the center of the Universe.

Johannes Kepler, a devout Protestant, was similarly ostracized by members of his church after he calculated the motion of the Earth and other planets around a stationary Sun; a heretical notion at the time which now makes space travel (and my work as a space architect) possible.

Baruch Spinoza's controversial concepts which challenged tenants of the Hebrew Bible and nature of the Divine led to his expulsion by religious authorities from Jewish society by age 23, and the inclusion of his writings on the Catholic Church's *Index of Forbidden Books*. Nevertheless his ideas came to have profound influences on Albert Einstein and other prominent contemporary thinkers.

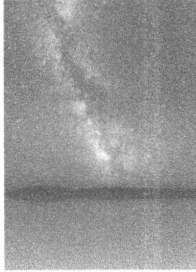

An Intelligent Thing to Do

WHEN CONTENDING THAT *Deus sive Natura* (God is Nature), Spinoza envisioned a God that does not rule over the Universe through Province in which a Deity can make changes. Rather, he envisions a God which itself is a deterministic system by which:

> ...*things could not have been produced by God in any other way or in any other order than is the case.*

In Advayavada Buddhism, Spinozism is viewed as a philosophy in which all reality is held to consist of only one substance, typically again referred to as God or Nature. Both material things and thought (e.g. body and mind) are matching attributes mirroring each other. Here, what Man and other sentient creatures share with the rest of existence is not thought of any kind, but rather their *conatus* of which sentient cognition is but one element.

From a human perspective, this conatus is experienced in the form of *progress*, which is similar to *Te*, the *virtuous power* of the *Tao* in Taoism.

My very cursory exploration of religious doctrines has led me along different paths, always producing more questions than answers. No single religion yet encountered has fully satisfied my curiosity about God's true Nature or Nature's true God. Admittedly, since there are more than a thousand separate religious groups registered in America alone, I have doubtless overlooked a few possibilities.

I once naively expected that quests for such lofty answers motivated most scientists...physicists in particular. Any such assumption was dashed when as a university student taking a freshman-level physics class I became excited about some now-forgotten metaphysical implications of Michael Faraday's 19th century ballistic cannon experiments. Accordingly, I arranged an appointment with a Nobel laureate physicist in the department.

He listened attentively with only slight traces of amusement as I discussed the great significance of my observation at length. When I had finished, he gently told me that he really never thought about such momentous matters. He then explained that he just enjoyed solving puzzles.

I later concluded that he had shared an important lesson with me after all. Maybe the perplexities associated with Nature and God should be regarded as special challenges that make life more interesting and fun. Perhaps that is exactly what the Creator has in mind.

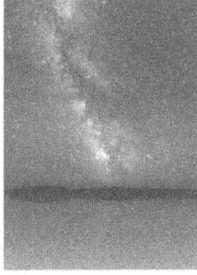

Your Unique and Timeless Self

HAVE YOU LIVED before, and will you live again? Most certainly, yes.

And when you are reincarnated, will you recognize yourself? Without a doubt. You just won't know who you are.

So just who are you? What personal qualities that make you uniquely yourself would you wish to bring into another mortal life? In considering your answer, try to look at yourself from inside your mind's eye.

Your self-awareness becomes active long before you ever leave the womb. As a fetus, you begin to experience yourself through consciousness of your mother's sudden movements and heartbeats that are amplified by the protective fluid that surrounds you.

Following birth you are flooded with new experiences. That comforting heartbeat is replaced by louder, more varied sounds, including your own voice. Blurry objects appear in your new field of vision, including your own hands and feet. You encounter other sensations for the first time, including tastes, smells and temperature changes. Some are uncomfortable, such as hunger and stomach gas. And you learn how to communicate your displeasure with your lungs, facial muscles, and tears to summon help.

It takes you a while to differentiate yourself from other objects and events around you to know where you end and everything else begins. But you soon discover that those things which are uniquely part of you can be directly controlled or experienced through your senses.

For example, you can move and make sounds on your own command. You can open your eyes to see, or close them to shut out light. You can feel things that touch you, but not things that touch someone else.

You begin to recognize yourself as *you*, distinctly separate from *them*. As the center of your own world, you feel very special; so special in fact that everyone and everything outside yourself seems to have been put there for your special benefit. Later you learn that this assumption is not entirely accurate. As you grow older, it becomes apparent to you that others also take their own existence and priorities seriously, and that to avoid problems, it's often a good idea to accommodate them.

Discoveries from Inside the Mind

THROUGH INTERACTIONS WITH the outside world you become more self-critical and introspective; and the in the process of growing, you accumulate information, acquire talents, develop relationships and record memories. You compare yourself against prevailing models and expectations and try your best to conform. Building upon these experiences, you continually mold and reshape your self-concept and visible identity...or *personality*, if you prefer to call it that.

Will your self-concept or personality be reincarnated into future lives? I doubt it.

You didn't come into this life with any old photo albums and scrap books, and that's probably a good thing. They would have just cluttered up your current life with old preconceptions, and probably would have limited your openness to new opportunities. Losing the past through rebirth or amnesia isn't the worst thing that can happen to you. It isn't like being dead. Being alive is what really matters.

Free your imagination now, and picture your child's mind and sensory connections in a closed box that is floating in perpetual time. Suddenly, a door in the box opens, and you see figures outside. All, except for one, are eating candy bars (which you can't comprehend), and you watch them unimpressed.

Then the other begins to eat, and you immediately experience the pleasant taste of sweet chocolate. Now you become interested in that figure, and through continuing involvement with it, additional experiences are revealed to you. You also learn that you can make that particular individual do marvelous things. Its physical form is unimportant, and you recognize and accept it as being yourself.

Now imagine that this present time when the door is open is a random sample of eternal time. What if the door opened to another time a few eons ago, or a few eons in the future? Wouldn't you expect to experience contact with a figure who is attached to your awareness then as well?

I do. I just can't conceive that experiencing a great present occurs only once.

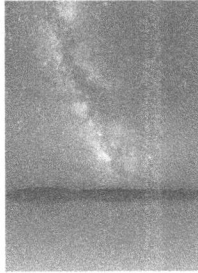

Filling Your Mortal and Spiritual Space

The opportunities you realize through life depend upon your vision and judgment. Select a reality that fits your dreams.

Sharing Nature's Soul

FROM THE TIME of our ancient ancestors, Man has looked to the heavens for guidance and inspiration. The Sun, source of all life, governed seasons for hunting and signaled time to prepare shelter, clothing and food for winter's sovereignty. The Moon was a calendar for planting and harvesting as settlers asserted dominion over wilderness. The stars were maps and compasses that led explorers on voyages which extended territorial domains.

In these ways, and many more, the sky expressed the majesty and will of great powers that controlled human enterprises and destiny. It presented mysteries that raised human consciousness and stimulated self-reflection. It was the true home of the human soul where mortal achievements would ultimately find reward.

Advanced telescopes and space travel have brought some aspects of the heavens into closer view, yet mysteries of the human soul remain to be as elusive as ever. We now realize that the Moon, planets, Sun and stars are far more distant than our forefathers and foremothers perceived with unaided eyes. If this is where souls reside, then the space available for them to occupy is enormous, extending throughout the Universe. Perhaps this offers the promise of interplanetary and interstellar space travel to us all!

Before we get too excited about roaming around heaven all day, it might be interesting to consider different possibilities regarding a soul's essential nature...and Nature's essential soul. It seems that most of us attach some importance to the idea of having a soul, because without one, life would just lead to a dead end.

Is the principal reason to live a good life to enable our souls to enjoy peace and contentment in an endless hereafter? If we believe the wrong things or behave badly, will our souls suffer eternal punishment?

I have some difficulty with these concepts because I favor the idea that mortal life is a blessing, not a test for something later. The important joys and sorrows we experience are influenced by ways that we respond to that reality.

I can't comprehend any way to reward a soul, or to punish one either, for that matter. If souls are part of the Universe, an essential aspect of Nature, they already have everything they could possibly need for satisfaction. And since I doubt that they have any corporeal nerve endings, eternal fires of damnation probably wouldn't hurt much.

Their biggest problem might be boredom, but then there wouldn't be any clocks to watch in a cosmic time frame.

Larry Bell

Helium Balloons and Jellyfish

AS A CHILD, I imagined my soul to be like an invisible helium balloon in my head. The balloon contained my personality and my experiences, including memories of wonderful times and friendships. When I died, I expected that my balloon would be released to float up into the clouds, maybe ever higher. It might be carried around by winds so that I could look down upon everything below.

I expected that there would be other balloons up there too, including all of the people I loved and missed who had died. If the balloons were transparent or ethereal, I would be able to see images of their former bodies inside, appearing as they looked when I knew them so that they could be recognized.

Unfortunately, without physical bodies we wouldn't be able to hug each other. That would be a sad and lonely feeling.

The foregoing visualization characterizes my interpretation of explanations presented by the church that I attended. According to that doctrine, each of us has an individual soul which imbues us with faculties of thought and emotion. This immaterial entity co-exists with our mortal body, and personifies our unique spiritual identity. Upon physical death, our soul continues to be separate and distinct from all others, with capacities to experience happiness or misery, as dictated by divine evaluation of our Earthly performance.

When I grew older, another possibility occurred to me. Maybe there is only one soul, the soul of God or the Universe. That soul would be like a big ocean containing all life. Like jellyfish, all creatures would be formed out of the water, as well as contain the precious liquid within.

If those creatures were rational and self-reflective, they would enjoy their own individuality, potentially believing that they *owned* the seawater inside them. In reality, they would only be borrowing nutrients from that cosmic fluid which would soon be returned for others to use.

That idea influenced me to realize that there is something more important to me than mortal survival. It is the promise that I am a spiritual extension of all life, and will continue to be so long as Nature exists.

Your Unlimited Inner Child

WHEN MY FATHER and mother passed away, I mourned not only for them, but also for parts of myself that seemed to have died with them. Their love had nurtured me. Now that they were gone, I felt diminished.

The importance that they attached to me influenced me to value myself more. Never again would I be able to engage in personal discussions with dad, or enjoy reflections of my achievements in his eyes. And never again would I hear mother express concerns that maybe I was working too hard, sleeping too little, or not watching my diet.

Also lost were the common recollections of countless times we had shared as a family, and expectations of new experiences that we would enjoy together in the future. The world without them in it was unimaginable.

The pain that I felt through these losses was centered in the child who lives deep inside me. Like all children, this part of me is quite selfish, concerned mostly with the way changes affect self. That child was now an orphan. Giving fuller credit that the child deserves, however, he is also the source of my capacity to love, to care about things that really matter, and to grow beyond the past. That child would now have to draw upon these resources and become his own parent.

As husband, father, and friend to others, my inner child goes for long periods of time with little conscious attention from me. Maybe his voice is lost in the clamor of people and activities that fill my life. Perhaps my concerns for his welfare have been diverted to other people around me who I care about, and who express their needs more insistently. And possibly that child has been forced to grow up somewhat in order to help me shoulder responsibilities that I have cheerfully and gratefully accepted.

I have observed that people who focus much of their attention on helping others, gain much more than they give in the process. They include parents, teachers, religious counselors and doctors to name only a few. On the other hand, people who live primarily for themselves may be inclined to pamper their inner infant excessively, resulting in a spoiled child that dominates their outlooks and actions.

Successful self-parenting seems to embody the same general principles that apply to all effective parenting. It balances appreciation of the innocent beauty of the infant with necessary discipline and guidance that encourage the child to accept appropriate responsibilities. To accomplish this, we must set good examples for our child-selves to follow.

Larry Bell

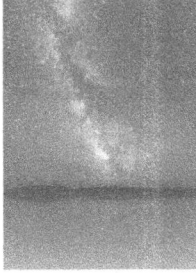

The Need for Self-Parenting

The Child in Me

Fragmented snapshots in my mind
obscured by faded memory,
reflections of my former self,
the innocent I used to be.

This tender soul lives on, I know
and shares my life continuously,
He is the source of all I am,
My true and good identity.

Open-minded, quick to learn,
full of fun and fantasy...
potentials unconstrained by doubts
that limit creativity.

He paints my dreams, directs my cares,
and drives my curiosity.
His trusting nature gives me hopes
That guide my goals and destiny.

My inner child is sensitive,
quite lacking in maturity,
with patience short and temper strong
I must instruct him constantly.

Yet through his faults his beauty shines,
I owe him a priority,
to be a father and a friend,
to know and love the child in me.

Seeing Your Outer Nature

THE CONDITIONS AND opportunities we recognize in life depend much more upon vision than location. Wherever we are, what we see is influenced by the viewing angles we choose and the ways we focus our minds. How we interpret what we see also reflects ways that we view ourselves in those settings.

Visualize yourself the way a sighted microbe would see you from inside your body—as an endless Universe of incomprehensible size. From an ant's point of view you might appear as a big foot that threatened to trample his or her life and handiwork. A small child looking up at you would see you as being bigger than you see yourself in the mirror, partly because they are shorter, and also because the spacing of their eyes makes *everything* appear larger.

All of these creatures might exist in proximity to one another, yet live in separate worlds quite unaware of the others'. Similar circumstances can apply to people who live together, yet view conditions from different perspectives.

Many of us tend to be either somewhat near-sighted or far-sighted by nature. Some direct their attention to immediate realities they see close at hand, focusing upon fascinating or troubling details. Others direct their consciousness farther away to survey distant dreams and landscapes. And there are those among us who, like seagulls, readily and regularly re-focus their vision to do both.

Yet even if we have 20:20 mental acuity, the images we see are often incomplete. By looking out at the world from inside our heads, important figures are missing from the picture. We don't see ourselves. As a result, we may forget our presence in the scene that surrounds us, and experience much of life as spectators rather than as active participants.

When you observe photographs and videos of yourself, are you often surprised by the way you look? Do you usually accept that image as the person you imagine yourself to be? And when listening to a recording of your own voice, does it sound the same as it does when your hear yourself speak? Are there unexpected nuances of your speech patterns and inflections when you hear them coming back to you?

If so, how do you feel about that person that you are now experiencing as others do?

Views from Clouds and Canyons

AS WE LEARN to see ourselves from the outside, we can begin to observe our relationships, opportunities and choices within more objective frames of reference. Focusing close-up, is the self that you witness cheerful and enjoyable to be around? Does he or she appear to be interested and involved in what they are doing?

Stepping slightly back, are you honoring friendships? Do you see yourself acting upon possibilities which are within arms' reach? Are you proactive; or rather do you appear to be sitting at life's sidelines waiting for opportunities to be presented by someone else?

Moving to another vantage point high above enables us to view our lives in a broader perspective. Do you like the scenery where you are? Are you out in an open field, or enclosed in a canyon? Are you alone, or are you involved in a center of activity? Are there places in sight where you would rather be? Can you see any paths that lead there? What obstacles are in your way? Are you pointed in the right direction?

Now let's at least pretend that the self you have been observing from these different vantage points is someone you really love and care about. As your own friend, you can excuse yourself for being less than perfect because any weaknesses are overshadowed by many qualities you admire.

On the other hand, you want to help your friend-self achieve a happier, more fulfilled life, even if it means that you sometimes risk being critical. Based upon your outside view of yourself, what advice would you offer to be helpful? Would you listen to yourself, and would you be motivated to trust and act upon that advice?

It isn't always easy to be your own trusted friend. It often requires that we step outside ourselves and take responsibilities for the realities we see. Still in doing so, there are rewards beyond measure. We can discover a person who has capabilities that we have never recognized, potentials we never appreciated, and a new friend we enjoy being with.

Unleashing Your Natural Curiosity

DANGERS OF CURIOSITY have been well recognized by Mankind ever since a snake-in-the-grass tempting Adam and Eve with an apple of wisdom got them kicked out of a ready-made Paradise, albeit for an opportunity to help construct a new one just as good.

History is also replete with other curious examples: including Benjamin Franklin's dangerous thunderstorm kite-flying experiment, a peeping Tom in Poughkeepsie who was nearly bludgeoned to death by an irate husband, and a cat that curiosity reportedly killed for some unexplained reason somewhere.

In fairness, however, there have also been episodes when too little curiosity has caused serious problems...like when Trojan soldiers failed to look a large Greek gift horse in the mouth.

One of the most troublesome aspects of curiosity is that you can never be certain where it will lead. When allowed to get out of hand it can cause people to challenge conventional wisdom, and in extreme cases, even question the wisdom of conventions. It can seduce us to think about things that are recognized to be of no importance, diverting attention away from subjects that authorized experts tell us we should concentrate on. Really curious people face the risk of not *fitting in*.

Of course most of us realize that curiosity within bounds is okay. Babies and young children, for example, have a lot to learn, and we don't always have time to teach them everything ourselves. It's very cute when they ask us questions about big things like sex and death, even when it makes us uncomfortable that we can't offer simple, elegant and profound answers.

We also know that scientists usually have lots of curiosity, and that they occasionally stumble onto discoveries that are useful. Since they spend almost all of their time in laboratories or attending conferences, there isn't much opportunity for them to get into trouble.

Artists often have curiosity too, and seem to question just about everything most of us take for granted. Sometimes they come up with ideas and observations that are interesting, even beautiful. The rest of the time they usually stick to their own misunderstood and unappreciated business.

Questioning What You Believe

IN TRUTH, NEARLY all of us have both of these characteristics to some degree, although it is often socially and politically correct to keep some curiosity under wraps outside the bedroom.

Let's face it: people with overactive curiosity tend to be a bit eccentric. Others who pretty much know what they believe about everything are much more solid and reliable. In fact we might think of them as concentric, because we can invariably understand where they are coming from, where they are going, and where they are likely to wind up.

Of course we all believe things. By this, I am referring to things we really care about. So I'm not addressing those sorts of circumstances when we might say, for example:

> *I believe that I will have another helping of that delicious pecan pie.*

No one particularly cares about that, unless it's the last piece.

Instead, I'm referring to the kind of belief that represents true faith. For instance, we believe in certain people who we have learned to value and trust. We believe in lessons and ideas that inspire and guide us in seeking higher, more productive possibilities in our lives. We believe in dreams that give us hope and motivate us to pursue challenging and worthwhile purposes.

All of these beliefs offer foundations and references for understanding ourselves, as well as compasses to help direct us in ways that are valuable to others. They also provide frameworks for defining priorities.

Are curiosity and belief polar opposites? Is curiosity, by nature, open, and belief, by necessity, closed? I don't *believe* so.

Curiosity reveals experiences and options that enable each of us to make more informed choices about what to believe. Then when what best passes a truth test comes along, we have a better basis for recognizing and applying it. Belief, on the other hand, gives curiosity substance to work on. Belief, in fact, can motivate curiosity to explore broader dimensions of meaning. In this sense, belief should really be an open system too.

Perhaps the greatest danger of curiosity occurs when we neglect it and allow ourselves to accept unsupported precepts and preconceptions. Without curiosity we are also likely to miss out on unexpected adventures of thought and experience that enrich life and make it more exciting.

So why not go ahead, accept curiosity's lesser dangers, and just enjoy the adventure—wherever it leads?

Creating Room for Dreams

LIFE IS A voyage to meet a new person we are always in the process of becoming at each successive port along the way. Each leg of the journey offers challenges and lessons that change us.

Near-term concerns often press us to concentrate on the present, and let future selves deal with tomorrow. For now it may be all we can handle just getting to the next safe harbor.

Why dream about that person we want to eventually become, knowing that such illusions will probably be dispersed by unpredictable winds and tides of fate anyway?

One reason is because if we don't think about what we really want out of life, we won't have any basis for setting our course in the right direction. Another is because when we have some understanding of what we want, we can avoid wasting time and energy on routes destined to nowhere. A third is because understanding what we want can energize us to do something about it.

Dreaming about the future probably came easier in childhood. That was before setbacks and other disappointments challenged our confidence, before we forgot how special we are, and before magic was disproven. Maybe our expectations began to wither when our parents and teachers warned us about how difficult it is to convert hopes into realities, and stressed the importance of looking at life from a *practical point of view*.

Predictably, years of experience have caused us to be much more discriminating in choosing goals and plans that temper adolescent idealism with mature rationality. In any event, we have learned to distinguish between idle fantasies and feasible possibilities and between casual desires and worthwhile commitments...at least sometimes.

I won't argue that this hard-earned objectivity isn't necessary and beneficial in large part. But what if we go too far, allowing pragmatic conservatism to rule us completely?

Along with the innocence of youth, aren't we in danger of losing something else? Aren't we at risk of giving up those exciting visions of unbounded potentials that our child-selves naturally and wisely recognized? And if so, aren't we more inclined to abandon our expeditions of growth and discovery at readily accessible, yet marginal destinations?

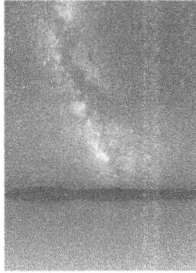

Voyages of Self-Discovery

HAVE YOU SETTLED for less than is possible? Do you know what is personally most important? Can you imagine what an ideal life would be like as forward as you care and dare to visualize?

What would you be doing from morning to night? How do those activities relate to your interests and pleasures now? Would the activities become repetitious and boring over time? Would you be working for someone else, or for yourself?

In that future life, are you married? Children? Is earning a large income a big priority? Would you settle for less income and security if required in order to do what you enjoy most? In the balance between time for family, recreation and work, which are most vital? In the balance between desire for outside recognition and personal satisfaction, where do you fall?

Now, if you are truly brave, compare those observations with your life now. Are you happy and agreeable to be around most of the time? Are you missing out on many of the things you care most about? If so, is this okay? Is your life voyage moving in a direction that really interests you? If not, who is steering your ship?

Dreaming about the future may be a forgotten art we must relearn from our inner child-self. Of course we also need to apply subsequent lessons of experience which help us understand what we value most in ourselves and our lives. Assuming that visions control realities, and I believe they do, then dreaming is something we can't afford to abandon or postpone.

If we do, our ship of opportunity may leave port without us—piloted by others.

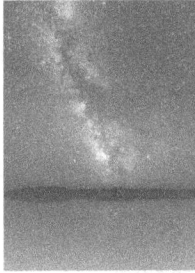

Expecting All Life Can Offer

It is not selfish to expect everything possible in life. When you deny yourself, you also diminish your ability to enrich others.

Owning Your Expectations

IT PROBABLY COMES as no great revelation that you are surrounded by people and establishments that are constantly telling you what you should want out of life. Some actually have your interests in mind, even though their priorities and circumstances may be different from yours.

Others are less generous, primarily motivated by concerns about ways your life and desires impact their own. Using powers of seduction and threat, both subtle and explicit, they entice you with images, shame you with superior performance examples, and cajole you with arguments in efforts to persuade you to accept their role models.

Few, if any aspects of your being are off limits. You are presented with standards of beauty to aspire to, symbols of success you should acquire, types of work you should pursue, approaches to parenting you should apply, fashions of clothing you should like, and even satisfactions you should enjoy.

If it is any consolation, you probably impose your models on at least a few people also. That's only fair.

We may like to think that, being of strong minds and resolve, we know what we want and can stand up to contrary positions. Or maybe we often just accept those influences, enjoy them, and then go with the flow.

The real rub seems to occur when some important concepts about what we want out of life are at odds with people we share interdependent relationships with. It is one thing to inform your friends that you have decided to become a Sahara camel driver in a nomadic tribe, and quite another to spring that surprise upon your spouse and children. You may find that those camels will have to fulfill an important family niche that you have just opened.

So, truth be known, it isn't prudent to determine everything we expect out of life without also considering others we are responsible to and responsible for. If they are important to us, then they already represent part of what we desire our lives to be. If we love them, we also want them to fulfill their dreams as well.

The challenge is to plan things so that everyone wins.

Visions of a Would-Be Camel Driver

Some of this may require compromises. For example, maybe the would-be camel driver settles on getting a large homely dog and moves with the family to a sandy beachfront home. Still, I doubt that this solution would address the root issues.

Perhaps the real solution is to frame our expectations more upon what we most want to experience and less upon any particular form those experiences take. Maybe that would-be camel driver feels a need in her life to have more time for quiet reflection. Maybe she desires an element of change and adventure. Maybe she yearns to simplify her life by going to a place where she won't have to bring her makeup kit, designer clothes and television set.

Maybe she has visualized the person she is becoming, and wants to leave the road she is on to explore less traveled pathways. And maybe all these possibilities are available right where she is.

If we live by ourselves we are free to act upon our expectations in any way that doesn't land us in jail. We should not be overly concerned when others, however well meaning, disagree with those choices. After all, our lives are ours alone to live.

If, on the other hand, we have chosen to make our lives interdependent with others, there are solid and necessary grounds for negotiation. When any member of a partnership is unhappy, all lose in the bargain.

Any successful negotiation process begins with understanding and defining essential expectations of the participants. If the would-be camel driver had done this, her family might have recognized that the real changes she desired could include her freedom and opportunities to become more, not less, than what she currently represents to them.

In return, she would become more responsive to their needs. And the nomads and camels would just have to go on without her...just as they always have.

Valuing Yourself

IF YOU WERE to sell part of your life for a lot of money, would you consider it? Let's imagine that a research center offered you $1 million to be a subject in a five-year-long suspended animation experiment starting next week which they told you would also reduce your life expectancy by the same amount?

Okay, what about $2 million?

Or imagine that you didn't have to actually shorten your life, but were offered money to endure a long experience that you really didn't want. For example, you are offered five times your current income, or at least $450,000 to collect specimens of penguin excrement in Antarctica for research dealing with eating habits of polar birds. The work would require you to live in a tent on an offshore ice floe for a year. All basic food and clothing would be provided, but you wouldn't have any means of communication with loved ones back home.

And, oh yeah, the one person you would be living with was a jerk who smells worse than the penguin excrement and snores.

Or if this example is too extreme, what about collecting cow chips in Montana, and they give you a cellular telephone? What would that be worth?

The point is that many people seem to sell large portions of their lives in exchange for doing things that they don't enjoy, and sometimes even detest. We hear them tell us that they are overworked, underpaid, and unappreciated; their job is boring, and their colleagues are offensive. Or they are alone by themselves without friends and nobody calls or visits them.

Because they feel abused or neglected by others, they tend to devalue themselves. When they do this, people around them also value them less, causing their self-esteem to continue in its downward spiral.

Do they have any choices? Not if they don't seek any.

Of course there are vast numbers of people who are thrust into unsatisfactory, even tragic conditions that they have no control over. Examples are those who suffer incapacitating injuries and illnesses, war victims who are confined with their families in refugee camps or worse, and aging homeless people who have no caring families at all.

What Are You Worth to You?

THERE ARE ALSO many people who voluntarily accept dangers and hardships in order to serve needs of others. They probably do this because they place a very high value on all life, and enjoy rewards that most of us never experience.

The payments received in return for contributions we make take many forms. Money is one, and we often associate our worth with the amount that our time commands in the market place.

Others assign a value to services and work products, and either accept that exchange price or seek other options.

Consider also that some people would and do enthusiastically welcome the opportunity to conduct research similar to the penguin project for modest payment, and invest years of intensive study preparing for just such possibilities. They might do this because they are very interested in understanding more about effects of pollution upon the aquatic food chains in Antarctic waters which affect nearly all life on our planet.

In doing, so they are rewarded by the satisfaction of doing something they rightly regard to be important and insightful. That work may also advance their professional careers and legitimate sense of self-worth.

As individuals, we measure our own worth according to

varying personal priorities and criteria. Some equate success with money and security, some with respect and recognition, some with professional interests and challenges, and some with contributions they make to the lives of others. These measures, of course, are not mutually exclusive. Many influence the ways most people see themselves to some degree.

It may be useful to reflect upon which of these and other measurements are most important to you. Is it possible that you sometimes undervalue yourself because you are using the wrong measuring stick?

In all probability, you are worth more than you think.

Don't sell yourself short.

Anticipating Joys

DOES IT SEEM that you spend most of your life waiting for good things to happen? And has it occurred to you that this in itself may be one of life's greatest joys? Think back, if you will, and consider that possibility.

Can you remember times when anticipation was better than the ultimate reality? Maybe when you looked forward to your grandchildren's visit before they tried to teach your parakeet to fly by tying its leg to a blade of the ceiling fan? A birthday gift from your husband that you thought was a dress you showed him, but it turned out to be another blender? A romantic evening you had planned with your wife before your son got the flu? An exciting blind date that your best friend arranged who had a *Born to Lose* tattoo on his neck? A non-refundable trip you won to the Bahamas before the hurricane hit? A promotion you had been promised before your boss's nephew joined the firm?

Disillusionment   notwithstanding,   isn't   anticipation wonderful?

Life would probably be a lot less interesting if everything worked out the way we expected. In fact, things often turn out for the better.

People who are less than we had hoped for introduce us to

others who are more. Positions we aren't accepted for leave us open for opportunities that prove to be much more worthwhile. Detours we are forced to take lead us to fascinating new places. Even the largest setbacks we experience are often blessings because they encourage us to adapt, and we become stronger in the process.

Of course really bad disappointments are traumatic and discourage us from trusting hope. Examples are when important relationships we desire go awry, and when people we love don't recover from injuries and illnesses.

These pains are recorded in our minds among lesser memories of fingers burned by hot pans. As a result, we may develop emotional reflexes that pull us away from dangers of expecting too much. We brace ourselves against pitfalls of optimism.

Recognizing that anticipation of joy invariably presents the risk of disappointment, the rewards still outweigh the dangers. It is difficult to reach out for happiness when our arms are wrapped protectively around ourselves, or to experience relationships from inside a shell. That is why we seldom see a turtle smile. Joy is most fully experienced when soft tissues and nerve endings are exposed.

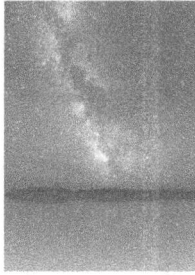

And Enjoying Anticipation

WHAT DO YOU have to look forward to right now?

If you can't think of anything, then create something. Since this may require some practice, you might want to begin at the entry level.

For instance, you might put a seed in a glass of water on your bathroom window sill and watch it grow a little day-by-day. Maybe plan a surprise for a friend and think about how good it will make them feel to know that they are special and appreciated. Write a letter to that person you care about most and tell them why; then send it to them by regular mail, even if they live in the same house you do so that they won't receive it right away. Go ahead and order a ticket for a trip or event you have been considering. Then plan to purchase some new clothes for the occasion, but don't get them right away so that you have more time to enjoy the idea. If there is something that you planned to make, go out and get the materials and imagine how terrific it will look when it is finished.

When you feel that you are ready, you can move on to more ambitious and adventuresome levels of anticipation.

Write to your children that you haven't heard from for a long time and tell them that you have just met a wonderful person at a nudist colony who is helping you revise your will...then wait for them to call.

Relish plotting the demise of your wife's *Spandex* exercise outfit that you hate to take place next Tuesday night when she is at jewelry class, leaving a shredded trail of evidence leading from the crime scene to your dog's bed. (A similar scenario might revolve around a certain shirt your husband wears.) Send that person that you have been mooning about an invitation to attend a hunting and fishing show, and let fear of rejection be damned! Get together with some friends and organize a fencing or motorcycle club for senior citizens in your community.

There is really no need for me to continue. At your advanced level, I'm sure you will dream up your own ideas.

Larry Bell

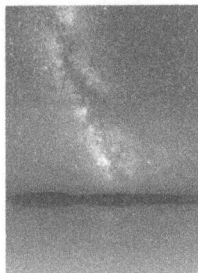

Capturing Opportunities

Possessing wings and marvelous eyes,
but disposed of fussy taste,
sea gulls swoop down from the skies
and snatch the scraps that others waste.

For strong persistence and insight
it's hard to beat the polar bear;
he'll watch an ice hole day and night
to nab a lunch that's lurking there.

Sea otters concentrate on fun
and seem to have their rules down pat;
don't work until all play is done,
and even clown around at that.

A porpoise is the kind of friend
you really want to be and know,
defending others to the end
with loyalty that's more than show.

Though baleen whales are mammal kin,

their manners really aren't the best;
they filter tons of good stuff in
and casually spit out all the rest.

The octopus is slow to act,
and probes to see if all is right,
but when convinced a hunch is fact,
holds on to it with all his might.

While sharks are enterprising fish
who sense where bounty can be found,
they're loners who do what they wish,
and aren't that great to be around.

And smaller fish should watch their backs
when barracudas are in sight;
they hunt in gangs for helpless snacks
and have a very nasty bite.

Larry Bell

Lessons from Aquatic Predators

*Romoras look for a free ride
on any passing host they find;
they suck up closely at their side
and seize whatever's left behind.*

*The triggerfish takes careful aim
at dragonflies that flit above;
good marksmanship is not a game
if that's a meal you truly love.*

*Anglerfish strike rock-like poses,
apparently don't even have to try,
they simply wiggle lures on noses,
then snap up fools as they swim by.*

*The halibut wants to just blend in,
and does this very well indeed;
he doesn't really care to win,
but is content to bottom feed.*

Hiding out in offshore reeds,
the snake sneaks up on resting prey,
he moves and strikes at lightning speeds
and is successful in this way.

Now please consider carefully,
from your objective point of view-
of all these creatures in the sea
do any seem at all like you?

Yet unlike snakes, or birds or fish,
or mammals of a different kind,
if you don't see the chance you wish
you can create it in your mind.

Wherever there is unmet need,
and caring thoughts and hopes abound,
there's always chances to succeed
in making choices that are sound

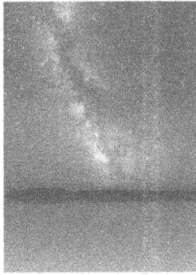

Recognizing Successes

A BIG PROBLEM with success is that you often can't be certain when you have acquired it—at least not by comparing yourself to others. Of course you can usually visualize that you have achieved more in some areas than most people have, but others might properly view you in the same light.

Then you, in turn, might look back at them and ask:

- *Yeah, but are they as happy?*
- *Are their children as wonderful as mine?*
- *Are they as popular as I am?*

Then you've got to go back and evaluate those things.

Some people appear smart enough to just know they are well off and let it go at that. I probably envy them.

When I was a young boy I put a lot of ants in a large jar with grass and leaves at the bottom and watched them. Most seemed pretty content, or at least didn't openly express displeasure, as they busily organized their new home.

A few, however, crawled up the inside of the container and roamed around the lid. Imagining that they had some special goal in mind, their intent was unclear. Were they trying to escape? Were they members of a scouting party only doing their job? Did they wish to get away from the crowd? Were they simply seeking a change, or rather, seeking a higher purpose?

It's often difficult to know exactly what ants think about, and it might be somewhat disappointing if we did. Yet it occurred to me that maybe those ants, whether they climbed or not, had valid priorities, and that life in that jar might have some parallels to our human existence. Since we can't escape it, we are well advised to try to make the most of it.

During subsequent years, I have enjoyed a large variety of interesting and informative acquaintances along life's highway. They include a number of astronauts and cosmonauts, many of whom have become close friends and professional colleagues. All of them are popularly recognized to be highly goal-oriented and successful. Otherwise, they wouldn't have accepted the dangers and hardships leading them to walk on the Moon, to establish time records for orbiting the Earth and working outside their spacecraft, or to conduct difficult and complex experiments.

Observing Ants and Astronauts

WHILE THEIR NATIONAL origins and backgrounds vary, some similar personal challenges astronaut friends have faced, both before and after their missions, may offer lessons for all of us.

Being selected to represent their native country in historic space efforts was an honor that signified they possessed a surplus of the right stuff, but that was only the beginning of some real tests. In addition to learning and being evaluated on what they would need to know, they also had to pass challenging tests of patience and optimism as they waited for an opportunity to fly. If married, both they and their families often had to endure years of uncertainty under conditions which weren't very glamorous or financially rewarding.

Life was like an endless countdown until finally their time arrived, they realized their dreams, and many cheered.

Following a possible ticker tape parade or meeting with the President (at least for those earliest space missions), these public heroes had to experience the world as life-size mortals again, wondering what to do next. After viewing your planet and the heavens as God sees them, what do you do as an encore?

Many, in fact, went on to do very well. Some, for example, pursued careers as space program administrators, public representatives, business executives, artists, and writers. And regardless what they chose to do, many gained deeper personal and spiritual insights from their space experiences that made them stronger and better people as a result. All had to adapt and move beyond original goals that had motivated them, and learn to apply their successes to support new ones.

So how can we interpret what success means? People do this in different ways.

For some, success might represent an elusive goal that motivates them to grow. Just when you think that you know what it means and are getting close, something, possibly yourself, moves the peg up a notch.

Alternatively, maybe recognizing success is a matter of maturity; an ability to understand that you already have it, to apply what you have learned in the process of getting it, and to have the wisdom to appreciate it. Both scenarios are open-ended, directing lives which are interesting, exciting and valuable to others.

Pursuing Mortal and Moral Progress

The biggest issue isn't whether something can be accomplished, but rather, whether it should be, and who will do it.

Purposeful Living

A BIG CHALLENGE of life for many of us is to seek a win-win relationship with self and others which balances the special interests of both. This is not to imply that these interests are mutually exclusive. Most often, particularly in the longer term, they are very much the same. It's best not to learn this the *hard way*.

German philosopher Friedrich Nietzsche defined living correctly as a full life based purely on personal reason and conscience—independent of religion. He said every person should live his or her life for the sake of living it and not be influenced by a concept he rejected: afterlife.

Nietzsche's German scholar contemporary Immanuel Kant

saw things differently. He believed that there can be no morality without religion as defined by a universal *Categorical Imperative* whereby a person is duty-bound to act in a certain manner to avoid serious consequences. Here, the action was just as important—if not more—than the outcome.

Kant supported what is now referred to as *foundations of retribution,* or *just desserts,* meaning that a person who commits a crime should receive nothing more or less than the penalty called for. This idea prominently appears in most cultures and religions. Christians refer to it as the *Golden Rule,* namely to *Do onto others as you would have them do onto you.*

Another translation is *What goes around, comes around.* For better or worse, it works both ways.

Pope John II broadly characterized a universal moral law as being written by the human heart. Two modern religions, the Baha'i faith and Unitarian Universalist Church strive to promote universality as a central tenet.

English novelist Aldous Huxley argued that there is a *perennial philosophy* or core of moral principles that exist in every time and place throughout history.

Indian independence leader Mahatma Gandhi advocated self-suffering, nonviolence and a search for truth as universal values. American philosopher William James believed that love is a singular foundation principle of all ethics. Charles Darwin speculated that the desire for approval is a primary moral root.

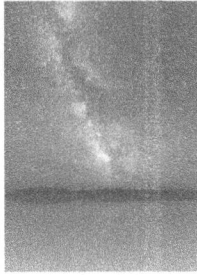

Blessings and Boomerangs

IN 2000, RICHARD Kinner and Jerry Kernes in the Division of Psychology in Education at Arizona State University-Tempe, along with Phoenix counselor Therese Dautheribes, compiled a short list of universal values taken from texts of major world religions. Included were Judaism (the *Tanaka*), Christianity (the *New Testament*), Islam (the *Koran*), Hinduism (the *Upanishads* and the *Bhagavad Gita*), Confucianism (the *Analects of Confucius*), Taoism (the *Tao Te Ching of Lao Tzu*), and Buddhism (the *Dhammapada*).

The study also consulted with and reviewed materials of several secular organizations, including the American Atheists, Inc. (*Atheist Aims and Purpose, Atheism Teaches That,* and *Introduction to American Atheists*), The American Humanist Association (*Humanist Manifesto I, 1933* and *Humanist Manifesto II, 1973*), and the United Nations (*The United Nations Declaration of Human Rights, 1948*).

Here's what they came up with:

- *Commitment to something greater than self: To recognize the existence of and be committed to a Supreme Being, higher* principle, transcendent purpose or meaning to one's existence; and to seek the truth (or truths) and justice.

- *Self-respect, but with humility, self-discipline, and acceptance of personal responsibility: to respect and care for oneself; to not exalt oneself or overindulge; to show humility and avoid gluttony or other forms of selfishness and self-centeredness; and to act in accordance with one's conscience and to accept responsibility for one's behavior.*

- *Respect and caring for others (i.e., the Golden Rule): to recognize the connectedness between all people; to serve humankind and be helpful to individuals; to be caring, respectful, compassionate, tolerant, and forgiving of others; and to not hurt others (e.g., do not murder, abuse, steal from, cheat or lie to others.)*

- *Care for other living things and the environment.*

Fueling Passion's Light

I ONCE HAD a somber occasion to contemplate what priorities dominated a purposeful life during a conversation with a very close family member who was then in hospice care. He was someone I regarded to have lived a fine one, and wished to communicate my appreciation of what this meant.

I told him that if one day I find myself reviewing my own achievements in the face of known near-term terminal realities, three questions will emerge above all:

- *Did I have any fun?*
- *Did I do any good?*
- *Did I live my life with passion?*

With regard to the first, in light of the apparently incredible genetic odds stacked against our arrivals on the scene, it would be a terrible waste not to celebrate opportunities to enjoy it.

Joie de vivre (joy of living), a French phrase often used to express this priority, is characterized by *Robert's Dictionary* as *sentiment exaltant ressenti par toute la conscience,* a sentiment that involves one's whole being.

Psychologist Abraham Carl Rogers recognized a sense of playfulness—fun, joy, and amusement—represents an important part of a self-actualized personality:

> *...the quiet joy in being one's self...a spontaneous relaxed enjoyment, a primitive joie de vivre.*

In my view, doing good in summarizing one's life fundamentally prompts each of us to ask whether or not we have attempted in good faith to respect that previously outlined list of *universal values*. It doesn't really have much of anything to do with having achieved wealth or fame.

Rather, it asks us to contemplate: can I be trusted to be a good spouse, parent and friend?; do I have a generous nature when it comes to sharing credit and effort which recognizes the worth and contributions of others?; have I touched the lives of others in a constructive way simply because I could?; and am I comfortable with that person that inhabits my own skin?

That third item...the *"passion"* word, is what to me sets humans apart from other perfectly wonderful creatures. Some might just as readily refer to this as *"love"*.

It should be apparent watching puppies and kittens play that experiencing joie de vivre is not by any means unique to humans. As for *doing good*, Darwin's theory attributing pursuit of reward or approval as a primary motive isn't entirely unique to our species either.

Our Unlimited Human Resource

I BELIEVE THAT passion ratchets things up to a whole other level. It is what drives us to express our highest human potentials: to have empathy and truly care about others; to set goals; to meet challenges and seek excellence that sets exceptional examples; to create music, art and literature that lifts our intellect and spirits; and to believe in the power of worthwhile ideas and our God-given abilities to make them real.

A prerequisite for passion is the ability to deeply care about something, or more preferably, lots of somethings and someones. This quality drives nearly everything else, including motivation, curiosity, understanding, creativity and persistence.

One big advantage of those who have passion about something is that they are often too preoccupied with what they care about to become sidetracked listening to experts who are all too willing to tell them otherwise. In fact the very reason many people become successful is because they became interested in a possibility or discovery that nobody else paid much attention to or thought would work.

When is the last time that someone advised you to give

importance to any special interest that fascinates you even though they didn't happen to share it? Be sure to thank them. They are true friends.

Have you done the same in encouraging others to pursue theirs?

I would guess that most interests are not fixed affinities we are born with. Instead, they are more likely to arise through exposures to a wide variety of people, ideas and experiences.

Sometimes they come to light through problems and obstacles we confront. They often relate to talents and other qualities we acknowledge in ourselves and others. They are contagious, and can be shared to forge bonds with kindred souls who share our values.

Pursuing passions stimulates our curiosity, inciting us to courses of inquiry and action that reveal unexpected possibilities. We should appreciate them, nurture them and enjoy them.

Have fun with your passions, and yes, apply them for good. A well-lived life deserves no less.

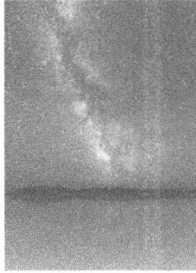

A Japanese Father's Letter

MY DEAR FRIEND Itaru Tanaka was an exceptionally fine man who enjoyed a fascinating and distinguished well-lived life. His childhood exposure to death, suffering and destruction in Tokyo during World War II and later experiences as a well-known war correspondent and companion-biographer of important world leaders undoubtedly helped to shape his strong values, character and insightful international and human perspectives. Cancer ended his life in 1994.

In June, 2013 I posted a Forbes article which contained the following letter that Itaru wrote to his son Makoto in preparation for the time he would be spend living with my family upon moving to the U.S. as a student at the University of Houston. The wonderfully wise advice it contained drew appreciative responses from many readers along with heartfelt expressions of gratitude from Itaru's family.

May, 1989
Dear Makoto,

You may find it helpful for me to set forth our aims for your visit so that you can refer to them. I hope you will promise to keep a daily record of your experiences, however short those memos may be. It will be useful if you will include dates, times, and places.

I am making it materially possible for you to go to the New World so that you may gain first-hand experience managing your life outside the discipline imposed by school and family, and so that you may have a long and meaningful stay. This will enable you to gain direct knowledge about one of the largest, richest and most powerful countries in the world. Your life and career will be greatly influenced by this important experience.

Herein are some hints you may find useful in making a great success of your stay.

Getting the Most Out of Your Experience:

You must meticulously plan your days throughout the entire program. This is not only because good planning means good discipline, but also to enable you to get the most out of the time available. Another cardinal principle which will be useful to you, not only during your visit, but always, is that living a good life requires that you do nothing in excess.

Be genuinely interested in people. Remember every person——be they young or old——has unique lessons to offer. Encourage them to talk about themselves and their families. When conversation lags you can always ask a sympathetic question or offer a thought-provoking statement.

Loving Advice to a Son

Remember that a listener is always more appreciated than a talker and avoid boasting. On the other hand, don't fall into the other extreme of being too self-effacing or frightened to contribute to a conversation. Since I know that you do not suffer this problem, I find no need to stress it.

Making friends involves being genuinely interested in people, their problems and their experiences; avoiding selfish and provocative acts; offering consideration and helpfulness; and being clean and well turned-out.

The best way to have a good time when you are with a group is to make sure that everybody participates and enjoys themselves. Don't be selfish in not caring what happens to others present so long as you are alright.

A great deal of experience in life can be obtained by closely observing the behavior and reactions of others, measuring their conduct against your own, and determining what standards you should apply.

If the group you are with engages in bad practices, either in drink, sex or any other matters, there is no need for you to go along with this. If some members ridicule you about this, tell them that you gave a pledge to Professor and Mrs. Bell as well as to your parents and insist that you intend to stick to that promise.

Observing the USA:

You will be living with an American family, reading their newspapers and watching their TV. You will find that many people are extremely ignorant about Japan, just as you and your father are ignorant about other countries. When you hear criticism about Japan and the Japanese people, avoid getting into heated arguments, but carefully listen and consider what they say.

Read newspapers and other publications available in the English language. Mark in pencil any word or expression that is unfamiliar and check it in the dictionary.

Try to meet people of all ages and backgrounds. Get involved in sports activities and youth clubs on and off the university campus.

Loving Advice to a Son

Make it a point to learn something about US history. This is absolutely essential to understand America's political actions and motivations, at home and abroad.

When you ask questions about the United States, keep the following in mind: "I am interested in how its people live, their expectations for the future, and what they expect regarding my appropriate behavior."

Personal Behavior:

Adjust to your host's lifestyle. Express your gratitude when you are kindly treated. It may be a good idea to give them flowers when you meet and leave them, or have them delivered by a florist. The value of the flowers might be between $5 and $10, or you might purchase an equivalent value on chocolates. In addition, write a brief letter of gratitude with whatever nice personal remarks you can think of addressed to all members of the family that will participate in looking after you.

Wake up at least one and one-half hours before your first class starts. I do not know how much time it will take from home to the university, but plan accordingly and allow for this.

Be sure to clean the wash basin and bathtub each time after use. In the evening, always be cautious about making too much noise, such as by playing a radio or tape player, heavy footsteps, and slamming doors or windows. Try not to create extra troubles for the Bells or others in the community.

On Mondays through Fridays, come home immediately after classes to study. Tell yourself: "Since I have good holidays during the weekends, today I will work hard."

During the weekends, allow some free time to spend with the Bells. When you go out to meet friends, tell Professor Bell and Mrs. Bell beforehand where you will be and with whom.

Always plan to come home before the Bell's bedtime. In case you should miss that limit, telephone them before 8 or 9 pm. Don't use the telephone for long chit-chats with friends. When necessary to contact us, call collect.

Loving Advice to a Son

In classroom, always tell yourself, "I am curious." Do not think that learning is like filing documents in a cabinet, but be sure to use your brain for reasoning.

We all need wisdom along with knowledge. I believe the Bible is one of the most essential sources for this. Try to read at least one chapter of Proverbs and five from the Book of Psalms. This can be accomplished within a one-month period.

Health and Safety:

Take good care of your health and avoid getting into unnecessary dangerous situations. Always calculate whether the risks you are taking are commensurate with the rewards. Think about ways that risks can be minimized; for instance, by sitting in the back of a car if there is no safety belt next to the driver's seat.

Be proud as you abide by traffic rules and school regulations. Some people boast about breaking rules of society. Do not be one of them.

Avoid carrying large sums of money on your person or flashing money about. Also avoid going into public parks at night, or any parts of large cities which are seedy or ill-lit.

—Your father

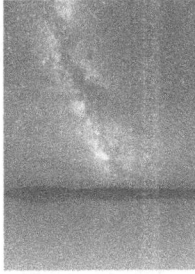

Recognizing Priorities

IT SEEMS TO me that we tend to respect people who appear to know what they want and are determined to get it. Somehow they project an air of confidence and decisiveness that we may feel we lack. They move on opportunities when we falter. They let us know without any doubt what they think is most important for themselves, and also for us…often even persuade us to agree. We tend to look to them as leaders and may typically assume that they are smart.

I have observed that pigs can be like that.

While I personally believe that pigs are a bit overrated in many of these areas, their behavior has earned them admiration among some prominent authorities. An observation attributed to Winston Churchill recognizes their strength of character and forbearance. Comparing different animals, it was noted that cats are often aloof, egotistical and arrogant. Dogs are often too dependent and ingratiating. But a pig will treat you like an equal.

I confess that virtually all of my personal experiences with members of the porcine species is limited to one individual, a *pet* (although she would have been offended by that description) named Priscilla. To be more species specific, Priscilla was a member of the small *pot-bellied* (no offense intended) Asian variety, and was actually quite attractive (after one became accustomed to special standards of pig beauty).

More than just another pretty face, she also had other fine qualities. She preferred to be very clean, respected house rules against messing the floor, and enjoyed human companionship to a fault. Above all, she always knew exactly what she wanted, as well as how to get it.

If Priscilla was representative of her kin, pigs don't seem to want anything very unreasonable. But when they care about something, they really care a lot. And there were two things that Priscilla (who had been spayed) cared about most.

First, she cared about eating, and cheerfully spent a great deal of time supplementing her diet foraging for tiny, defenseless grass sprouts in our back yard. Few survived.

Second, she cared about where she sat. And when that place happened to be on your lap while you were reading a book or absorbed in other matters, she didn't handle rejection graciously. Perhaps this related to an excellent sense of self-esteem and entitlement. Yet she wasn't one to fawn on you after you had been away for several months if she had other more immediate sitting matters in mind.

Learning from Pigs

SURE, PIGS ARE pretty smart when they are motivated to learn something. If you want them to apply their native intelligence, a bribe of food can be inspirational. I have concluded, however, that a key reason we assume they are smart is because they are pig-headed about getting their way by making us accommodate them.

Maybe there is a lesson in this. Possibly, if we were more assertive in making our priorities known, people would be more inclined to think that we deserve some measure of respect and accommodation also.

This suggests that we first need to be quite clear in our own minds about what is most important. Sometimes we may expect others to understand what we want intuitively, but that's not realistic. Maybe they're preoccupied with thoughts about where they're going to sit...or other priorities of their own.

What is most important to you? Which of these needs and desires are negotiable, and which are not? Are you prepared to do whatever is required to achieve those which are not negotiable?

It's often difficult to understand our priorities until we are presented with options in life that force us to make choices. Then, maybe we evaluate best and worst-case scenarios for each in terms of benefits and risks.

In reality, our priorities are most frequently expressed through the relatively small decisions we make every day which all add up to define our total life experiences. Those little choices have a way of sneaking up on us and appearing to be of limited consequence at the time.

But don't let them fool you. If you don't have a good idea where you want them to lead, you may ultimately wind up sitting out in the cold.

Keeping Life Moving

ARE YOU BORED? Does the high point in your day occur when the newspaper arrives with new coupons to clip, when your dog greets you as you arrive home from work, or when your kids finally go to bed in time for you to watch your favorite television program? Is everything in your life pretty comfortable and predictable? Have you become so proficient at what you do that there's no challenge anymore? If so, it may have occurred to you that you're in a serious rut.

Being bored might seem like a great gift to less fortunate people whose lives are full of turmoil and strife for reasons they can't control. They represent the majority of the world's population.

Unlike them, you have other options, and boredom is a luxury you can't afford. Given a choice over the matter, life is too short and valuable to waste.

How do you get out of a rut? You probably had to do this with your car a few times. Maybe you can use the same approaches.

If your rut is shallow, you can try to drive out slowly, taking care not to spin your wheels and just get stuck deeper. That happens when you try to escape boredom by doing the same things you are already doing, only more intensely. For example, you are dissatisfied in your work and try to compensate by working even harder or more hours; or when the children are driving you to distraction and you focus even more attention on them.

The best way out might be to gradually change your living pattern to bring in some fresh elements. This could involve making a point of getting to know one new person every week or so, perhaps even someone you have been around for a long time and possibly never thought you had much in common with.

If that is true, so much the better. Take an interest in them. Be a friend for no reason at all. Get out of your own shell.

You can also break your routine by planning something new to do at least every week—then increase the frequency.

Order some season tickets to something.

Take the initiative to get together for breakfast, lunch, or dinner with people you met at the party.

Take an evening class.

Get a dog and get up early to walk it in the morning.

Get a babysitter, and give yourself and those kids a break.

Strategies for Muddy Roads

FOR DEEPER RUTS you may need a tow or push. Attach yourself to something that is moving. Get involved with an organization and volunteer to chair an active committee. Accept responsibility for getting to know and help someone who really needs it. Pull yourself out of yourself.

Set a new goal to accomplish, and give yourself a schedule. Create something, write something, learn something...change something. Work to make your life more valuable to yourself and others. Become indispensable.

If you can see that the road ahead is full of more ruts, you may even consider an alternate route. That decision may require negotiations with one or more traveling companions, but then, they might welcome a change also. Discuss destinations that are attractive to everyone.

Decide if your priorities are scenery along the way, or whether you care most about arriving quickly at a place that is interesting and challenging. The journey might involve exploring ways to improve current relationships to make them more vital, seeking a different career opportunity, or physically moving to a new setting.

Do something that forces you to adapt to new possibilities

and experiences. Take some worthwhile risks.

It isn't easy to get out of ruts because change is never easy. If you are in a comfortable rut and can't imagine any way out that justifies the efforts and risks, then just enjoy it and stop feeling sorry for yourself.

If, however, it isn't acceptable to you, then get yourself together. Get motivated to do something about it. Become excited about possibilities.

Get unstuck—and just keep moving!

Recognizing Life's Gifts and Living in Your Place and Time

If we don't always receive what we want, it may be because we don't take time to think about what is really most important or to appreciate the wise and generous intentions of our benefactors. The world reflects you, just as you reflect it. If conditions that influence you aren't perfect, then make them better.

Rediscovering Friends and Family

DOESN'T IT SEEM that we often expect a great deal from people who are closest to us, yet also undervalue many of their special qualities and the importance they represent in our lives? Perhaps we fail to recognize the significance of those gifts to us because we had hoped for something else. Then, after these people are gone, we realize that they gave us something very special—the shared love and experiences which remain among our most valued treasures. Unfortunately, by then it is too late to tell them what we have discovered. When it comes to critical expectations, many of us are probably toughest on our parents. As children, our mothers and fathers appeared larger than life. We looked up to them and feared their disapproval. Then, as we became older, we may have begun to realize that they actually possessed mortal flaws. We might have even become angry at them for betraying our former illusions of perfection.

Later, as adults, and possibly even as parents ourselves, we usually come to realize that our expectations as children were unrealistic and unfair. Yet our inner child selves might still never agree, harboring disappointments and resentments regardless of how hard we try to persuade him or her otherwise. We can also be pretty rough in our expectations for a brother or sister. Their flaws may have always been apparent, at least in regard to their relationships with us. Worse, we may have even experienced envy when they seemed to be free of certain short fallings we perceived in ourselves.

We know that we are supposed to love them, and might sometimes feel guilty sometimes when that sentiment seems to require more effort than it should. Maybe both of us find it difficult to discard childhood concepts of each other that neither of us currently identify with. It can be uncomfortable to be reminded of those embarrassing aspects of our young lives that we would prefer to forget.

Spouses can be a challenge too. We may both believe that we know each other very well, but each may disagree at least to some extent with our partner's clearly inferior and unreasonable assessments of certain perfectly wonderful and logical things we do and believe.

Strong Currents in Deep Waters

MAYBE WE BOTH feel that those inaccurate or incomplete evaluations don't incorporate adjustments for our growth and efforts to improve. Or maybe each of us senses that the other doesn't see them in all of their full natural colors because the lenses they are being viewed through are filtered by stereotypical perceptions and variant priorities.

Both of us may expect unconditional tolerance and understanding, yet neither of us may be prepared to give it in return. We share much, but never completely merge. If we did, life would be a lot less fun and interesting.

Friendships come in a great variety of sizes and forms. Some of the more casual ones can be quite tolerant and forgiving because we have less of an investment in them. Others involve considerable trust and are governed by higher expectations and stronger rules.

Since friendships aren't bound together by birthrights, exclusive life-long commitments, or shared responsibilities such as children and mortgages, we might tend to regard them to be somewhat fragile. This condition may be a factor in the level of importance that we attach to them, recognizing that they must be constantly earned and nourished to remain meaningful. Still, we expect true friends to be loyal, valuing us even when we aren't at our best. It's painful when they aren't.

The depth we feel for family and friends is often most exquisitely revealed in periods of hardship and sorrow. These times help us to recognize how trivial their imagined faults really are.

Instead, we appreciate how vital they are in our lives as we draw strength from their care and company, seeking solace in their company and comfort in their presence. We are reminded that through knowing them we have shared joys and survived difficulties, have come to understand ourselves and others better, and have been greatly enriched in the process.

Are tragedies necessary to bring such truths to our consciousness?

Hopefully not.

Maybe we can rediscover them by releasing filters that obscure our vision, letting unreasonable expectations and disappointments drift away in the tides of time.

Maybe as we look upon those waters of experience, we can recognize their beautiful reflections in ourselves and smile.

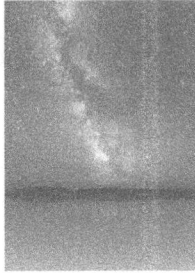

Being at Home Where You Live

ONE DAY MANY years ago when I was with my sister and brother-in-law, our conversation somehow turned to the somber question of where we would want our mortal remains to be put. When queried on this, I replied that it really didn't matter at all. Just find any pretty place to scatter my ashes, and that will be perfectly fine.

It then occurred to me that this subject was really part of a larger issue which revolved around where I considered my *real* home to be. If I were to choose one particular place that is most important in my life, where is it? I'm still thinking about that.

Many places have been very special to me. All evoke memories of wonderful people, happy and trying times, landscapes and buildings—a flood of clear and half-remembered images.

Each of those places represents important experiences that are part of me. How could I choose between them?

Would I pick the small Midwestern town where I spent my childhood through high school years? That's where I first discovered joys and challenges of friendship, flirted with romance, acquired formative lessons and values, was first exposed to responsibility, and enjoyed fun and adventures which were not all known to my parents.

And what about all those other places? Places where I was stationed in the military, attended universities, fell in love and became married, experienced my own children, pursued interests and achievements, and encountered people and possibilities that have had strong and lasting influences. That place where I live now holds many of those memories, along with similar current realities.

Over the years, for one reason or another, I have visited locales where I once lived before, often with hopeful anticipation of rediscovering the home I once knew. Each time I was disappointed to realize that it no longer existed. Most of those people I had known were gone. Settings that I had enjoyed had changed beyond recognition. Even broader landscapes seemed unfamiliar or alien due to a wide range of subsequent developments.

My feelings of attachment and disillusionment have been strongest when I have returned to my home town. There are powerful attractions that draw me there. The farmlands and natural countryside are as beautiful as ever.

Scattered Ashes and Memories

OF SPECIAL PERSONAL importance, the private airport that my parents built and operated there still exists, now as an active municipal facility. A circular paved and landscaped memorial site that I created for them originally contained two sentinel trees to symbolize my parents still together, standing side-by-side. The earth containing those trees, now harsh winter casualties, berms up to the top of a curved retaining wall which forms a bench overlooking a runway; a place where people can rest and watch airplanes. Mom's and dad's ashes are buried there, and I feel comforted and close to them when I visit that place.

But the area has changed in many ways that are difficult for me to adjust to. Just up the highway from the airport where I had spent many youthful years, a large indigenous Indian-owned and operated bingo gambling casino has been built on formerly rural land. The place is packed with people throughout the day and night, and has become a major employment center where small town residents work among bow-tied blackjack dealers and net-stockinged waitresses.

The near-by state park where we roamed freely and partied boisterously at all hours is now crowded with tourists. It once had private cottages which are gone, and is now publicly controlled with tightly regimented rules that include closing hours. I doubt that many local residents go there anymore.

Fast food franchises and big commercial outlets have drained business away from the friendly mom-and-pop restaurants and stores that I remember, and most of them have disappeared. So much for nostalgia!

Maybe it's a blessing that we really can't go back to recapture our pasts. After all, what's so bad about the present?

As wonderful as those memories are, they don't offer the vitality and excitement of anticipation that we experience in our current lives. The past is like a marvelous book we have already read. We have enjoyed it and learned from it. And perhaps some new discoveries are revealed when we read it again.

One of those lessons is probably that we can't ever go back.

Another is that *home* is really where we live among people who still need us and events that we are still part of.

Let the ashes fall where they will.

Our National Treasures

I HAVE HAD the great fortune to travel extensively and to enjoy close friendships in many countries. These opportunities have opened my eyes to discover great beauty in people and cultures that had once only been foreign caricatures in my mind.

Interestingly, a number of my international friends who have visited the United States for the first time have told me the same thing about us. And while my travel experiences have immensely deepened my appreciation of wonderful advantages and privileges we often take for granted, they have also made me more aware of some parodies and paradoxes in the images we communicate abroad.

Viewed from an international perspective, we North Americans are sometimes difficult to understand, and sometimes even harder to be around. We are friendly, open and enthusiastic people who have a tremendous amount of pride which can be interpreted as arrogance.

It is evident that we regard our country to be the greatest on the globe: the most democratic and free; the wealthiest and most powerful; the most scientifically and technologically advanced; the most creative and productive; the most righteous and generous; the model for all others to follow.

On the other hand, we are preoccupied with enormous problems that constantly erode our sense of well-being. Included are: crime and violence; deteriorating public education standards; rampant drug and alcohol abuse; poorly served indigent and homeless populations, growing cost burdens of quality health care; and chronic national underemployment.

Meanwhile, popular print and broadcast media bombard world audiences with unflattering snapshots of our national character which desensitize us to these contradictions. We abhor human abuse and violence, yet reward entertainment sponsors who produce extreme examples featured to sell movie tickets, attract television viewers and market video games.

We exalt personal liberty. Yet, at the same time, we respond complacently as we are asked to support new laws and regulations that limit choices on the assumption that career politicians and appointed bureaucrats know more about what we need and exercise better judgment to achieve it than we do. We love peace and liberty, but forget that those benefits which have been purchased at the expense of countless lives sacrificed must be preserved with ongoing commitments.

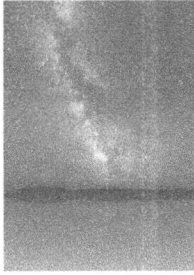

The America I Know

CHARMING NEWS PERSONALITIES compel and distract us with local and national trivia, while important yet abstract world events slip by with scant notice. We become mesmerized spectators of conditions and fictions that surround us.

Is this the way we really see ourselves? Is this the way we really are? Maybe partially, but certainly not impartially. It's not the true America I witness.

The America that I celebrate is a federation of states governed by a representative Republic which is united by shared and cherished principles enunciated in a wise founding Constitution that guarantees rights to exercise free speech and pursue bountiful treasures of liberty and happiness. If that freedom brings out the worst in some people, it brings out the best in most. Compulsion doesn't produce virtue.

The America that I believe in encourages people to dream what they can accomplish and accomplish what they can dream. This spirit rewards wise choices and risk-willingness in combination with hard work to achieve worthwhile goals. Its free enterprise legacy has produced an extraordinarily high standard of living for ordinary people. Even the poorest among us fare far better than most populations of the world.

The America that I love is a beautiful land, rich in resources, where kind, generous and environmentally conscientious people care deeply about ensuring clean air, water and land have made great progress in protecting the wellbeing of its people and ecosystems. Our natural environment is improving and people are living much healthier and longer.

The America that I honor recognizes and celebrates successes achieved through enrichment by ethnic, racial, religious and cultural diversity, social mobility, and a judicial system which aspires to provide justice for all. Learning from egregious errors of its past, the nation proudly elected a black president to lead it following abolition of slavery less than 150 years earlier.

Sure, America may not be perfect in a utopian sense, but as 19th century French historian of American governance Alexis de Tocqueville observed:

> *The greatness of America lies not in being more enlightened than any other nation, but rather in her ability to repair her faults.*

As it turned out, de Tocqueville offered another free enterprise observation that serves as a very prudent warning:

> *The American Republic will endure until the day Congress discovers that it can bribe the public with the public's money.*

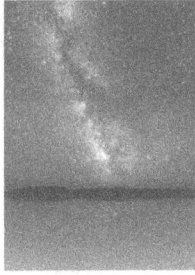

Appreciating Our Timely Advantages

ONE OF THE great things to remember about the present is all the work that has been done by others to get us here to realize the benefits. Were it not for their efforts and sacrifices, many of us would not be around at all.

Consider if you will, that if you had been born a few decades earlier, your life span and health quality would be reduced significantly. The 50-year-old U.S. life expectancy in 1900 is now about 75.

The same holds true if you had been born in other parts of the world that don't have comparable standards of medical treatment and nutrition. There is a strong possibility that you wouldn't even have survived the birth process or early childhood diseases, including some that are still around, but are no longer considered to be very serious.

If you had been fortunate enough to reach what we now envision to be *"middle age,"* (old age then and there), your prospects for prevention, early detection and recovery from heart problems, strokes, cancers and other ailments would be dramatically reduced. I, for one, would not be here to write this.

We have a lot of scientists and medical practitioners to thank for these advancements.

People of vision and courage have provided us with an American free enterprise system of government that offers unlimited possibilities to enjoy our extended and healthier lives. That system recognizes our value and rights as individuals, and provides a fertile field for seeds of progress.

It may not be possible to sense the vast breadth and depth of our advantages until we have observed life in parts of the world where they are absent or lacking. If our streets are not paved with gold, they are nevertheless paved with golden opportunities. This is demonstrated by millions of formerly oppressed and impoverished immigrants who build constructive and rewarding lives here, often in remarkably short periods of time.

The next time you are stuck in highway traffic, perhaps spend some of those moments thinking about how lucky you are. All those cars reflect the prosperity and mobility we often take for granted. Pay particular attention to those elevated cloverleaf structures that form the spaghetti bowl confusion that is frustrating when you lose your way. Realize how much work went into building them so that you could have more time at your destination.

And also, what about those incredible bridges over rivers and amazing tunnels through mountains! Think about the engineering, technology and labor that went into creating them.

Gratitude to Road Builders

OF COURSE WHEN we wish to travel significant distances, there are easier and quicker ways to go. We can simply drive or take public transportation to the nearest airport, check our baggage, and relax until we arrive a few hours later.

Other people designed and constructed those comfortable airlines and facilities for us. Imagine that it once required many weeks of perilous sea voyages at enormous personal expenses to travel to places we now go for brief holidays, and at costs which amount to what we can earn in months, days, or sometimes even less.

Only a couple of generations ago it would require many months, sometimes more than a year, to send a letter or parcel abroad and receive a reply. Think about how easy it is now. For less than it costs to buy a shirt or necktie you can send one to Japan and have it delivered to the recipient's front door in a couple of days. You can email a picture of your new baby or grandchild to that same person in seconds for free or call them to hear their voice, or Skype a visual conversation with them to include other family members and friends.

When I was young (before television), we avidly listened to radio sports announcers as they described blow-by-blow boxing matches. Now we can watch live action of all sorts from optimum vantage points in our living rooms, including real-time events which are taking place in locations around the world...even in space.

If you are more selective about information you want, (and hopefully you are), your choices are fantastic. Your daughter no longer needs to rely exclusively upon an encyclopedia or even a local library to obtain material for her report about a particular artist. Now she can access recent data, even animated images, from the Louvre in Paris and other major museums along the Information Superhighway connected to her computer and phone.

The world and neighboring parts of the Universe have been brought to our eyesight and fingertips over less than a half-century...less than a cosmic blink in the 4.5 billion year history of our planet. Imagine what the next 50 to 100 years may bring.

Isn't it exciting to be able to witness those wonders, and maybe even have opportunities to contribute in some way to new possibilities for others to follow?

Larry Bell

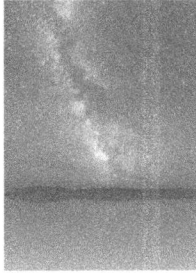

Weathering Global Climate Change

ARE WE HUMANS wrecking the climate? Hasn't it always been repeatedly changing without any help or hindrance from us?

In 2016 I sat next to a woman on a flight from Houston which began with pleasantries regarding the purposes of our trip. When asked whether mine was for business or pleasure, I said that it combined a bit of both. I explained that I was on my way to do a media interview. That led her to ask what it was that I do, to which I answered that I'm in the habit of writing quite a lot about topics that vary considerably, but frequently address stuff about climate and energy…often many politically incorrect aspects.

She asked:

> *You aren't like that guy in Ohio that doesn't believe in*
> *climate change, are you?*

I responded that I don't personally know of anyone who doesn't think that climate changes, but there may be one in Ohio that I have yet to meet. Seems to me that climate change has been going on for quite a while…billions of years in fact.

Global temperatures were at least just as warm about 2,000 years ago during the *Roman Warm Period*. Conditions were much the same again during the *Medieval Warm Period* about a thousand years later. That was when Eric the Red and his Norse pals sans-sandals, raised sheep and goats on southwestern Greenland's coastal grasslands.

Around 1350, Red's Viking descendants pulled up stakes and high-tailed it out of there for friendlier climes with the coming of a *little ice age*. That big chill lasted until shortly after Washington's troops spent a brutally cold winter at Valley Forge in 1777, and Napoleon's beat a frigid retreat from Moscow in 1812.

Incidentally, the warming that followed began before the Industrial Revolution brought CO_2-belching smokestacks and SUVs, and has continued in fits-and-starts ever since.

Still, U.S. temperatures between 1910 through the mid-1940s were warmer than now, and then cooled again for about three decades. By the late 1700s many "climate experts" heralded the arrival of the next real ice age. That alarm vector reversed entirely about a decade later when Senator Al Gore's steamy 1988 Senate hearings concluded that the planet is on fire, and that we are the guilty culprits.

She: *We must be. How can anyone deny the influence of the record levels of CO_2 we are polluting the atmosphere with?*

Me: *Satellite temperature records which have been available only since 1979 show that other than naturally-occurring 1998 and 2015 El Nino temperature spikes, no statistically significant global warming has occurred for nearly two decades.*

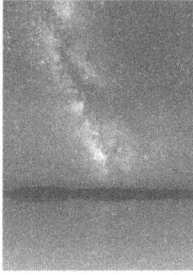

A Politically Incorrect Conversation—Continued

Me: *On the other hand, satellite imagery shows that the plant-fertilizing CO_2 "pollution" you referred to has increased global greening by 25 to 50 percent since then...lots more veggies for all God's creatures.*

She: *Then why are glaciers melting faster than ever, and causing oceans to rise and coastlines to flood?*

Me: *Yes, the Arctic, which goes through regular 60 to 70 year-long warming and cooling cycles, has most recently been losing some ice mass, while most of the vastly larger Antarctic continent has been gaining.*

A National Academy of Sciences report attributes a primary cause of those thunderous West Antarctic Ice Sheet iceberg collapses we often see featured in the media to geothermal heat from seabed volcanoes below. This coastal melting has been operating at time scales of hundreds to thousands of years.

There's also no reason for feverishly overheated concern regarding glacial melting causing a rapid sea level rise. It's another natural phenomenon that has been occurring over eons. The rate of that increase has stabilized over the past few hundred years at about 7 inches per century.

She: *Why then are increasingly frequent and severe weather events occurring which scientists predict will become even worse? How can you possibly claim that we aren't causing all of this to happen?*

Me: *If we are, might we then also take some credit for good news too?*

No category 3-5 hurricanes have struck the US coast since October 2005, a record century-long lull since 1900. There has been no recorded increase in the severity or frequency of floods, droughts, thunderstorms or tornadoes in recent decades either.

She: *Well what about all of the real climate scientists who say otherwise? Al Gore got the Nobel Peace Prize for telling us differently. Do you think you are smarter?*

Me: *I admitted to real professional limitations on that last point. Being more a rocket scientist than true climate scientist like him, I falsely assumed he got the award for inventing the Internet along with an Oscar for his sensationally dramatic science fiction horror movie acting performance.*

That abruptly ended our chat. My seatmate promptly returned to reading a *Rolling Stone* Bernie Sanders feature and the rest of that flight was very quiet.

I even got some sleep.

Worlds of Possibilities

We are citizens of a tiny global village that faces daunting problems and challenges. The only possible future is one we will all realize together.

Observations from Space

MY ASTRONAUT AND cosmonaut friends all seem to share common personal reflections regarding their views of Earth from space. They are deeply moved by how beautiful our blue planet looks set remotely in a vast field of darkness.

They are also struck by how fragile and vulnerable it appears. The thin life-supporting layer of atmosphere that surrounds it is proportionately no more than the skin of a grapefruit. Erosion of topsoil caused by land clearing can be easily observed as it infiltrates rivers and seas. Deserts are visible in areas that once contained lush vegetation...changes brought about by deforestation, poor conservation and agricultural practices, and other human land use impacts.

It is clear that we all share a tiny global village. We breathe

the same air and depend upon the same oceans as our primary life resources.

Current technologically avoidable nuclear accidents and true pollutants, (not the bogusly misrepresented and vital plant-nourishing carbon dioxide "climate pollution"), know no nationally or politically defined boundaries of consequence. They cannot be compartmentalized by high walls that separate land areas, divide the oceans or extend into space to protect us from our neighbors.

At the same time, no single technological innovation, however dramatic, will offer a cure. No nation alone controls the intellectual or financial resources to develop and implement effective remedies. And no society acting alone enjoys a monopoly on the moral wisdom and character that authorizes them to impose drastic solutions upon others.

Add to this that it is human nature, not the infinitely broader cosmic variety, which embodies both mankind's greatest threat and hope. It may be instructive to remember that international space programs and developments were born out of the ashes of war...the German V-2 buzz bomb attacks on London during World War II. Those terrors have since expanded with intercontinental missiles topped with nuclear warheads deployable to planet-wide targets.

A more encouraging view of mankind's presence in space is mentioned in my recent book Beyond Flagpoles and Footprints coauthored with Apollo XI Astronaut Buzz Aldrin (Stairway Press, 2017). Global audiences watched on July 17, 1975 as TV images showed Soviet Cosmonauts Alexi Leonov and Valery Kubasov shake hands with NASA Astronauts Thomas Stafford, Vance Brand and Donald (Deke) Slayton high above the Atlantic Ocean.

Global Perils and Promise

THE HISTORIC DOCKING of an American Apollo Command and Service Module (CSM) and Russian Soyuz vehicle joined two habitats and crews together which had been launched from distant continents within two hours of each other two days earlier. One had departed from the Kennedy space Center in Florida…the other from the Baikonur Cosmodrome in Kazakhstan.

The political timing of that Apollo-Soyuz mission was no accident, highlighting a new policy of détente, a symbolic act of peace between superpowers. The US was engaged in a Vietnam ground war at the time, and Russia's adversarial proxy involvement in the conflict added to Cold War tensions.

Buzz, a former F-86 Sabre pilot who in 1952 shot down two Mig-15s over near the Yalu River, observes:

> *In Korea we knew we were really fighting the Soviets as well as the North Koreans, and a strong sense of competition on our part carried into the space race. We were determined not to let the 'Ruskies' beat us in Korea, and we certainly weren't going to let them get the upper hand in space.*

Buzz later realized: *It's high time now to raise our vision and commitment to loftier, more far-reaching goals.*

Soviet leader Leonid Brezhnev shifted his previously hostile public position to extol peaceful diplomatic benefits of the Apollo-Soyuz experiment, and by extension, its importance to global cooperation in space to make the world safer. He providently said:

> *The Soviet and American spacemen will go up into space for the first major joint scientific experiment in the history of mankind. They know that from outer space our planet looks even more beautiful. It is big enough for us to live peacefully on it, but is too small to be threatened by nuclear war.*

That joint U.S.-Russian space mission was to be the last flight for an Apollo spacecraft and also the last manned U.S. space mission until America's first Space Shuttle launch in 1981. The diplomatic and technical Apollo-Soyuz experiment paved the way for future Shuttle-Mir Space Station and International Space Station programs that followed. Humankind's brief international experiments with space development and exploration reflect and project conflicting prospects of peril and promise. Our wisdom and willingness to confront great challenges will shape national and global progress, influence individual qualities of life and opportunity and determine the substantive value of lessons and legacies bequeathed to future generations.

The good news is that as the new millennium is well positioned to take advantage of a mutually recognized urgency of cooperation between former superpower enemies. Together with all willing nations we must work in space and on Earth to ensure that our tiny, interconnected global village is a peacefully sustainable place to live.

Lessons from Extreme Environments

THE SASAKAWA INTERNATIONAL Center for Space Architecture (SICSA), a research and teaching entity I established at the University of Houston, conducts planning and design for human facilities and operations in space, polar stations, offshore underwater and surface locations, natural and man-caused disaster areas, and other extreme environments.

SICSA is funded in part by interest profits yielded from a large endowment gift granted by the Japan Shipbuilding Industry Foundation headed at that time by the late philanthropist Mr. Ryoichi Sasakawa (now renamed the Nippon Foundation). Other financial support is provided by grants and contracts from public and corporate entities in the US. Some of that money finances SICSA's globally recognized and unique degree-granting Graduate Program in Space Architecture within the UH Cullen College of Engineering.

In 1990, soon after the collapse of the Soviet Union opened borders to visiting academics, I made arrangements through a Russian friend to take twelve of my students to Moscow for meetings with government and academic professionals who shared similar interests.

In addition to special discussions with representatives at several space and polar organizations, my colleague, Olga Zakharova, also organized a joint seminar titled Architecture in Extreme Environments that was held at the USSR Union of Architects headquarters. Participants included leading experts from many fields, including aerospace engineering, architecture and construction, energy, environmental sciences, medicine and others. Their backgrounds involved a variety of environments and problems, including areas which had been impacted by the Chernobyl nuclear disaster.

It became apparent that most of the very same priorities and ideas we had been addressing in the US paralleled theirs in the former USSR. They wanted to examine ways to advance peaceful human space exploration and apply scientific and technological spin-offs to improve conditions on Earth. They shared our concerns about impacts of technology and development upon the condition and future of natural environments and ecosystems. They were highly motivated to discover more efficient and effective energy and housing answers to meet the needs of their people.

Many of the participants presented studies they had conducted, as well as theoretical proposals and experiences with projects they had implemented. We were impressed by several of the innovative solutions they revealed to us, and were also surprised when some were similar to concepts we had pursued.

Connecting Global Minds and Solutions

IT BECAME OBVIOUS to all of us that since extreme environments pose difficult problems, they often motivate science and technology advancements that can benefit all environments. We all concluded that by working together, we might help prevent our entire planet from becoming an extreme environment.

In 1991, my Russian host joined me in co-chairing a much larger extreme environment conference that was held at the University of Houston. Called the *International Design for Extreme Environments Assembly* (IDEEA One). That four-day event attracted strong international and interdisciplinary participation, involving more than 400 attendees from a dozen countries to share experiences and ideas. Approximately 250 scientific and technical papers were presented and later published in a report containing nearly 1,000 pages.

The Houston IDEEA One conference led to other international exchanges. A second conference, IDEEA Two, took place in Montreal in 1993, where again many valuable experiences and provocative ideas were exchanged.

That meeting, along with subsequent events stimulated many cooperative relationships between public, corporate and institutional organizations by providing forums where professionals of like interests can discover and network with each other.

Our participation through SICSA, for example, has resulted in international student and faculty workshops and exchange programs that still continue. One is a graduate-level program co-sponsored by SICSA, the Rice University Baker institute for Public Policy, and the aerospace college of Bauman State Technical University that takes place in Moscow every summer.

Global cooperation to solve common problems is imperative.

As political scientist John Bryson noted:

> *We're all sleeping on a water bed, and we're not alone in that bed. When anybody moves in bed, we all wake up.*

I will add that the time has come to wake up to this fact.

Larry Bell

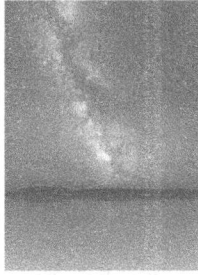

Living beyond Earth

A VERY FORTUITOUS invitation to a 1985 Tokyo meeting with Japanese philanthropist arranged by my astronaut friend Colonel Jerry Carr, Commander of America's 84-day-long 1973-74 Skylab-4 mission has led to the realization of a personal dream which has fundamentally impacted the lives and career paths of many others.

During the course of that discussion I suggested a need for an international academic institution dedicated to advancing peaceful and beneficial development and applications of space and space technology. Thanks to Mr. Sasakawa's concurrence and generosity, an organization named in his honor is accomplishing those goals.

Founded in 1987, the University of Houston's Sasakawa International Center for Space Architecture is the world's only advanced degree-granting program of its kind and a recognized leader in research, planning and design of space missions and habitats.

A central key SICSA priority is to educate diverse groups of students, including those who are previously non-space and from new-in-space faring nations, about emerging space development opportunities including Earth-orbital initiatives and joint human and robotic exploration of the Moon and Mars. In doing so, it introduces and engages participants in holistic, big picture problem-solving approaches as well as detailed conceptual design practices.

Technologies and approaches derived from space are often transferrable for beneficial Earth applications. Important examples include enhanced energy applications, advanced materials, and building construction technologies. Many lessons are particularly applicable to extreme environments, including offshore surface and underwater facilities, polar research stations and emergency accommodations for natural and human-caused disasters.

SICSA's three-semester-long MS Space Architecture curriculum is designed to inspire those next generations of innovators and explorers for opportunities and challenges presented by emerging government and commercial development initiatives. An interdisciplinary and multi-environmental emphasis attracts graduate students with backgrounds that include aerospace and mechanical engineering, architecture and industrial design, human factors and biomedical fields.

Larry Bell

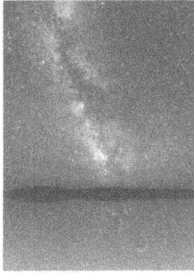

Architectures in Space

THE MS SPACE Architecture designation as a Science, Technology and Math (STEM) program signifies SICSA's commitment to support local, state and national high-technology workforce goals. Courses prioritize awareness and connectedness of widely ranging needs and issues gained through comprehensive project-focused activities. Practical hands-on experiences stimulate creative yet also practical approaches which are applicable to address complex challenges anywhere.

Program activities include diverse research, planning and design studies connected with Earth-orbiting space stations, crew and cargo transit vehicles for missions beyond Earth, and human facilities for the Moon and Mars. Special emphases are directed to requirements and means to enhance human comfort and safety throughout all aspects and phases of construction and operations.

SICSA's unique programs and activities draw upon expansive and diverse space science and advanced technology resources within the university and Houston region which includes the NASA Johnson Space Center and its industry network. Recognizing much to share and learn, SICSA constantly works to establish mutually beneficial relationships with other national and international institutions.

After more than four decades of abandonment, the Moon remains waiting for a return...this time by international explorers conducting experiments and possibly harvesting surface resources (including water) in preparation for future habitation on Mars.

Space exploration and development presents complex challenges. Examples include: the design and testing of advanced spacecraft propulsion systems to deliver people, equipment and supplies to those remote places; special high- capacity landers to deploy them on the surfaces; habitats and rovers to safely support crews over extended periods; means for radiation protection, particularly during solar storms; technologies for surface mining and processing of useful materials; and an endless variety of other essentials.

Such developments will provide enormous career opportunities for new generations of competently prepared innovators. I believe that SICSA will offer important ongoing contributions to help these adventuresome space pioneers succeed.

Larry Bell

Buzz Aldrin's New World Vision

BUZZ ALDRIN, MY friend over a time span surpassing four decades, is without doubt the most passionate advocate for space exploration and development—Mars in particular—that I have ever encountered. Even more, he continues to tirelessly devote his life, experience-based knowledge and bold creativity to make that happen.

Buzz believes that another space race back to the Moon would be counterproductive. Instead, the U.S. should chart a course toward global leadership without huge expenditures of taxpayer money to put and support people there. America's primary lunar focus should be to put robots on the surface for scientific, commercial and other private sector work.

Lunar science and development should optimize use of automation for hazardous jobs in combination with the perception, dexterity, versatility and innovation afforded by humans. Many lessons and technologies can draw upon routine uses in other extreme environments such as deep-sea pipeline maintenance operations applying high-definition video cameras, sensors and manipulators.

The Moon will provide an excellent place to practice and perfect these technologies and operational techniques on Mars, undertaking activities to scout out mining opportunities, pre-position and connect large equipment elements, and conduct tasks that would present dangers to surface crews.

Buzz proposes that a "Global Low Earth Orbit Lunar Coalition" be created to combine mutually beneficial international cost and service-sharing efforts in a manner similar to the 16-partner International Space Station arrangement.

Coalition organization and operations can also draw instructive government-to-government lessons from a successful history of international programs in Antarctica. The U.S. has interacted with other nations on that continent since 1956 with visiting exchanges of researchers involved in glaciology, biology, medicine, geology, oceanography, astronomy and astrophysics.

A recently established Aldrin Space Institute at the Florida Institute of Technology in Melbourne, Florida is working to advance student and professional interest and research that will support commercial and international development of lunar resources and promote eventual Mars settlement.

Headed by his son, former director of strategic planning for Boeing's NASA Systems Division, Dr. Andrew Aldrin, the Institute actively collaborates with faculty, researchers and students at other institutions including the University of Houston's SICSA.

Larry Bell

Cycling to Mars

AS WITH AIRLINES that don't throw away their airplanes upon reaching destinations, Buzz is the inventor of an interplanetary *Aldrin Cyclers* which will glide endlessly along space expressways within the inner Solar System. This approach is conceived to afford major cost economies over traditionally proposed one-shot Mars launch approaches by efficiently taking advantage of gravitational forces of the Earth and Moon to sustain the special orbit trajectory.

Such a network can form a celestial tract between worlds to support a constant flow of space science, and commerce. The idea is somewhat analogous to cruise ships that drop off and take on passengers without pulling into harbor, except that Cyclers don't stop when they fly by Earth. Instead, passengers access the spacecraft via speedy space taxis that intercept them.

Imagine that it's like running fast to catch a slow bus that repeats the same rout over and over. In this case, one must travel very, very fast to catch that space bus. Intercepting it from Earth requires a rendezvous velocity of about 6 kilometers per second (13,400 mph).

The Aldrin Cycler uses a special trajectory between Earth and Mars which enables crew and cargo transfers every two Earth-

Mars synodic periods (approximately every 4 2/7 years), with one intermediate Earth fly-by. By using two Cyclers, the frequency of Earth-Mars encounters for back and forth crew and cargo transfer opportunities is reduced to about 2 1/7 years.

Buzz acutely recognizes that bold plans demand bold commitments to the future. As he emphasizes in our co-authored book *Beyond Footprints and Flagpoles*:

> *We are at an important inflection point in human history. The decision is whether to look upwards and gain strength from vision and commitment to worthy goals beyond ourselves—beyond the here and now.*

That future will also depend upon national leaders with bold visions. Unfortunately, Buzz observes:

> *In my frequent travels around the world, I observe with sad irony that American leadership in space is appreciated more in foreign lands than it is within our own country. Many people I meet ask why we should invest huge sums of money going to space at times when there are so many important serious problems and needs at home.*

Buzz then reminds us who we really are:

> *My friends, there always have been such problems and needs, and there always will be. Great nations, great people, have always faced them, confronted them and triumphed over them. That is the bold spirit and confidence that made them great. That is the true character that defines America.*

Exploring Far Horizons

BUZZ ALDRIN BELIEVES Mars represents a new world destination of opportunity and discovery. He reflects:

> *It has been flown by, orbited, smacked into, radar-examined, rocketed onto, bounced upon, rolled over, shoveled, drilled into, baked, and even laser-blasted. Still to come: Mars being stepped upon. The first footfalls will mark a historic milestone.*

Buzz urges that those first Mars footsteps should lead a path to permanent presence. He adamantly argues that "success at Mars cannot stop with one-shot forays to the surface." This philosophy is far different from Apollo expeditions to the Moon where voyagers do some experiments, plant a flag, and then claim success.

Buzz is painfully aware that his views regarding permanent human presence are considered by many to be very radical, if not simply controversial and a political hard sell. He notes that a common response to this idea is: "Lifetime trips to Mars? That's a big pill to swallow!"

Nevertheless, he asks those skeptics to consider:

After investing billions and billions of dollars of world assets in getting them there, why have them turn around and rocket back homeward?

Having them go to the Red Planet and repeat this, in his view, is senseless. Since great distance between Mars and Earth makes a feasible return timing window very narrow, it makes far more sense to transport people there who plan to stay.

Buzz emphasizes:

When you go to Mars, you need to have made the decision to go there permanently.

In his view, having them repeat their voyages is dim-witted.

Why not allow them to stay there? Did the pilgrims on the Mayflower sit around Plymouth Rock waiting for a return trip? They came to settle. And that's what we should be doing on Mars.

As exemplified in the popular movie *The Martian*, preparations for long-term survival far beyond Earth lifelines pose a variety of innovation challenges. The new settlers will require an ability to live off the land, a circumstance that 102 other adventuresome souls once faced upon leaving England for a previous New World onboard a Mayflower voyage.

Permanent Mars settlers will be 21st century pilgrims, pioneering a new way of life. That will indeed take a special kind of person. Instead of the traditional pilot/scientist/engineer, Martian homesteaders must be selected more for their personalities…flexible, inventive and determined in the face of unpredictability. In short, they will be the survivors of a two-planet species.

Planetary Pilgrims

MARTIAN SETTLERS, HOWEVER, will face much stiffer challenges. As illustrated in the popular movie, a crop failure could bring disastrous consequences. Survival will challenge ingenuity and adaptability to evaluate and respond in real-time situations…to improvise, and to prevail over surprises.

The Mars settlers will quite certainly be immigrants from many Earth nations whose success will depend upon substantial international scientific, technological and economic investment. Much research is needed to develop and test unique facilities, equipment and methods to grow crops such as potatoes, beans, and wheat in the thin Martian atmosphere. This challenging area of study should involve scientific collaborations with Russia, China and other countries that are known to share this interest.

Means will also need to be provided that enable the new pilgrims to live "off the land" to the greatest extent possible in order to minimize costly Earth resupply dependencies.

One good candidate resource-rich destination is the Cebrenia quadrangle site located in the northeastern portion of Mars. NASA's Mars Orbiter Laser Altimeter satellite surveys indicate that this location contains water ice about 4 inches below the surface, plus soils with an abundance of silicon, iron, magnesium, sulfur, calcium and titanium.

Space radiation shielding will be required to protect crews and equipment from dangers posed by solar flare emissions during long journeys outside the Earth's protective magnetosphere and atmosphere. Possible solutions might apply solar storm shelters using Mars-sourced water (which contains hydrogen) and other indigenous shielding materials.

Inevitably, Mars settlement will invoke risks and casualties, just as other pioneering ventures have. As Buzz somberly points out:

> *Unfortunately, pioneers will always pave the way with sacrifices. Over the decades, we have lost numbers of individuals—several of them close personal friends of mine—all intent on pushing the boundaries of exploration and seeking new horizons. Risk and reward is the weighing scale of exploring and taming space.*

So why do it? Why accept these enormous challenges and risks?

A NASA report observes:

> *...a strong motivating factor for the exploration of Mars is the search for extraterrestrial life.*

Maybe what we will discover there is us. Maybe what we will discover are human potentials that we can now only dream about.

Choosing Relevant Realities

We can choose to see our personal world any way we wish...both from the inside out and from the outside in. We also have the power to change it through our priorities and vision.

Recognizing Where We Are

HOW WE VIEW ourselves and the world we are part of depends upon our point of view regarding where we imagine ourselves standing.

The Austrian-born philosopher Ludwig Wittgenstein observed that just as the eye, which is the source of the visual field but not in that visual field cannot see itself, so is the "I" which is the source of our consciousness.

As I discuss in my book *Cosmic Musings*, this condition is analogous to a GEICO insurance commercial, where we see a gecko lizard character walking through a stone tunnel towards an opening. When he approaches it, we witness him looking out searching for Mount Rushmore from the entrance connection in one of George Washington's eyes. He was unaware of this from the inside. Such tunnel vision can often obscure glaring realities in life that surrounds us. Looking from our place in the world from the outside, we often view ourselves through mirrored images and filters that present other misconceptions. A passage in William Shakespeare's Julius Caesar tells us:

> But by reflection, by some other things...And since you
> cannot see yourself so well as by reflection, I, your
> glass, will modestly discover to yourself that of yourself
> which know not of.

There are many people around you who will happily volunteer to be your mirrors, whether you invite them or not. Choose them wisely, and trust them cautiously from world perspectives which take into account where they happen to be standing as well.

Plato's Phaedo likens our limited understanding by which we perceive the world as analogous to prisoners chained in a cave since childhood. Their sense of reality is shaped by watching vague shadows projected dimly from flames onto a wall which they believe to be coming from outside. They have no way to understand that those shadows are actually being cast by showmen carrying objects and puppets behind the wall that they are chained to.

The shadow forms of perception in Plato's allegory are both non-physical and non-mental, actually existing nowhere in time, space, mind, or matter. They form our limited and often misguided understandings of the outside world and our places within it.

Aristotle argued that in order for animals to perceive and for humans to reason, perfect copies rather than shadows of forms are required. He reasoned that the human mind can literally assume any form being contemplated or experienced, and is unique in its ability to become a blank slate with no essential form.

Views from Mount Rushmore

PLATO AND ARISTOTLE both influenced writings of Saint Thomas Aquinas during the early Middle Ages which has been integrated into Roman Catholic doctrine. Like Aristotle, Aquinas perceived the human being as a unified substance embodying two substantial principles: form and matter.

During the mid-17th century, the dualism philosophy of Rene Descartes envisioned the perceptive and spiritual mind as a non-physical as a nonphysical substance capable of consciousness and self-awareness separate from the brain as the seat of intelligence. In his *Meditations of First Philosophy* he writes that while he could doubt whether he had a body (it could be a dream or illusion created by an evil demon), he could not doubt that he had a mind.

Descarte's mind was perceived as a "thinking thing" with the essence of himself with doubts, beliefs, hopes, and contemplates. This led to his best known philosophical statement; "Cognito ergo sum", or "I think, therefore I am."

So, is reality and self-perception truly in our minds? In a physiological sense the answer appears to be largely "yes."

While we depend upon our biological preceptors to inform us about what is "real," such realities are really just convenient illusions. Although we tend to think that stones are hard, snow is cold, and grass is green, laws of physics inform us otherwise.

Everything that we perceive as hard is composed of energetic stuff that has no solidity at all. The temperature we sense is but specific electromagnetic frequencies and wavelengths detected by neurons and calibrated by our brains to inform us about our surroundings.

Color perception is an interpretive phenomena as well. Yellow light, for example, describes transversal electromagnetic wavelengths in the neighborhood of 590 nanometers.

Those images we see in front of us are actually illusory constructs which are assembled behind our eyes in our material brains. The sensory impressions of taste and smell depend upon specialized chemical receptors that differentiate between presence of different molecules or ions. Hearing, a mechanical process, relates to how our brains interpret various vibrations within our audio detectors when something moves air around.

So just go ahead, enjoy those illusions, and above all, imagine something nice about where you are.

Expanding Opportunities in a Shrinking World

THE WORLD SEEMS to be a lot smaller today than it appeared not so many years ago. For one thing, the airplanes that carry us around are bigger and faster, even though the meals haven't always kept pace. And just about all of the populated places that we can imagine are connected together by meaningful electromagnetic wave signals that bounce off satellites orbiting 22,300 miles overhead.

Unlike the Stone Age era when I was a child, we can now exchange all kinds of information—even images of our latest cave paintings—over long distances without the effort required to transport those big rocks. It's remarkable that our early civilization even survived before the new era of cellular telephones, television, computers and a World Wide Web instantly connected us with global hilarities and horrors.

Yes, if his invention of global warming wasn't spectacular enough, Al Gore really outdid himself when he came up with the Internet. Being swept up in its midst, it's difficult to conceive how rapidly and expansively this transformative technology revolution has already altered broad aspects of our daily lives, much less how it will continue to shape our future.

Orbiting satellites have erased communication boundaries, spawning a world-wide information-sharing network which enables anyone with an inexpensive hand-held device to conduct personal and business transactions from nearly anywhere. E-mail, texting, Facebook, Twitter, Skype and many other platforms immediately connect us without geographical limits.

Applications are expanding exponentially; professionals and amateurs have formed information exchange networks around special interests of every conceivable nature; job-seekers and employers have established specialized matches, as have student applicants and academic institutions; small product and service providers have accessed the global marketplace; and singles have found compatible, life-long partners. We looked, we found each other, and we expanded our outreach beyond anything imaginable even a decade ago.

More and more entrepreneurs and other professionals are now telecommuting from homes or other locations of choice based upon various business, family and personal preferences, conserving time and fuel costs in the process that would otherwise be spent on crowded freeways. Parents are afforded more quality and supervisory time with their children in value-priced suburban and rural neighborhoods with schools and other amenities that best meet their needs.

Connecting with the Internet

EVEN LARGER CORPORATIONS can now decentralize management operations and/or relocate to outlying areas where lower land costs, employee labor rates and taxes offer strong attractions. Corporations can conduct meetings with overseas divisions, affiliates and clients from local facilities; scientific and technical organizations can hold workshops and conferences from distributed locations; and academic organizations can extend distance learning opportunities to remote and economically-challenged populations.

Small hand-held devices now enable us save time and money shopping for items with best prices and terms from limitless sources. Telecommunications and teleconferencing are reducing needs for national and international business and professional travel time and expenses.

Immediate on-line information services are replacing print media at a spectacular rate. Consider the impacts upon pulp companies which provide the newsprint and higher-grade paper for the many billions of daily, weekly and monthly newspapers and magazines that arrive at our homes and markets with dated information.

There are also costs required to deliver that paper to the

presses, transport the countless tons of finished product to distribution centers, and deliver smaller batches and individual pieces to points of sale and residences. All of this, of course, consumes energy...power to cut down trees, process pulp, print the publications...and fuel to haul the raw materials and finished parcels by truck, rail, air and van to readers.

Now add more fuel and power needed to recycle or dispose of the countless tons of paper after we read or ignore most of those news, entertainment and ever-growing advertising content. Come to think of it, with electronic options available today, it's difficult to imagine a more economically-obsolete scenario.

We can be certain that the Internet revolution will continue to change the world in ways we can't presently imagine, and very likely, do so for the better.

Perhaps the greatest gift is to connect all members of our planetary community with clearer understandings of common values that can bring us together...bonds of peaceful and mutually beneficial possibilities that make future wars unthinkable.

It becomes difficult to conceive of foreign societies as enemies after coming to know and share personal friendships with one or more of their citizens. Perhaps think of the Internet as technology with a human face. Use the opportunity to take a selfie, send it to someone far away, and request that they return the favor.

Experiencing Our Children

NO EXPERIENCE IN my life comes close to being as marvelous or challenging as the process of being a parent. How can anyone be prepared for such a responsibility?

There we are, selfish and independent individuals in a hedonistic partner relationship, and suddenly a new person pops out, takes over, and immediately starts to make demands. They may look innocent and helpless, but have no doubt about it, they know how to assert control from the git-go.

You immediately realize that your personal life has gone down the tubes as soon as you see the beautiful glow on your partner's face as they hold the little critter. Forget about anything else you might have had in mind for the next couple of decades or so; all plans are off until further notice.

Remarkably, you may even come to admit to yourself that everything you thought was important before. Free time, tranquility and spousal attention can wait. Like it or not (and you probably do), you have just been transported at warp speed into a whole new era.

Driving home from the hospital with our first tiny triumph bundled all snugly, I tried to imagine what he was thinking as he witnessed sunshine, trees, birds, cars and other wonders for the first time. This was clearly a historic event: ground zero; square one; the beginning of a great human adventure.

I felt greatly honored to share his discoveries. Like an anxious host receiving an important foreign Head of State, I hoped that he approved of what he saw. I looked forward to showing him much more.

Similar realizations attended the birth of our second son nearly two years later, with two notable exceptions. By that time, we had absolutely no illusions about returning to our pre-parent lifestyle in the foreseeable future. Yet we did not anticipate another big change that was in store for us. Now we were not only parents, but also peace negotiators and dispute arbitrators as heated battles were waged with the regularity of a goat in a plum orchard.

Being loved by a child is a joy that can make all other achievements in life pale by comparison. I doubt that any elixir known to mankind can match the rejuvenating power of their hugs and kisses when our morale is dragging, even when they are the cause. These gifts are also pretty great when they mature to ages when overt signs of affection between males are inhibited by social norms associated with rites of passage into adulthood.

Larry Bell

Unfamiliar Voices on the Telephone

ONE OF THE selfish advantages that being with children affords is the opportunity to vicariously experience childhood again. We must recognize, however, that it is their childhood, not a return to our own, that we are observing.

Their world is very different now, in large part due to special circumstances that we have worked hard to create for them. Do they appreciate our efforts? Probably deep down they do, but are too angry at us to show it much of the time. In any case, they have their own problems to deal with, including our own unreasonable expectations for them.

Our family like most has survived a lot of basic child-rearing experiences. We have endured the teasing, fighting, yelling and flatulence. We have contracted an impressive variety of contagious maladies that our children have brought into our home, and have contributed to retirement accounts of numerous doctors, dentists and orthodontists.

We have attended endlessly long PTA meetings, squeezed our bodies into little desk chairs at school open house functions, and participated in other obligatory institutional rituals.

We have clapped with pride when our boys appeared in school plays as trees and bumblebees, ministered to bruised knees and egos following sports events, and thrilled at treasures they made for us in art classes.

We have suffered their impatience on long car trips, cajoled and assisted with homework, dressed them for Halloween , and marveled at how fine they looked (or didn't) on their way to school dances.

We have laughed with them, played with them, argued with them, and even more frequently, worried about them.

It's difficult to comprehend how quickly time passes. One day we are introducing the world to a newborn baby, and sooner than we can imagine, that person is revealing new aspects of that world to us through their own perceptive observations.

Or we one day call home and hear an unfamiliar voice which, as we soon realize, now belongs to a son. Soon they will leave us and we can return to our original plans. If only we can remember what they were.

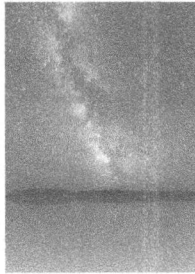

Unconditional Caring

IF YOU ACCEPT the premise that trust is a transaction, caring about someone or something can be a fine way to earn that trust. Yet when we truly care, we often do so without any external motives at all. Caring, as with parenting, is something most of us do at one level or another nearly all of the time.

The ability to care is both our greatest human gift and reward. It is most rewarding when there are no conditions and we expect nothing back in return. We care because we care. It is as simple as that.

We support charities because we care that they help people who need support.

We care about the natural environment because it holds the future.

We care about animals and other creatures because we are capable of being kind.

We care about our parents because we love them.

We care about our children because we feel responsible for them and they represent our unselfish hopes and dreams.

We care about lovers and friends because they have touched our lives.

Though basic levels of caring come naturally, people seem to get better at it with practice. Most parents and teachers become very skilled at it. So do many who take care of people who are old, infirmed, and others requiring special help. Sometimes caring is expressed at heroic levels, for example when someone donates a kidney, or when a soldier risks or forfeits his life for a buddy.

What causes us to care about others? Maybe it's partly influenced by our *dermal permeability*—the extent that we allow them to get under our skin. We may not always want to, and possibly don't always even like them very much. Yet somehow they get our attention, we open up, and they penetrate inside of us.

Maybe this sometimes begins when we feel that we owe them something and are obligated. Perhaps they are lovers and friends that we have been close to. Or perhaps they are just people who need help and we respond to their problems. Whatever the circumstances, we become involved, and they become important parts of our lives.

Some people protect themselves from involvements by striving to remain independent of demanding relationships and commitments that might take control. If they want to go to the same Chinese restaurant four nights in a row, why not? There is no one that they need to negotiate with. Should they decide to take off for a month-long tour of Brazilian bat caves—who cares? No one else will be affected.

Transcending Ourselves

YET TOTAL FREEDOM and independence come at a price. Their potential value to others is diminished, and they become more dispensable.

Of course, caring imposes costs too. There will often be times when we are compelled to put someone else's interests above our own. Some sacrifices may be relatively trivial, like going with them to see a really inane movie they want to see.

There are also circumstances that require major personal life adjustments. For example, deciding to attend to an incurable mentally or physically incapacitated parent in our home rather than having them institutionalized. Or encouraging someone we care a great deal about to accept a career or other lifestyle relocation opportunity that we recognize to be in their best interest, but will be seriously disadvantageous to ours.

What are the alternatives? Being self-protective can get to be pretty lonely and boring. When people concentrate most of their thoughts and energies upon getting what they think they deserve, others around them often build up defenses. A selfish attitude is worn like a garish tie that is impossible to overlook and difficult to ignore.

In business, as well as personal relationships, people put

greatest trust in those who subordinate their own private agendas to achieve the greatest benefits for a partnership. Those who succeed at the expense of others are likely to experience hollow victories and empty lives.

I have observed that people who practice caring relationships develop a habit of bringing that character into all of their endeavors. Others trust them, and for good reasons. They have developed the capacity to focus their minds and energies upon helping to create a worthwhile result for everyone rather than concentrating on ways they can receive the greatest benefit, including claiming the most credit.

Truly caring people are willing to contribute more than their share without keeping a ledger to demonstrate that they deserve more. Often they don't have to. Their generosity is usually recognized and valued by recipients who reward them far beyond their greatest expectations.

Through caring we experience life most fully.

When we permit others to become integral parts of ourselves, we become more whole.

Trusting Transactions

I BELIEVE ONE of the most valuable gifts we can bring to or receive from a relationship is trust. It's similar to issuing a credit voucher that holds the debtor responsible for repayment, using the relationship and borrower's self-respect for collateral. By issuing the voucher, the lender is demonstrating that they regard the relationship to be a worthwhile and solid investment.

How do we know if we can trust someone? One indication is their credit history. Have they defaulted on other obligations? Are they morally and ethically solvent? Have they already made significant contributions to the relationship? Are terms of agreement clearly spelled out and understood?

And when is it in our best interests to trust someone? Here are some additional factors to consider.

How vital is the deal to you? How much personal capital are you prepared to put at risk? Can you afford to lose? Are there some incremental loan agreements that can be provided to enable the borrower to establish a stronger credit line?

In my experience, all important transactions impose certain risks. Some people play it safer by simply settling for less. They want guarantees on almost everything in life, and are willing to invest little of themselves. Perhaps they have experienced serious disappointments in the past. Maybe they are just naturally suspicious and cautious. Or possibly they don't feel they have much of value that they can afford to commit.

I have observed that such people miss out on wonderful opportunities which are readily available to everyone.

Trust risks are often most difficult to accept when the stakes are highest. These large transactions typically involve commitments of our most prized assets, including our dreams, expectations, self-esteem and long-term plans. Others, such as children, may be impacted if the relationship is unsuccessful.

Sometimes people pull back from these deals because they seem to be too good to be true, electing to withdraw before they get in too deep. Sometimes we wait too long to commit, and the opportunity is lost to someone else. And sometimes they prepare so many guarantee and penalty clauses in the agreement that they scare the other principal party away.

It is also sometimes difficult to invest trust in people who have limited credit histories.

Children are a key example.

A Guide to Cost-Benefit Analyses

ON ONE HAND, we may often expect them to earn our trust before we grant it. On the other, without the currency in their credit accounts they don't learn the importance and satisfaction of repaying it.

They may occasionally disappoint us because responsibility requires practice. We must consistently, but constructively, correct them when they make mistakes, exercising care to avoid labeling them as being untrustworthy so that they don't begin to identify with that image and perpetuate irresponsible behavior. Instead, it is more useful to help children learn through earned successes by recognizing their achievements, and gradually extending their credit lines accordingly.

An even greater challenge is to help children learn how to trust wisely. It is a sad commentary upon present conditions in our society that they must be repeatedly warned about bad people who will steal and abuse their innocence if they aren't vigilant. They are constantly warned to distrust anyone they don't know (defined unilaterally as "strangers"), or risk terrifying consequences.

Children aren't the only ones who are put on alert. Epidemic outbreaks of sexually-transmitted diseases, violent crimes and predatory lawsuits are engendering a general atmosphere of suspicion and fear in our society.

Our wariness of contacts and relationships can take on a variety of forms. Examples are a prospective lover's sexual background, unfounded suspicions about a prospective business partnership or opportunity, and broad apprehensions regarding people who fall into racial, ethnic and economic categories exploited by identity politics that differ from our own.

Sadly, those years of innocence have passed for all of us.

So finally, how can we conduct cost-benefit analyses to determine when to invest in trust? I guess we have to rely heavily upon intuition along with two other important resources; intellect and courage.

Our intellect can guide us to gather available information, review our personal assets, and understand the possible upside and downside of each option.

Courage is needed to act upon a decision, one way or the other. Let intuition be your arbitrator, and if you decide to invest in a relationship, then go for broke!

Inspirations from Others

There is great beauty and wisdom all around us. None are so blind as those whose hearts and minds are closed.

Embracing Beauty and Wisdom

IMAGINE HOW BORING life would be without inspiration. Then again, where do you find it? Sometimes it sneaks up on us unannounced when we're not looking and missing it when we search in the wrong places. Sometimes it shows up within ourselves and we reflect it on others. Inspiration assumes an infinite variety of definitions and forms. The *Merriam-Webster Dictionary* describes it as: *Something that makes someone want to do something or that gives someone an idea about what to do or create.*

The *Open Dictionary* characterizes it as: *A sudden feeling of enthusiasm, or a new idea that helps you to do or create something.* According to the *Cambridge Dictionary*: *Someone or something that gives you ideas for doing something.* The *Free Dictionary* defines it as: *A sudden good idea; the excitement of the mind or emotions to a high level of feeling or activity.*

However incomplete and inadequate our attempts to define it, inspiration is something needed to fill an otherwise human void. It is something that guides our quest for understanding and practicing higher values. It is something that reveals forgotten beauty of nature and wisdom. It is something that provides examples of excellence we can aspire to and learn from, including generosity, courage, creativity, tenacity, and true life achievements. It is something that arouses our senses...something you feel when it touches you, sometimes prompting you to touch back.

Inspiration is all things we can imagine, and much, much more.

How do we recognize it?

Sometimes it arrives in our consciousness as a thunderclap of WOW! Or, as a silent, unexpected tear shed when inspiration softly touches our hearts. Sometimes it appears in the form of provident dreams upon which we construct marvelous thought castles of promise to house realities much larger than ourselves. Sometimes it is a force transmitted through bonds and connections of love and friendship that empower us...and humble us as well.

Sometimes we are its agents. Without meaning to we inspire others through shared experiences and lessons. Sometimes inspiration transforms...other times it instructs. Sometimes it enriches a moment...at others, influences a lifetime.

Oftentimes we let it inspiration find and recognize us.

It's not always auspicious...people say something honest and simple we sort of knew but needed to hear expressed more clearly. Knowing someone else sees this gives us courage to admit that maybe it's okay to share the same view. Sometimes it is discovered later with long-forgotten wisdoms remembered from others...like teachers, for example.

Open Eyes and Minds

OUR CHARISMATIC HIGH School band director, Irv Hansen, once told us: *Don't be afraid to blow a sour note...be prepared to make it a loud one everyone can hear. Otherwise, we will never make music.*

Those who know me will recognize that I continue to heed this wisdom. Yet many years later, when I reminded him of this important advice, he said he didn't remember. Maybe he just didn't want to accept blame on my behalf.

It's great to receive gifts of inspirational wisdom and thoughtfulness from others with much experience and insight to share. I will pass along a just a few that you may appreciate as I do:

> *Keep love in your heart. A life without it is like a sunless garden when the flowers are dead.*
> —Oscar Wilde
> *The best and most beautiful things in the world cannot be seen or even touched—they must be felt with the heart.*
> —Helen Keller
> *Keep your face always toward the sunshine—and shadows will fall behind you.*

—Walt Whitman

Clouds come floating into my life, no longer to carry rain or usher storm, but to add color to my sunset sky.
—Rabindranath Tagore

It's not what you look at that matters, it's what you see.
—Henry David Thoreau

If you can dream it, you can do it.
—Walt Disney

Nothing is impossible, the word itself says 'I'm possible'!
—Audrey Hepburn

Perfection is not attainable, but if we chase perfection we can catch excellence.
—Vince Lombardi

There is only one corner of the universe you can be certain of improving, and that's your own self.
—Aldous Huxley

Wherever you are—be all there.
—Jim Elliot

Be happy for this moment. This moment is your life.
—Omar Khayyam

And finally...at least for this moment...from Kevin Aucoin:

Today I choose life. Every morning when I wake up I can choose joy, happiness, negativity, pain... To feel the freedom that comes from being able to continue to make mistakes and choices—today I choose to feel life, not to deny my humanity but embrace it.

Written Words

ALTHOUGH IT'S DIFFICULT to be certain who invented writing because it occurred before patent offices were established, it really accelerated human understanding and progress.

Imagine that it had taken our early ancestors thousands of years to learn they could make a stone implement or weapon more than twice as sharp by chipping away material from both sides of the cutting edge.

Then maybe someone scratched an illustration of the idea (possibly using that wondrous stone invention) in order to take credit for conceiving it, signed his name (which might be difficult for us to properly enunciate—or grunt) using an "X", gave one of the improved spears to a friend (the first lawyer) as a bribe to help him defend his claim, and everything took off from there. This, however, is only a rocky theory.

Graphic images, which took a lot of time to draw (or scratch), became simplified into symbolic forms, and before long (in cosmic time) those symbols became so abstract and specialized that only a few people in the most elite classes could understand them. This undoubtedly suited them just fine because they realized even, then—particularly then—that information is power, and they often used it exclusively to their own advantages.

Paper and ink came along so that it became easier to record ideas, document events and communicate without the need to send graffiti-covered rocks through the mail.

Printing presses followed, and then information really began to flow, making it possible for large numbers of people to gain access.

Like all good things, everybody began to want some.

Through insurrections, social changes, and education, the general citizenry wrestled control of information away from those who had used it to exploit them, and people began to communicate more freely with one another.

Finally, some later inventors came up with ideas for photocopy machines and digital electronic data transmission, and you know the results. Our lives are buried in papers containing treasures and trivia. Our email files are jammed with male-enhancement ads and images of our grandchildren. Text messaging has reduced artful literacy to four-letter words.

I am adding to this by contributing one more book to the hardcopy and cyberspace glut.

Silent Conversations

STILL, I WILL also confess that I regard the opportunity to access virtually limitless sources of information to be an enormous privilege of our time. It's a wonderful gift to be able to read information on virtually every subject known to mankind; be stimulated by wisdom, insights and creativity of thoughtful minds; be touched by poetry; be inspired by stories of commitment and courage; be captivated by adventures and fantasies; and be entertained by observations that remind us that life can be silly and fun.

Consider how convenient it is to have information presented in a form that gives us unlimited time to digest facts, understand complicated principles, and sometimes pen notes to ourselves in the margins.

Writing has opened up new worlds to us in space and time. It enables us to communicate across oceans and continents, and connects us to minds and feelings of people who lived many generations before us with no dilution of clarity.

Literature reminds us that circumstances people have encountered everywhere and always, often parallel those in our own lives, offering lessons of wisdom, courage and compassion. Included are first-hand accounts of important ideas and events in history that are described by the very same people who created or participated in them.

Written words offer unique opportunities to communicate in a very personal way in a direct mind-to-mind level. They enable us to avoid self-consciousness and embarrassment that we may sometimes feel when we want to address private and emotional subjects and are afraid that we may perform poorly. They remove distractions caused by irrelevant physical characteristics and mannerisms of the author. They enable us to think about what is really important that we wish to share, express our thoughts carefully, and make revisions if necessary. And they leave a record which enables us to rediscover and mentally return to special moments and feelings that bring comfort and joy.

Reading is a highly valued pleasure in my life. It constantly reminds me how creative, interesting and good people are, and I am grateful when fine writers reveal products of rich experiences and imaginations.

I am flattered when someone loans or gives me a book that has particular meaning to them that they wish to share, and I enjoy extending the same recognition of caring and friendship to others. I can think of no finer gifts.

Visual Expression

EXPERIENCES WITH DESIGN and art have been important parts of my life, both as a practitioner and as one who enjoys works of others.

It may be relevant to mention that prior to founding and directing the University of Houston's Sasakawa International Center for Space Architecture, I headed the Graduate Program in Industrial Design at the University of Illinois for eight years and served on the national *Industrial Designer's Society of America* (IDSA) and on the editorial staff of *Industrial Design* magazine. My professional projects during that period included the design of automobiles, urban transportation systems, furniture, and a wide variety of other products and systems.

And yes, I am also an architect and professor, with significant experience in this design field as well...plus an endowed professor of space architecture.

Art, sculpture in particular, has been a personal passion. I have taught college-level art classes, exhibited my sculpture in numerous one-person and group shows, have been represented by an excellent Chicago gallery, and have works in public museum collections.

While I identify closely with both spheres of activity, there is a clear distinction between art and design...at least from my personal point of view.

The principal difference has to do with motivational priorities. In this frame of reference, designers must respond to special requirements attached to specific end product uses, with appropriate levels of concern for such factors as aesthetics, functional utility, user-friendliness, comfort and safety, economy of manufacture, durability and maintenance, and overall market appeal.

Artists, on the other hand, are entirely free to define their own priorities and objectives, which can be every bit as challenging and demanding.

Assessments of the quality and value that others attach to particular design and artistic creations are a different matter. Art, just like design products, is often treated as commodities, whether or not that was the intent of the artist. And if that intent influenced the artist to divert away from personal priorities I will argue that they are really practicing design.

Both art and design can be beautiful, enriching and inspiring, and I certainly do not wish to suggest that either is of greater intrinsic importance. But since I regard art to be a more personally involving subject, I prefer to share special impressions and pleasures that both have revealed to me.

Frozen Moments in Time

VISITS TO ART museums and galleries evoke many different kinds of discoveries and emotions. It is incredible to be able to witness people and scenes captured in frozen moments through drawings, paintings, photographs and three-dimensional pieces that transport me to other times and places.

It is marvelous to see great works of perceptive, imaginative and talented artists; be touched by their creativity and genius; and have opportunities to examine broad strokes and details that reveal their passion, energy, spirit, sensitivity, intelligence and skill.

It can be overwhelming to come in contact with an enormous variety of works, all assembled in proximity, that: reflect different attitudes, styles and social circumstances; some of which are quiet and contemplative; some bold and powerful; some cheerful and humorous; some dramatic and tragic; some pragmatic and noncommittal; some esoteric; some illuminating and profound; and some that challenge any interpretation or response whatsoever.

While I am very grateful that these wonderful places exist, I must also admit to occasionally having uncomfortable feelings when I see art in formal settings. One is the sensation of being in a mausoleum where the solemn, differential and pristine surroundings are excessively reverential, a condition which seems out of character with the vital and often disordered lives of those interesting people that created the works.

Visit the studio of most any artist and you will appreciate the contrast.

Highly selective deification may be interpreted to suggest that "real art" is somewhat elevated above mortal experience, rather than a product of vigorous and searching lives. It may also influence us to undervalue creative artists and works that have not been sanctified with such tributes, or even to sometimes distrust our own judgment regarding what is okay or not okay to appreciate.

A great joy of art can occur through personal discovery of beauty, intelligence and meaning in unexpected places. We recognize it when it communicates something to us, whether others attach value or not.

My home is filled with paintings, sculptures and drawings created by people that I have had the good fortune to know, as well as by artists that I have never heard of before. Some are works I created myself which reflect special frozen moments in my own life.

The works that I prize most highly draw me back repeatedly as I rediscover them among the clutter of my experience.

They remind me how lucky I am to have them silently waiting there.

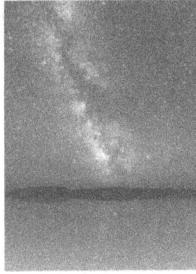

Music

LUDWIG VAN BEETHOVEN believed:

> *Music is a higher revelation than all wisdom and philosophy.*

Aldous Huxley described it as that, which after silence:

> *...comes nearest to expressing the inexpressible.*

Victor Hugo observed:

> *Music expresses that which cannot be said and on which it is impossible to be silent.*

Friedrich Nietzsche warned:

> *Without music, life would be a mistake.*

William Shakespeare harshly judged:

The man that hath no music in himself, nor is not moved with concord of sweet sounds, is fit for treasons, stratagems and spoils.

Sure, but what about the rest of us in our everyday lives? Can you possibly imagine what our existence would be like without it?

No soothing melodies to put crying infants to sleep. No inspirational hymns to awaken and revive you during long church or temple sermons. No excuse for embracing and swaying with someone you are attracted to, even if you don't know them very well—or releasing your natural inhibitions in public as you move your body in a wild suggestive manner in front of total strangers. No signal that something very exciting or frightening is about to happen in a movie. No marching or pep bands at high schools and college sports events. No instrumental groups, vocalists or genre to enjoy most or argue about. And no sentimental bookmarks or nostalgic mood generators to flash you back to special times and events.

Music is such an integral part of our life experience that we often forget it is present. Yet even if unaware, it can touch our deepest inner feelings, and can stimulate our full range of human emotions.

When we are attuned to it, music can amplify the beauty we experience in ourselves, in others, and in the world around us. And if written words communicate directly from mind-to-mind, music communicates directly from heart-to-heart. There can be little doubt that it is the true language of love. Even birds, frogs and crickets recognize this.

When humans leave our planet, music is typically one thing they don't want to leave behind. U.S. astronauts who are severely rationed in terms of personal items they are allowed to take have been known to smuggle a few extra cassette tapes and CDs aboard spacecraft.

Voices of the Spirit

THE RUSSIANS HAVE always been aware of the influence of music on crew morale and performance, and have actually programmed it in orbit to complement various types of activities scheduled for particular times.

Music is an international language that transcends boundaries of geography and dialect. It is probably impossible to really appreciate the true nature of people anywhere independent of their musical culture.

How can anyone begin to understand a Russian without experiencing the powerful passion and romantic spirit of their symphonies and ballads? Or appreciate the incredible transformation that occurs when polite and reserved Japanese business executives pack tens of thousands of Tokyo Karaoke bars, all taking turns in crooning popular and sentimental favorites to recorded instrumental backgrounds until and past wee morning hours?

During a year I once spent on a small U.S. Air Force Base in Greenland, I enjoyed the honor of being adopted by a hardy group of Danish construction workers who were living there as well. They had built a ramshackle shack called the *Dirty Shame* which boasted an old out-of-tune piano and an endless supply of beer.

None of my generous Danish hosts spoke English, and in concert with my total lack of any foreign language skills, any probing verbal conversations were somewhat handicapped. Yet with someone pounding out mutually familiar tunes on the piano, words weren't all that important after all.

I could improvise any forgotten lyrics without fear of embarrassment or contradiction, and overall, I thought that we sounded at least tolerable. The excellent Danish beer might have influenced my opinion on that matter, but we all became good friends without exchanging a controversial word.

Music is always within and around us if only we will but listen. It reveals and affirms the vast dimensions of our human spirit. Its voices and themes are infinitely diverse, and its language is universal.

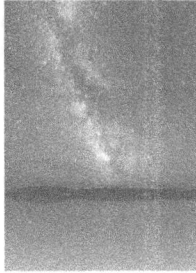

Dance and Drama

THEATER ENABLES US to indulge our voyeuristic nature. It invites us to witness other people's fantasies and experiences—portrayed through animated drawings, or acted out by human pretenders.

Our own lives dissolve with the house lights as our attention is directed to different places, times and possibilities that cover our visual field.

Figures appear before us who may represent virtually any character type we have known in our dreams and nightmares. We see morphological oddities, like mice and rabbits as large as children who walk on two legs, wear clothes, and talk in comical voices we understand.

Mechanized monsters and convincingly realistic aliens express human emotions.

Beautiful and handsome dancers seem to defy gravity as they leap effortlessly and move gracefully through magical settings. Others, reflecting the full range of humanity, may confront amusing and tragic situations that make our own circumstances seem lackluster by comparison.

The characters that we see may often remind us of ourselves and others we know—but there are also some usual differences. It may be more apparent, for example, whether we should regard them to be heroes or villains, generous or selfish, wise or stupid. It's not always quite so easy to make such evaluations of people in our general population because the contrasts are typically less obvious.

In the theater we can frequently identify the more virtuous individuals because they are generally the most attractive, or at least the most interesting characters. Lead female roles are often reserved for women who are more than just slightly attractive. Let's face facts…they are knockouts! No extra pounds of flab (at least not below the sternum), no irregular features, and no skin blemishes.

The leading men usually look pretty good too. However this is less important if they are very strong, smart, successful, funny, or have other endearing qualities. Fortunately, this provides more choices for us fellas in the audience to salvage remnants of our self-esteem.

There are also some other noticeable departures from life as we know it. Unlike us, the characters on stage almost always seem to know where they stand in dealing with an opportunity or problem. They respond decisively and take amazing risks in dangerous and complex situations where we wouldn't have a clue about what course of action to pursue.

Imagination Brought to Life

OUR THEATER ROLE models know exactly what to say, and they don't fumble the words as we do. In addition, they often possess physical abilities that are astounding, whether it involves dancing, acrobatics, fighting, or surviving injuries that would promptly dispatch most mortal souls. And they never have to interrupt what they are doing to go to the bathroom.

Theater has probably influenced our ideals and dreams more than we can ever begin to comprehend. We have loved and identified with those wonderful characters it has created for us. It has inspired our passion and compassion by connecting us to that kind and caring person within us. It has dared to create the impossible so that we can visualize and believe in the possible it as we once did. It has entertained us, provoked us, taught us and enriched us.

There are many to thank for this. Watching entranced in our comfortable popcorn butter stained seats we are unaware of grand behind-the-scenes efforts which have brought those experiences to life: the tens of thousands of individual drawings required to create those film animations; the years of disciplined training and months of rehearsals that made those dancers appear so natural and graceful; the long filming sessions involving numerous retakes until one finally appeared to be just right for each sequence; the stunt people, special effects artists, costume makers and cosmetologists who transformed relatively ordinary people into superior beings; the daily live performances where actors and actresses relived each scene over and over, yet conveyed the impression that each was a new and fresh experience; the set designers, constructors, lighting experts and camera crews who made places and events more exciting, believable and enchanting; and all the others including script writers, film editors, choreographers, musicians, directors and investors.

Illusions can come hard!

While it is great to just sit back and enjoy the shows that those serious efforts have created for us, it may be healthy to occasionally remember that it's okay if our lives don't seem to match up. Since we don't have all that support, we have to stage our own low-budget productions, improvising the scripts as we go along, with no opportunities to rehearse, and only one chance to get each scene right.

And we can't even restrict the camera angles.

Recognizing Our Own Importance—The Pleasures of Our Own Company

Go ahead and do it. If you don't, who else will? Some of life's most satisfying adventures are solo journeys that lead to self-discovery. You can go anywhere you want, and travel as light as you wish.

Depending Upon Ourselves

MANY YEARS AGO my dad, who was a flight instructor and charter pilot, gave me flying lessons out of our family airport. With his hands and mine both on the dual controls, our mental and muscular commands seemed to merge in a way that made it impossible for me to be certain which of us was really responsible for causing the aircraft to bank and turn, or climb and descend.

One day after we had landed, he unexpectedly suggested that I take my first solo flight. Before I fully realized what had happened, I suddenly found myself looking down upon the miniaturized landscape below, and suddenly became conscious that I was more alone than I had ever been in my life. It was immediately clear that I was the one doing all of the flying, and that I would have to be the one to do all of the landing as well.

At that point I experienced very mixed emotions. It was exhilarating to enjoy new sensations of freedom and independence as the 140 Cessna responded to my wishes on that beautiful summer afternoon. Yet, I also felt considerable apprehension that maybe I wasn't quite ready for the challenge of returning to the security that I had taken for granted only a few minutes earlier. There was no longer anyone else who could help if I needed it, and no option except to succeed. The landing wasn't as smooth and easy as I had wished. I circled the pattern and lined up for my final approach at the proper distance and altitude according to plan, but my airspeed was excessive. As a result, I hit the surface pretty hard and fast, bounced high, and could see that I was rapidly running out of runway. Finding myself airborne again following my brief contact with terra firma, I advanced the throttle and pulled back on the controls to go around for another try. In my determination to do this I reacted too aggressively, nearly causing the plane to stall out and execute an unscheduled encounter with the tree line ahead.

That wonderfully resolute craft was not about to surrender its own future to my incompetence, and pulled us both back towards the clouds. Grateful for another chance to get it right, I circled the field again, landed without incident, and apologized to my tolerant host. After the Cessna and I both arrived back, each in one piece, I asked dad if he thought I should go up for another spin. He smiled somewhat painfully and suggested that maybe I had experienced enough excitement for that day. I am sure that he was actually speaking for himself as well. And I think that we both appreciated and respected each other a little bit more after that shared adventure.

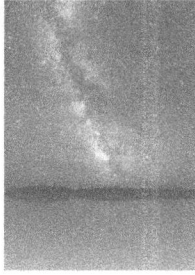

Experiencing Solo Flights

I HAVE OBSERVED that others close to me have known parallels to my first solo flight experience.

At times, we may feel a need to separate ourselves from outside influences that cloud our awareness of who we are and what we are able to accomplish by ourselves. Acting on that need can be lonely, frightening and risky, but also tremendously exciting, satisfying and enlightening.

Life circumstances sometimes put us in the cockpit alone when we would prefer to have company. We have no choice but to take hold of the controls and at least pretend to ourselves that we know what to do...to believe that we can fly, and to recognize no other option.

Solo flights can take a large variety of forms.

They occur when a young person strikes out on their own for the first time, leaving family and friends behind.

They happen when people leave controlling relationships where their lives have been dominated by a jealous, selfish or overly demanding partner.

They result when someone gives up a secure but unsatisfactory work position to create their own new business.

In fact, they are experienced whenever we suddenly find

ourselves facing a major new challenge alone, whether intentionally or not.

Risks in solo flights also take many forms. Included are possible loneliness, loss of familiar support systems, criticism and rejection by people we like, financial debt, and risks with uncertain success.

Yet, regardless of the outcome, we learn that we can survive and are strengthened by that knowledge. Then, before we know it, we're airborne again.

Self-Discovery

I HAD DEFINITELY not volunteered to spend the final twelve months of my four-year U.S. Air Force tour of duty in Sondrestromfjord, Greenland. As someone who values the warmth of mild climates and warm female companionship, that was one of the last places I would have chosen. Unfortunately, neither the U.S. Department of Defense nor Father Fate had solicited my preferences in this matter...and there I was.

Trained and licensed as an air traffic controller, it was my responsibility to "talk in" aircraft under low or even zero-visibility conditions using radar systems that had been developed to support the Berlin Airlift during World War II. The airbase at Sondrestromfjord presented a special challenge because the single runway was flanked on both sides by high mountains, and terminated at the base of another. This meant that there was no option for planes to execute a "missed approach" and circle around again if anything went wrong during landing.

Since air traffic levels were low, we weren't overworked. In fact that was one of our problems.

Sondrestromfjord (or as we called it, Sondey) was primarily an emergency refueling base for the much larger and more active Thule Air Force Base which served as a radar surveillance site during the Cold War with the Soviet Union. Located near the edge of the edge of the ice cap about 90 miles inland from the Davis Straits, there was no soil on the rock surface to support trees or other vegetation.

Temperatures during the long Arctic night sometimes dropped to -60 degrees Fahrenheit, and frequent high wind conditions made the effects of the cold even more penetrating. During this period we were virtual shut-ins. This circumstance was particularly depressing during our several-day-long work shifts at the radar site location which was remote from the main base of about 100 airmen.

There, at the radar site, our two-man teams were confined in a tiny one-room standby shack while waiting to assist inbound aircraft. Our only other company was an occasional Arctic fox that observed us in the dark as we waded through drifted snow to and from the radar unit—or, since we had no plumbing, as we went out to answer nature's call. The latter mission had to be performed quickly in peril of frostbite injuries which would cause sitting to be painful, or potentially impact any future family plans.

An Isolated Example

LACKING NORMAL OUTLETS for recreation we spent much of our excess free time engaged in ping pong, card games, recorded music, and some Japanese Godzilla movies that had been brought in by someone with either bad taste or good humor. Mail was infrequent, about every month or so, and I regret to say that morale was generally very low.

I have since come to know the Arctic and Antarctic explorers and scientists who have happily endured incomparably worse conditions, but the difference was that they did so to achieve important personal goals. Most of us felt that we were wasting a year of our lives cut off from everything we really cared about for no good reasons that we could understand. Some fellows psychologically dropped off the deep end of depression, and to a man, we all had extremely negative opinions of that place.

Then, one day, I hit upon the idea of getting into the portrait painting business. Since we didn't have commercial services there to rely upon, just about everyone took up an avocation to help earn a few extra dollars. (My first experiment as a barber was a failure that left my victim nearly bald.)

Using pigments left over from scavenged paint-by-number kits and scraps of tarpaulin stretched over plywood for improvised canvasses, I began to produce paintings of friends' loved ones from photographs that they supplied. Before long, I found myself sitting outside for hours on end, fingers numb with cold, trying to capture the magnificence of those mountains that I had previously cursed.

That landscape which had seemed so barren and brutal began to reveal itself in a whole new way. Its scale and rugged beauty demanded my respect, and that recognition illuminated something inside me.

I realized that there was a very good reason to be there after all. What better place to discover the excitement of my own fragile existence?

I learned important lessons during that unplanned year in Greenland. One is that changes that are forced upon us can provide unique opportunities to discover unexpected aspects of who we are. Another is that the wonderment we often fail to see around us may lie hidden behind mental blocks of ice and mountains of stone.

Contacting Our Human Spirit

WHEN I WAS a young member of the University of Illinois faculty in Champaign-Urbana, Illinois, I lived at the edge of town—at least it was then. Immediately beyond my home the area opened up to flat farmlands bounded by a limitless sky which stretched as far away as eyes could see.

Although I had previously been stationed fifteen miles away at Chanute Air Force Base for two years, and had lived in Champaign-Urbana for several more as an undergraduate and graduate student, I had always preferred a rolling or mountainous landscape.

But that was before I bought a motorcycle.

The 400cc Suzuki wasn't big and powerful by Hell's Angels standards, but it was plenty fast for me. That lean and beautiful mechanical steed became an extension of my mind and body as it propelled me forward in great surges of energy.

With almost no thought or effort on my part, it tilted its angle of attack on curves as I unconsciously shifted my balance, and hurtled me through wind and space. Or, when I wished, I could hum along at a leisurely pace and absorb the sights, sounds and aromas of the surroundings.

Unlike cars, which enclose and isolate you from the outside

world, motorcycles put it right in your face!

Within seconds after mounting my bike, I was part of that rural panorama at my doorstep. Life was different there. The sky, which was primarily regarded as just a weather source in the city, revealed its fuller character, constantly being transformed by a changing display of cloud formations, colors and light conditions.

Rain had a richer aroma out there also, often mixed with the somewhat acrid smell of ozone and heavy scent of wet humus. And those raindrops didn't just fall; experienced on the motorcycle, they became projectiles that stung exposed skin with ballistic force that punctuated their individual importance.

The land was constantly changing as well. Blankets of snow and ice dissolved to reveal rich black topsoil, purple rocks, and scattered patches of vegetation that had survived hard freezes. Sounds of tractors became audible over the steady putter of the Suzuki, and farmers dutifully waved back to me along country roads as they cut furrows for another planting season.

Motorcycle Rides in the Country

FIELDS AND TREES budded into blue, yellow and brown-tinted shades of green that gradually covered the earth and contributed sweet fragrances, finally becoming dominant forms on the surface and horizon. Cornfields eventually reached heights where they obstructed views of road intersections and traffic, requiring that my riding become more vigilant.

I felt contented and free, and was moved by the fertile richness of those Illinois plains.

Country life along those small asphalt and gravel roads added a special human dimension to the experiences. People appeared to be going about their affairs in the same general fashion that has characterized life there for generations. Farms expressed family cooperation, stability and pride that warranted admiration.

Old homes and businesses in various states of repair reflected histories of dreams, plans, lives and relationships that stimulated imagination. Residents in roadside towns where I stopped for coffee pursued timeless conversations and repartee which will continue so long as neighboring friends meet. I had no desire to interrupt them with my presence, but was happy to be among them.

When I gave up that motorcycle, I felt like I was abandoning part of my spirit. It had transported me to wonderful places, experiences and realizations that could never be repeated in quite the same way without it.

Upon moving to Houston, however, it became evident that all of my personal experiences might come to a premature end on a crowded freeway if I continued that love affair. I'm a lot older now, and my reflexes aren't nearly as good as they once were. I also don't have any mortal time left to risk.

Still, I would like to believe that much of that old motorcycle spirit part of me is still there. I am occasionally reminded of this when I walk or drive in the country, or eavesdrop on a conversation in a small town grill en route to somewhere else.

At times, at least for a few years, I even half expected to find my old friend waiting for me in the parking lot, ready to leave with me on a new adventure. Maybe someday that motorcycle spirit will carry me to new wonderful adventures and places that I can't even imagine.

Maybe it was always there within me, always will be, and just carries me along for the ride.

Illusory Reflections in Time

I HAVE ALWAYS greatly enjoyed going to movies, and I still do. As a result, I have fallen in love with countless actresses, and have envied as many leading men. I have been inspired by acts of bravery and compassion, have laughed myself silly at comedies, and have tried to conceal tears of sadness and sentimentally when situations turned out wrong or right.

Those characters and events provided models which I have undoubtedly influenced what I expect from relationships, ways I think I should behave in various circumstances, and concepts of alternate lifestyles that I may subconsciously desire. All lurk somewhere in my psyche, and I probably identify with some of them more than I can ever fully recognize.

My wife often gives me a hard time when I sit engrossed watching an old movie on television which she regards to have little contemporary merit. This is particularly true when the film is a Western cowboy or war story where the plot and outcome is as predictable as tomorrow's whiskers.

She asks:

> *Haven't you already seen that a hundred times? What*
> *possible satisfaction can you get out of watching it*
> *again?*

I usually sit there in a stupor and grunt something unintelligible so that she will know that I heard her, yet not have to interrupt my attention long enough to formulate a real reply.

So, okay, honey, this is the answer you have waited for so long.

Movies are like time capsules that document attitudes, ideals and circumstances which have shaped the ways many of us think today. If the old plots and characters seem simple by current standards, it is at least partly because people wanted and expected clarity in their lives.

Heroes and heroines were consistently confident and brave because it would have been unthinkable to have them let us down. Wars were fought for love and good of the country, and no one would question their purposes and validity. Good always prevailed over evil because any other outcomes would have been travesties to justice. Romances occurred between two people because we believed that this was somehow preordained if they were naturally just right for each other.

Sure, everyone pretty much knew what was going to happen, and when it did, we could leave the theater comforted and secure with our hopes intact. What's so bad about that?

Of course, times, as reflected through more recent movies, have changed. New lead characters have appeared, and familiar film personalities have aged before our eyes.

Larry Bell

Watching Old Cowboy Movies

MANY OF OUR former film idols have adapted to new roles, just as we have. When we first met them they were young, attractive, idealistic and adventuresome. Now, the men appear as wiser, battle-hardened veterans, paunchy and colorful detectives, parents of a new breed of romantics, and elderly folks contemplating life's final scenes. Fewer of the female stars continued in significant roles, or any roles at all for that matter, after their bloom of youth faded.

We have also witnessed the popularization of anti-heroes who help us make peace or war with our subsequent loss of innocence. Lead figures can be alcoholics, drug users and criminal types that evoke empathy because they are presented to have experienced hardships and express sensitive, humorous or other redeeming human qualities. We watch them as they return bitter and confused from senseless wars; as they make serious mistakes that hurt themselves and others; as they engage in sexually explicit, yet meaningless relationships; as they encounter and react to bigotry; and as they voluntarily—or not—live or work under depressing and hopeless conditions.

Glamour is often associated with power and wealth achieved at the expense of ethical principles. Killing and suffering are made exciting, yet mind-numbing, through the use of special effects, slow motion and close-ups.

Blessedly, there are many kind, positive and beautiful movies that capture better aspects of our nature. Less fortunately, we may often have to go to specialty theaters featuring foreign films with subtitles to see them.

Maybe it is sometimes good for us to see movies that depict the seamy side of life and highlight human frailties, if only to illustrate how vulnerable we can become if we're not careful. Perhaps they also remind us that life can still be worthwhile even when conditions that surround us are far from perfect. And possibly, it is constructive to put some of those old romantic fantasies behind us and boldly look reality in the eye with appreciation for opportunities bestowed on us.

But isn't it fun to occasionally return to those simpler and more idealistic attitudes and experiences of the past? To watch actors and actresses we have admired become young, hopeful and determined again, and to remember those we have loved who are now gone? To revisit the youth and dreams we once knew as they are replayed over again?

Isn't that okay once in a while?

Joys of Sometimes Being Alone

WHILE I CERTAINLY don't consider myself to be a recluse, there is a lot to be said about sometimes being alone. Just in case you've forgotten, I'll offer some examples.

First, as a point of clarification, let's assume that "being alone" is considered to be a state of mind, but not necessarily of body. There are some excellent being alone opportunities when you are among strangers. Public places, such as restaurants and airports, are fine places for this.

Think about the times that people near you had children who behaved badly and annoyed everyone in the vicinity within their screaming and crying range. When you are alone, you can be grateful that those kids aren't your problem. You can glare at the parents with an indignant air that suggests that your child-raising skills are superior. You can also be thankful that your rascals aren't around to firmly disprove that myth.

When you are alone in a crowd, you can enjoy anonymity and just dematerialize into the environment. Many of us learned to do this in military basic training camps to avoid being picked for a work detail. Children who haven't been listening in class also get pretty good at it so that the teacher won't call on them for an answer.

Becoming inconspicuous is also a useful skill when you see an interesting person and don't want them to know that you are studying them. There is probably no special gender trend here, although it may possibly correspond somewhat with elevated hormone levels.

Others tell me that the trick here is to look as innocuous and expressionless as possible, fix your eyes on some imaginary object a few feet away from the human target, and work the hell out of your peripheral vision. That ability reportedly comes in very handy when you are in the company of the "significant other" in your life who is using the same technique to keep an eye on you.

When you are alone in both body and mind, other opportunities open up. Freedom to be compulsive, for example.

You can stay up all night with the television or radio on to any program you desire. You can eat anything or everything in the refrigerator, and not feel guilty when that includes the last two pieces of pie or scoops of ice cream. You can walk around half dressed—or hell, naked if you prefer—if it suits your fancy, or wear clothes that your spouse hates in blissful silence.

You can write something, build something or clean something on the kitchen table without anyone moving it or complaining about the mess, and leave dirty dishes in the sink for a few days until the dog licks them or roaches carry them away. And if you're a couple of hours late feeding that dog, there's no one to tattle on you.

Tuning In and Tuning Out

WHEN YOU ARE alone, there is nobody to interrupt you when you are tuned in or tuned out. No one to tell you to pick up something at the market or drive the kids somewhere when you are in the middle of a good book, or worse, a television program that you have been waiting to see. No one to have to help with a homework assignment that was put off until the last possible minute when you had planned to relax after finally finishing your own project that you had put off until the last possible minute.

There's no one to use up all of the hot water when you were looking forward to taking a soothing bath or shower. And no one to tie up the home telephone when you are expecting an important call, or want to contact someone on theirs for whatever dumb reason.

When you are alone, you can adjust your car temperature exactly the way you want it, tune in a radio station that your kids don't like, and turn the music up really loud. There's no need to stop every fifteen minutes so that someone can use a restroom, but you can choose to stop to eat when, where and what you want.

You don't have to pack and repack all those books and toys you would otherwise need to take along to keep the urchins busy every time you stay at a motel overnight. And there's no one to warn you that you're driving too fast, except for public servants who do so after it is too late.

If being alone is sometimes a little lonely, that's not necessarily all bad either. Imagine how great it is to talk to a loved one on the telephone after being away from them for a few days. Think about how warm and sentimental it makes you feel about them when you are traveling and wish they were with you. Think about how nice it is to get back home again or to have them visit.

Reflect about how lucky you are to have them in your life to care about you, to make demands, and to put their priorities above yours.

After you spend a few minutes contemplating all of this, include some extra time with yourself to let those realizations really sink in. Then you can savor them in delicious solitude without any irritating distractions.

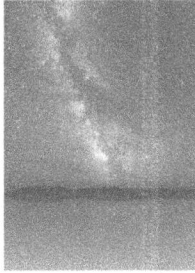

Enjoying Self-Acceptance

The best thing you have going for you is you. If you aren't perfect, think about how boring life would be if you were.

Laughing With Yourself

I DON'T KNOW about you, but I'm capable of doing some pretty dumb things.

I'm not referring here to situations where I've made reasonable, yet unfortunate decisions based upon the best available information at the time. No, I'm talking about occasions when I wasn't paying attention to what I was doing, didn't bother to get the facts straight, or just plain used poor judgment.

A lot of those events didn't seem the least bit funny at the time. But maybe recalling some of those moments now is similar to the way that my dad once described the enjoyment of eating black olives. "You don't really appreciate the great flavor until you get older."

Besides, having survived my errors, they couldn't have been all that serious. Now that I think of it in retrospect, I probably wouldn't change much.

Of the many dumb instances in my life, it's difficult to select those that stand out for being most noteworthy. Some memories probably died of terminal embarrassment. However, I will offer a few representative examples that may prompt you to recall and take pleasure in some of your own...recognizing of course, that such competition is futile.

Okay, here's one I definitely wouldn't want to repeat.

I once parked my car in neutral with the parking brake released on an incline in front of a barbershop located on a busy four-lane street. I'm sure that you have already guessed what happened.

There I was in the barber's chair, helplessly watching as my car backed slowly down the slope across all four lanes— miraculously without incident—as drivers frantically executed evasive maneuvers. Properly shamed, I changed barbers after that.

Lack of adequate planning for trips has gotten me into trouble on several occasions. One time, I didn't bother to recheck the date of an invitation to lecture at the University of Texas in Dallas. After waiting more than an hour for my hosts to meet me at the airport, I realized that while the day was right, I was a month early. So I asked my wife to fly in and join me, and we enjoyed an impromptu holiday.

I once flew to Tokyo and discovered upon arrival that having forgotten to renew my passport; I couldn't leave the immigration check point at the airport. The security officers contacted a friend who was waiting for me. We were both informed that before entering Japan, I would have to fly to another country where an American Embassy could correct the problem.

Surviving Dumb Mistakes

MY PAL OFFERED to join me, and we caught the next departure for Seoul, Korea. There, we experienced a new problem. As a Japanese citizen, he would not be allowed to enter Korea unless he was in transit to somewhere else. So he booked a ticket to go on to Singapore the next day.

The next morning, following a great evening together in Seoul, I was informed by the American Embassy that I would need to wait a day for my passport application to be processed. This created an extended opportunity for more time in that beautiful and interesting city. I would like to return there someday by intent.

There is one mistake that stands out in my mind as a whopper. When I was in the U.S. Air Force, my squadron headquarters relocated to another on-base facility. All of us pitched in to help the move, and I contributed by painting various signs for the new building and parking lot. Since my work drew admiration, it wasn't long before other squadron units asked me to paint signs for them. I obliged good heartedly—at least for a while, until I began to tire of this voluntary activity.

One morning, I was awakened by a telephone call from a colonel who, in a most pleasant manner, asked if I would be willing to paint a large sign to be placed in front of our regional headquarters, which was also located on the base. I politely declined, reminding him that as an air traffic controller, sign painting wasn't part of my job description. Doing so would also exceed the number of hours I was allowed to work in my safety-critical field according to regulations.

The biggest part of that mistake was informing him that while he could order me to do so, it would compel me to file a formal protest.

A short time later, I received transfer orders which reassigned me to the Sondrestromfjord Air Force Base in Greenland. As it turned out, that colonel was in charge of staffing overseas bases.

This experience turned out to be a teachable moment that has lasted a lifetime. Namely, it is that when someone in a superior position asks you to do something, it's a good idea to check their area of authority before saying no.

Yet, I can't help but smile when I think of the special joy that his one-upmanship must have brought to his life, and give him the full credit that he deserves for his victory over my recalcitrance.

Colonel, whoever and wherever you are, I salute you!

Trusting Your Intuition

I REGARD INTUITION to be our greatest intellectual resource....one that aggregates, integrates, correlates, and guides almost everything that we think and do, whether consciously or not.

Intuition requires a foundation and scaffold constructed of lots and lots of experience and information to build upon. That construction process begins right after we leave the womb...and probably even much earlier than that.

So exactly what is intuition? That depends a lot upon who you ask.

The Merriam-Webster Dictionary defines it as "...a natural ability or power that makes it possible to know something without any proof or evidence."

The Cambridge English Dictionary describes it as "... an ability to understand or know something immediately based upon your feelings rather than facts."

Some characterize intuition as a "gut feeling"...an unconscious reasoning that propels us to decide or do something without necessarily telling us how. Some lightly characterize it as a merely a "hunch."

Those gut feelings are sometimes capable of making us

hungry, or alternatively "sick to our stomachs."

International business consultant Francis Cholle, author of *The Intuitive Compass*, urges us not to disregard those hunches either. He observes:

> *We don't have to reject scientific logic in order to benefit from instinct...We can honor and call upon all these tools, and we can seek balance. And by seeking this balance we will finally bring all the resources of our brain into action.*

According to a Psychology Today report, only about 20 percent of our brain's gray matter is dedicated to conscious thoughts, while 80 percent is dedicated to unconscious ones.

Cholle describes a dialog between those two different parts going something like...

Conscious Brain: "What should I wear today?"
Unconscious Brain: "Red."
Conscious: "Red what?"
Unconscious: "I don't know, just something red."

As Sophy Burnham, bestselling author of *The Art of Intuition* described it:

> *It's different than thinking, it's different from logic or analysis...It's knowing without knowing.*

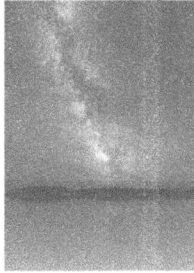

It's Smarter than You May Think

IVY ESTABROOKE, A program manager at the Office of Naval Research, told the New York Times in 2012 that intuition is a power the U.S. military is researching to determine the role it plays in helping troops make quick life-saving judgments during combat. He reported:

> There is a growing body of anecdotal evidence, combined with solid research efforts, that suggests intuition is a critical aspect of how we humans interact with our environment and how, ultimately we make many of our decisions.

A 2013 study published in the journal Perspectives on Psychological Science indicates that intuition can be practiced by working on your "mindfulness" which is described as "paying attention to one's current experience in a non-judgmental way."

Ultimately, intuition is challenging to describe, and impossible to confine in a bounded box. It somehow unexplainably bridges between the conscious and nonconscious parts of our mind, and between instinct and reason.

Our intuition enables us to fill in blanks of conscious understanding; to perceive patterns and relationships between things that others may not recognize; to connect dots; to notice trends and assumptions that do and don't fit our world experience perspectives; to provide early warnings regarding which people and ideas to trust; to alert us to promising opportunities and warn us of hidden dangers; and to guide personal priorities that keep us focused on things that matter most.

Intuition is something very personal...something we have often earned the hard way through painful errors...something that deserves our respect. It is our inner voice speaking to us: loudly sometimes; sometimes in a barely perceptible whisper. It is something that can appear as an inner sense of dark fear and foreboding, or as a bright flash of sudden insight. It can come over you unexpectedly as a cold chill, or a warm breath of promise.

Our intuition can be defiantly obstinate or fleetingly fragile when challenged by others who believe that they know better while offering little evidence of this. Our clarity on such matters can be clouded by strong agendas and emotions.

Intuition is the inspirational wellspring of creativity, and the ultimate arbitrator of differences between business winners and losers. Steve Jobs called it "more powerful than intellect."

Some will refer to intuition as common sense, but it isn't always all that common. Yours is unique to you...a major part of what makes you special.

Your intuition personifies you. Listen to yourself intently and intuitively.

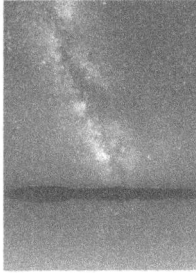

Satisfactions of Speaking Out

HAVE YOU NOTICED that people who are generally regarded to be successful typically express opinions and ideas freely? This has caused me to wonder if their willingness to speak out has influenced their success, or whether their achievements have given them the confidence and license to do this.

Most likely, it works both ways. Yet we can't necessarily assume that people who talk a lot have much to say. We know better by listening to politicians.

Nor can we assume that people who don't speak up are unsuccessful, as evidenced by some doctors who charge a lot, but never seem obliged to explain what is really wrong with us.

It might be noted that attitudes about speaking out are influenced by different cultures. For example, the Western adage that "the squeaky wheel gets the grease" stands in direct opposition to the Eastern caution that "the nail that stands up gets hit on the head."

This stark contrast in philosophies has been apparent in numerous international conferences and business meetings that I have attended. Those of us from the U.S., Canada, Australia, New Zealand and Europe tend to do a lot of our thinking out loud, expressing our viewpoints spontaneously, and often dominating conversations.

Since those from Japan, China and other Eastern societies are typically much more quiet and restrained, we might erroneously conclude that they are impressed, or maybe have little to share. In reality, as some of my good Asian friends have confided, they often think that we are presumptuous and impolite, and wonder if we will ever shut up.

We have all encountered inconsiderate people who have unrelentingly inflicted boring and self-aggrandizing monologues on us, and we obviously don't want to behave like that. There are also times when we may lean towards the opposite extreme. We want to say something that is on our mind, and are strongly tempted to, yet decide against it because we are afraid that it may not come out right, or that the audience will react disapprovingly.

How do other people rise above similar doubts? I gained some insights on this matter several years ago when I attended the Federal Executive Institute in Charlottesville, Virginia.

Although the Institute is intended for high-level administrators from all U.S. Government agencies, a few non-government employees like myself are sometimes invited to provide broader cross-fertilization opportunities. I was on a leave of absence from the University of Illinois at the time, pursuing a lead consulting role in a national *Crime Prevention through Environmental Design* program sponsored by the U.S. Department of Justice.

Nail Heads and Wheel Bearings

THE INTENSIVE TWO-WEEK-LONG program was designed to enable participants to examine personal goals and leadership skills through challenging exercises. A representative test involved assigning a complex group problem to be solved within a tight deadline, and requiring everyone to reach consensus on the solution.

No one was put in charge, but it was clear that someone would have to quickly assume leadership responsibility in order to accomplish the objective. While one might expect some resentment among the other competitive achievers when anyone took that initiative, this was never the case. In fact, there was often an apparent sense of relief when a brave soul put themselves on the spot, enabling everyone else to relax a bit.

It didn't matter very much if that volunteer wasn't necessarily best suited for the job, or that they hadn't been elected for that role. More importantly, they cared enough about achieving the purpose at hand to stand up and risk taking some heat.

I have observed that leadership is a quality we often may not recognize or act upon in ourselves until a situation we care about motivates us to take charge. When we do so, most others are likely to cooperate and support us.

It's natural to be nervous about speaking up as we wait for that hammer to strike from above. But when we rise above our fear and do this intelligently and considerately, others can be expected to respect us all the more.

Accept the habit of believing that your opinions are valid and that your ideas are important.

And, the next time that inner voice urges you to take the risk, let others hear it as well.

Writing Our Own Introductions

MOST OF US are raised to regard modesty to be a virtue. We usually feel uncomfortable in accepting praise, or when circumstances require us to say nice things about ourselves, and take a dim view of others who come across as conceited braggarts. Yet sometimes it is necessary to explain our strong points to people who don't know us, to help them understand how we can be of value to win their confidence.

After all, who knows our special virtues and qualifications better than we do?

Self-promotion is a practical necessity in many circumstances. It is a requirement in running for public offices, seeking work positions and business opportunities, and sometimes even in social situations when we want to make a favorable impression.

Some people are quite skilled at using generally accepted approaches, and we typically respect them for it. Political candidates, for example, refer to themselves by name as if they are talking about someone else when they tell us why we should vote for them. They also write testimonials highlighting their accomplishments which they have others present on their behalf.

Position applicants write resumes that also give appearances of being prepared by objective third parties that list their superlative qualifications. In fact, nearly all of us are compelled to toot our own horns at least sometimes.

I am routinely asked to write letters of recommendation for my former students when they apply for professional positions. In doing so, I invariably request that they prepare draft versions of the correspondence they wish me to submit. There are two important reasons for this requirement.

First, they usually have much clearer understandings of their prospective employer's interests and priorities than I do, and can focus the letters on aspects of their own experiences and abilities that will be most relevant. Second, they can provide specifics regarding their associations with me that I may have forgotten, along with particular achievements that they are especially proud of.

This procedure enables me to be a well-informed and effective advocate, plus give them practice in recognizing and presenting their contributing value. I seldom find it necessary to make any significant revisions for the final versions I send, and any changes I do make usually involve deservingly laudatory observations. It is always a pleasure to praise people who have earned it.

Just as Others Do

DO YOU EVER wonder who supplies all of the impressive background information about speakers when they are introduced at various public and professional assemblies? As someone who frequently lectures at such forums, I will confirm what you probably guessed all along—that more often than not it was those speakers themselves.

It's part of the routine to sit there and at least pretend to be somewhat embarrassed as everyone hears about our wonderful credentials, accomplishments and honors that we outlined for those occasions. But it is even more embarrassing to find ourselves on stage addressing groups that have no clue about our backgrounds or the legitimacy of our expertise.

Having been in both situations, I greatly appreciate the importance of having a good introductory send-off to facilitate audience interest and rapport.

Being good advocates for ourselves doesn't mean that we are pushy at the expense of others. Certainly we are familiar with people who are inclined to oversell themselves through egocentric behavior and misleading embellishments of their own abilities and achievements. They promote themselves so aggressively that their self-aggrandizing attitudes and actions warrant only contempt and distrust.

This has the opposite effect of winning confidence and respect by projecting our real qualifications in a tactful, open and honest manner. Doing this doesn't take anything away from others. Rather, it can establish a more meaningful basis for interacting with people who will benefit by understanding us better.

Boiling it all down, effective self-advocacy involves treating ourselves with the same level of regard and consideration that we would accord to others that we hold in high esteem. It isn't necessarily something we are compelled to talk about, and it's often better when we don't.

Nor is it something that we need to keep foremost in our thoughts, because in doing this, we become selfish and arrogant. All that is really required is to be enthusiastic, yet objective about what we have to offer, and possess the candor to communicate our strengths as circumstances dictate.

Who can fault us for that?

Joys of Being Different

IF YOU RECOGNIZE and enjoy that you are different from everyone else, there is a good possibility that you are motivated to expect a lot of exceptional things out of your life.

Of course, most of us want to comply with rudimentary social standards of behavior and appearances to some degree. Otherwise no one would invite us to nice parties, and children are apt to call us unflattering names.

But when people are so intent upon being accepted that they lose sight of personal priorities and goals, avoid worthwhile risks, and rely solely upon popular and proved ideas, then they are carrying conformity too far. On balance, I'd rather be unconventional than dull any day.

I believe that it is becoming more and more difficult to attain high levels of success with ordinary qualifications and approaches. For example, take professional careers.

Several years ago, it could be generally assumed that after someone received an advanced professional degree from a prestigious institution, a rewarding employment position was pretty much assured. This was before most professions became seriously overcrowded relative to market demands and corporate employers began to downsize. Still, universities have continued to produce diploma-bearing hopefuls at constant and growing rates, causing competition for available openings to be tougher every year.

By necessity, both young and experienced professionals are leaving their original fields to pursue other options that apply personal interests and talents. Many are creating new enterprises and services, a trend that requires those entrepreneurs to be much more versatile, innovative and adventuresome than was previously their norm.

More and more university graduates are coming to realize that while their university educations provide useful knowledge and skills, the degrees they have earned guarantee nothing. What matters most is confidence that they have something special to offer, an ability to recognize possibilities, and a willingness to accept essential risks.

Years ago, people who abandoned traditional careers might have been called rebels. Now they're often referred to as survivors.

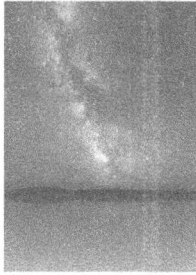

Releasing the Rebel Within

BREAKING WITH CONFORMITY in order to release the maverick side of our nature can often put us at odds with those who have more traditional outlooks. They may become uncomfortable when we dispute their more conservative models and repudiate certain values they espouse. They may experience frustration because they don't quite understand how to relate to us...or know how to control us. And consciously or not, they might secretly envy our self-assurance, strength and creativity.

Bosses and colleagues in our workplaces may think we are stepping out of line or on their toes. Even loved ones and friends might sometimes prefer that we be more predictable, independent, and less "interesting."

But acting upon strong spirits of individuality can also help sustain truly vital relationships. People who don't do so are typically dismissed as nonentities. They don't get respect, and others intentionally or inadvertently walk all over them. At best, they aren't considered to be very stimulating, except perhaps by those who are equally boring. There is probably at least a bit of rebel in all of us. That's the part that is never quite satisfied with ourselves or the circumstances around us; causes us to stand up for things we believe are right, and oppose things that aren't; and to recognize that we aren't exactly like anyone else—and really don't want to be.

Our rebel selves influence us to value reason over dogmatic authority; challenge unwarranted preconceptions and limitations; and explore unorthodox approaches when necessary in order to succeed.

When we surrender that rebel to others, or imprison it within us, we create conflicts with our unique and exciting natures. Those are battles that we can't afford to lose.

Honoring Our Own Achievements

Life's transactions often demand an investment of personal resources. Give yourself enough credit so that you don't need to borrow from someone else.

Earned Recognition

YOU CAN TELL that I'm an important person the second you walk into my office. It's very large, contains nice furniture and a jungle of plants, and has big windows with a desirable view. But the real clincher is when you look at the walls which are covered with certificates, plaques, and photographs of me with celebrities. It becomes immediately obvious that I must be quite wonderful.

While those accouterments and mementos may reflect some actual achievements in my life, they also probably indicate at least one human foible—namely that I like to feel valued. Granted, this desire can be justified in practical terms. I want people who are looking to me for particular services, to be assured that I have the right credentials. That rationale can help me account for the various professional licenses and prestigious organization memberships, honorary proclamations, awards and other official-looking regalia.

However, I would be less than wonderfully honest not to admit that most of the stuff is there for another reason as well. Basically, I like having it around as a reminder to myself that maybe I'm doing okay.

Some of those items do have special meaning to me. The photographs of my family represent, hands-down, the most important accomplishment in my life. There are symbols of recognition for things that I worked hard to achieve, and memorabilia associated with people and projects that bring back exciting and cherished memories.

Other tributes, which look just as impressive, involved very little investment of my time, effort or commitment. Those, for example, which signify that I attended a workshop somewhere or spoke to a group. And although I appreciate the sponsors' thoughtful acknowledgments of my participation, it doesn't necessarily mean that my contributions were particularly exemplary.

For self-recognition to be truly meaningful, it must involve something we really care about and believe we have earned. It doesn't always require that we are successful and that everything turns out as planned, or that anyone else is keeping track of our contributions.

It's great if others understand the efforts that we make, honor our intentions and applaud the results...but what if they don't? Wouldn't we have applied ourselves just the same anyway? And shouldn't it mean more to us that we did it because we wanted to, rather than because we cared about outside recognition?

Whether You Received it or Not

IT SEEMS TO me that people who do things primarily for approval are typically the least likely to receive it. Others detect that motive, and don't respect it.

On the other hand, dedicated and generous deeds don't usually continue long without notice. People who contribute unselfishly are the ones most likely to realize recognition. We respect them, and want them to succeed.

I experience real satisfaction when someone honors me with trust. Sometimes that takes the form of responsibility that is extended when there is a lot riding upon my performance.

It is gratifying when those I hold in high esteem regard me as a partner and friend.

I can also find pleasure basking in the reflected light of other peoples' achievements when I know that I have played at least some small part in providing opportunities and constructive support. For example, when a former student continues on in a field of interest that I introduced them to and makes a success of it. This doesn't take any credit away from their accomplishments, but makes me feel somewhat like a proud father, which I also am.

It's wonderful to receive recognition from others, and it can be disappointing and discouraging when we deserve it and it doesn't arrive. Wanting to be appreciated and acknowledged when we have done well is only natural.

But there's also a lot to be said for recognizing your own achievements so that you don't have to rely upon others to do this for you. Then, rather than having to wait for them to tell you that you're on a good path, you can just truck merrily along and make the most out of your time and energy.

And if there aren't any cheering throngs along the way, and they never name the road after you, does it really matter? Who cares, so long as it carries life in a worthwhile direction!

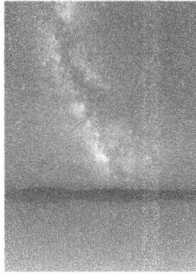

Influences on Lives of Others

EVERY ONCE IN a while, a former student stops by my office and says something nice about how I have helped them. Some of my involvements with them go back many years, and to be honest, it's often difficult to remember who they are, much less anything I may have said or done that they valued.

But it makes me feel very good when it happens, and it's also wonderful that so many of them appear to be enjoying their lives and progressing in their careers. A few have told me that they met their spouses in elective graduate-level classes that I have offered, and that these unions brought children into the world. When I learn of such things, I am reminded of how my life has influenced marvelous events that I am usually unaware of.

Of course, if I hadn't been around to offer those courses, those individuals might have enjoyed other equally terrific alternate relationships and experiences. Still, that doesn't change the fact of my importance in their lives, and I feel honored by this.

I'm certainly not unique in this regard. We all impact peoples' lives in ways we can't fathom. Some routinely do this through their work. Doctors make people well; teachers motivate and guide young minds; police and firefighters rescue people; employers enable people to support families and create personal and professional networks; attorneys help people get out of trouble; scientists, engineers and architects enhance our lifestyles; and elected officials influence circumstances of peace and war.

Unless we live alone on islands, we also affect lives of others just by being our natural selves. We may intentionally or inadvertently introduce people to each other who fall in love and have families. We possibly influence people to relocate or change jobs as a result of our advice or assistance, causing their lives to take a whole new direction. And most assuredly, we touch and affect loved ones and friends in countless ways, large and small, on virtually a daily basis.

A lot of those interactive events—probably most—are similar to "Brownian Motion", where like molecules, we randomly bounce off others, transfer energy, and change our own trajectories and theirs at least somewhat with nearly every contact. If these experiences are sometimes a bit bruising, they do help to keep things lively.

Molecular Events

JUST WHEN WE think we know where we're headed...wham! Someone comes along and shoves us into a new reality. And we do the same to others. Unlike molecules, however, we attempt to exercise some control over where we are going and the results of our encounters.

We try to avoid collisions which are painful for all parties (including ourselves), and make contacts as gentle, satisfying and purposeful as possible. We can never be certain about the long-term effects of our impacts on others, but even when somewhat misguided, we generally mean well.

People sometimes tell us when we make mistakes that cause them hurt or anger, when we could have done something better in our relationships with them, and when we offer advice that doesn't work out well. This can be disillusioning and discouraging.

Parents feel unappreciated when they hear chronic complaints from their children.

Teachers are frustrated by hostile and uncooperative students that they have tried to reach.

Doctors get sued by patients that they have endeavored to help who use them as scapegoats for unavoidable circumstances.

Employers are criticized for forced layoffs, regardless of how hard they may have tried to prevent business reversals.

Dedicated police and attorneys are tarred with the same brushes as their non-representative corrupt peers.

But despite all the hard knocks, isn't it gratifying to exchange kinetic and mindful energy with others, and to realize that our actions and reactions make a difference?

Think about people whose conditions have been altered because you are on this planet—including those who wouldn't otherwise have been born at all. Imagine that the chain reactions you have set into motion will continue throughout the future of humankind.

Then recognize how very important you are the next time you bump into someone.

Difficult Decisions You Have Made

WE INEVITABLY FACE situations which require us to make very difficult decisions that are important to ourselves and others. These circumstances often catch us completely off guard and unprepared. We may have little time or information to assess options and implications, and lack appropriate experience to direct us. Some of the choices may involve high-stake gambles that we can't avoid, where lives, relationships or financial survival might hang in the balance.

The really tough decisions that we make reveal our true character. They force us to confront our worst fears, come to terms with fundamental values, and take charge in the face of great uncertainties. Regardless of the outcomes, our responses to these challenges can teach us many important things about ourselves that we might otherwise never know; enabling us to develop, discover, test, understand and appreciate personal strengths that can be applied in the future.

The roughest decision I have ever faced occurred after a massive stroke left my mother in an almost totally unresponsive state with scant hope for improvement. Although she had signed a living will instructing that she never wanted to be kept alive by artificial means, my sister and I had a feeding tube inserted as a temporary measure to buy time for any chance of a partial recovery.

Mother did improve to the extent that she gradually became able to swallow small amounts of food placed in her mouth, although not enough to sustain her indefinitely. Tests indicated that a large area of her brain had been damaged, and that any significant gains in her awareness or intellectual functions were extremely unlikely.

Then, on two occasions, she pulled out the tube connected into her stomach and stopped eating for days at a time. Did this mean that she could actually reason, and was taking matters literally into her own hands?

By reconnecting the tube each time she pulled it out, were we violating her wishes and cruelly extending her suffering? If she did continue to live, trapped in a dysfunctional body and sustained in an uncommunicative condition, would that be preferable to death? What constitutes a minimally acceptable quality-of-life? Who can decide that for someone else?

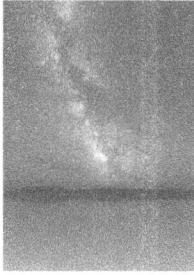

Practicing Tough Love

THE IDEA OF willfully letting someone you love die is terrible to contemplate. But, because we loved her, we decided that forcing her to continue in that tragic state would be inhumane and unconscionable. We were certain that she would not want this if she had a choice.

Shortly after we elected not to reconnect the tube, mom experienced a mortal stroke that was unrelated to our decision. While we will always live with the painful reality of that judgment call, it is one I do not regret.

Many people face wrenching decisions every day. How can we ever be sure what is the right thing to do?

Unfortunately, we can't. Still, recognizing that there are no universal answers, maybe there are some general considerations that can help to guide us.

For example, are we doing our best to understand and honor the desires of people who can't act in their own behalf? Are we responding with integrity, more out of love than fear? Are we influenced more by what we believe is right according to our highest intelligent and moral principles than by concern about how others may view our decisions? Have we taken into account all known factors so that we will be able to accept the validity of our decision later, even if the outcome isn't good?

In the final analysis, we just have to do the best we can to be courageous, compassionate and wise. Then we have good reason to respect ourselves for that, whatever the consequences.

Obstacles You Have Overcome

I'M NOT ALWAYS as sympathetic as I probably should be when people complain about disadvantages and misfortunes that they believe to have held them back. Others who have had it just as bad, and often a whole lot worse, have managed to move beyond their handicaps, celebrate life, and accomplish wonderful things.

I'll bet that you can draw many examples from your own experience.

This isn't to refute the obvious realization that a lot of people really deserve our empathy, compassion and help. But I don't have particularly charitable feelings for those who surrender to lethargy, exhibit antisocial behavior, and blame the world for failing them when they haven't worked to improve circumstances which are well within their responsibility and control.

Sure, some people seem to have it a lot easier than others from the very beginning. They start out with more attentive parents, better schools and safer neighborhoods. Maybe they're healthier than some, more attractive than most, and have remarkable talents that appear to come naturally. And possibly, they have inherited sources of income that give them a big jump-start.

So what? Think about all the exciting challenges that they are missing; those earned satisfactions that result from triumphs over adversities.

Whatever your background, you have undoubtedly had to overcome obstacles that have tested your courage, creativity and confidence. It's also predictable that you have come to understand yourself better and appreciate life more as a result. This is certainly true for one very special person that I have had the enriching fortune to know.

Eric was a student in my University of Houston graduate program several years ago—one of those many fine young people full of enthusiasm, idealism and sincerity who are always a pleasure to be around.

Although he enjoyed his time here, he looked forward to returning to Belgium to be reunited with his friends and family following graduation. Then, after fulfilling his military obligation, he would embark upon the professional career that he dreamed of.

Things didn't quite work out the way he planned.

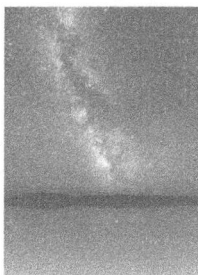

Getting On with Life

THE WEEK AFTER he completed his studies, Eric was severely injured in a car accident while vacationing with his brother and a pal. He was in a deep coma when I visited him in the hospital.

His father had flown in to be with him, and his doctor gave us terrible news. Eric had sustained extensive brain damage, along with severe traumas to other internal organs and limbs. It appeared to be extremely doubtful that he would regain consciousness, and even if he did, would probably never be able to talk, dress and feed himself, or lead a normal life in any respect.

Eric's father accepted that prognosis graciously and bravely, but said he would not abandon hope for a much fuller recovery. I tried to act optimistic too.

Eric and his father have visited me in Houston twice since that tragic time, and have proven the doctor wrong on all accounts. The road to recovery has been long and painful for Eric and his family, and intensive therapy sessions continued.

His progress was constant. In spite of the fact that he walks and talks with some difficulties, he has lost the use of one arm, has impaired vision, tires readily, and has also had to adjust and adapt to other daunting problems, his mind is not only functioning—it is marvelous.

Eric matured into an individual of truly admirable awareness and insights who speaks again and again about good ways that accident has changed his life. How, through that experience, he discovered the great importance of the love he has received from his family and friends. How it has reminded him never to take the incredible gift of life for granted. How the need to compensate for his inability to manually draw design concepts and construction details has motivated him to become highly proficient with computerized graphic systems, leading him to create successful business offices in Belgium and New York that offer these services commercially.

Hearing Eric tell it, that accident was a lucky event. And there's every reason to believe him.

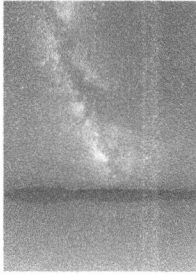

Accepting Responsibilities

HAVE YOU EVER turned down a big opportunity because you didn't want the additional responsibilities that went along with it? For example, a relationship that demanded an exclusive and permanent commitment that you weren't prepared to make? A job offer or promotion that would require you to work longer hours, be in charge of more people, develop new areas of business, or accept a commission or profit-sharing plan in lieu of a salary? An invitation to participate on the Board of Directors of a company that is facing challenging management or financial problems, or to accept a committee nomination or assignment which would require a lot of effort? An investment or a co-signature on a loan for an exciting and potentially high-yield venture that carried some unusual risks?

If you declined such possibilities, did you do so because you are a very selective and prudent person with many options to choose from? Or was it more because you like to be a free, unencumbered spirit and keep life simple?

Our attitudes about responsibility have enormous influences upon what we expect out of life, the way we view ourselves, and the importance we represent to those around us. Some people thrive on being needed, and routinely hold themselves accountable for more than their share of obligations. Others shun unnecessary entanglements, viewing life as a perpetual series of self-centered cost-benefit analyses.

It is sensible to realize that we do have accountabilities to honor our own priorities. Pressing outside demands may sometimes cause us to forget this. After all, obligation junkies have problems too.

For example, they can be vulnerable to those who would abuse their generosity; become overextended, overwhelmed and frustrated by taking on more than they can handle; and express overly efficient, aggressive and controlling behaviors that make them unpleasant to live and work with.

Trying to escape responsibilities can have some large downsides too. Where does that lead? Possibly to making do with yesterday's opportunities? Independence from people and experiences that can be enriching? More time to feel lonely with?

So how much responsibility initiative is enough—or too much? While I don't have any fixed answers, I will offer some personal guidelines that I apply in considering these vexing questions.

Perhaps they may be useful to you.

Larry Bell

Standing up to be Counted On

I HAVE TOO little responsibility when I find myself wondering what to do with my spare time and begin to reorganize my sock drawer; waste time waiting for someone else to do something that I can easily do myself; worry about silly and trivial things; don't have anyone to make unreasonable demands on me; and am not in the middle of at least one small or large crisis.

I have too much responsibility when I find myself fanaticizing about what I will do if I ever have any spare time; waste time doing things that others can easily do for themselves; rush through activities that I would ordinarily do more carefully and enjoy; feel that others are taking me too much for granted; self-righteously evaluate others more harshly than they deserve for doing less; and wish that some friendly aliens would whisk me away from it all.

But what if I went on that flying saucer ride and returned a year or two in the future to discover that everyone was getting along just fine without me? When they called rolls, my name would no longer be on any of the lists. All of the things that I had been working on that seemed so important would have been completed by others who had pretty much forgotten that I had ever been involved.

Sure, many might be glad to see me again. But they would

have learned a secret that I had been holding back from them and myself—that I can become dispensable.

I've decided to continue my masquerade, trying to convince people that I can save the world and do everything that I have persuaded them to expect from me. And when asked to stand up to be counted, I'm going to remind myself to be grateful for that chance, and whenever possible, rise to the occasion.

Celebrating Self-Indulgence

Mastering generosity may require some experience. Occasionally you can practice on yourself

Clinging to Fantasies

I'M MORE INTERESTING in my fantasies than I am in real life.

It's not that I'm totally boring—I do a lot of neat stuff. But while won't admit it, I probably get more respect from colleagues and students than I deserve.

There are many times, perhaps a majority, when I mostly paddle along, trying to keep my little boat on an even keel. Just an ordinary guy who gets ordered around by his wife like lots of other husbands do, blends into crowds, and is generally ignored by beautiful women and domestic animals.

Is this person really me? Unless I am mistaken, I wasn't always like this.

Inside, I don't feel any different than I did long before I was offended when cashiers at fast food restaurants began asking me if I was eligible for a senior citizen discount.

The self that resides inside my mind remains to be a young and idealistic sort, although his interests have changed just a mite over time. I can still remember how excited my child-self became when he built a raft—complete with a toilet paper tube telescope—and dreamed about great ocean adventures. How he encouraged me to swing from tree limbs and trumpet calls to friendly elephants after seeing Tarzan movies.

I still dimly remember how his attention later turned to attracting girls, or at least thinking about them constantly; to imagining enchanted relationships; to conceptualizing perfect career opportunities; and to anticipating fantastic adventures as that former and present me ricocheted like a pinball in an old arcade game through different life experiences.

Being extremely impressionable by nature, that self of mine can still be aroused into action by the slightest provocation, including sentimental music, a warm touch or smile, and a kind and thoughtful comment.

For example, when you have been anticipating for months how happy someone would be when you visited them, then spent the first hour after your arrival waiting for them to end a trivial telephone conversation with another friend.

When you had been anxious to witness someone's pleasure upon receiving a special gift you spent a great deal of thought and time locating, only to find they obviously didn't appreciate your effort.

Or when you were really pumped up about sharing a brilliant idea and received an incredulous response.

Starring Roles and Bit Parts

HAS IT EVER happened when someone looking at an old picture of you that wasn't really all that old asked who the skinny person with the dark hair is?

And call me a romantic fool, but I still cling to illusions that life is supposed to be full of poetry and grace. I still imagine that one day I will come home to an adoring wife who is waiting in suspense to know how I am feeling, and inquire about all the wonderful things that I have accomplished in tearful gratitude.

Soft melodic strains of a romantic ballad will be audible in the background. Conspicuously absent will be strident discords of complaint about everything that went wrong in endlessly frustrating efforts to get the garbage disposal serviced and the telephone bill corrected, what the dog did, and what I must do and when.

By coincidence, my wife Nancy has reported having the same outrageous fantasy.

The great thing about fantasies is that we can have any leading roles we wish, while real life often casts us in bit parts. In the outside world, others often typecast us according to scripts and supporting roles that best suit their interests.

Not wanting to disillusion them or introduce confusion into

established relationships, we may go along, concealing that exciting and enigmatic character within us.

Nancy often chastises me for tuning out from daily routines as I sail mentally off to some private place. I suspect that many other husbands are criticized for the same selfish indulgence.

In doing so, are we fleeing from realities? Or rather, are we seeking reinforcement in super-realities?

Who cares, so long as it enables us to rediscover our own youthful and vibrant faces, those skinny people with dark hair, even if they are mirrored in illusions.

Rising Above Perfection

HAVE YOU SOMETIMES been troubled by a small flaw in something you own which no one else would pay any attention to, yet is often the first thing you notice whenever you use it? A tiny dent in the door of your shiny new car, for example? Sure, it still looks good overall, and drives just the same as before. But it isn't perfect anymore; and maybe that bothers you a lot.

Many of us probably have tendencies to view ourselves in the same critical manner. We worry about flaws in our appearance and actions that bother us to the extent that it is way out of proportion to any logical significance.

Some of those imperfections may be outside of our control, so that all we can do is live with them. Others relate to things that we could change if we really cared enough to exert necessary discipline and effort. Then we can exercise one of three options: feel guilty about accepting the status quo; set an improvement plan into action; or make peace with the circumstances and rise above the need for perfection.

It may be constructive to sometimes be a little bit tough on ourselves so that we recognize possible areas for improvement, knowing that we could have done better at one thing or another, even when the results seemed perfectly satisfactory to others.

Then, we have to decide whether the objective is important enough to warrant remedial initiative, possibly at the expense of other priorities.

But let's remember that compulsive perfectionists often neglect to look at broad issues, fret about small matters, and can be difficult to be around. At least that's what other people tell me.

So, just how perfect do we really want to be? I frequently ask myself that question when I look in my wardrobe closet.

Maybe you're one of those people who can eat as much of everything you want and never put on extra pounds. I'm not. Or at least I wasn't until a successful medical cancer intervention considerably shortened my innards. Before that, my body fat exceeded standards established by ancient Greek sculptors by a fair margin.

I occasionally got serious about trimming down through a combination of starvation and discreet exercises and intermittently lopped off a couple of waistline inches. Then some holiday or celebration came along with more culinary temptations than I could resist, and I was right back to where I started—or worse. As a result, I still have several sets of wardrobe sizes with girth measurements that vary by about a foot in two inch length increments to where I am now.

Discarding Tight Clothes

I'M OFTEN TEMPTED to give away those former fat clothes that stand as haunting reminders of failed discipline. Yet perhaps they also serve as earned trophies of past triumphs as well...to demonstrate, once again, that self-improvement is a constant but winnable struggle.

Attaining holistic perfection, however, ups the effort ante a whole bunch. But as the artist Salvador Dali observed, "Have no fear of perfection—you'll never reach it."

Twentieth century English art critic, John Ruskin, wrote that obtaining imperfection wouldn't be that great in any case. As he notes his book, *The Stones of Venice*: "To banish imperfection is to destroy expression, to check exertion, to paralyze vitality." We certainly wouldn't want to inflict these curses of perfection upon ourselves.

And apparently, life really does imitate art after all. It can be difficult to resist the temptation to be influenced by the hopeless pursuit of illusory perfection portrayed by glamorous magazine and TV idols—and ads hawking weight reduction pills, diet plans and exercise equipment targeting our image insecurities. They tell us that we can pretty much kiss any real chances of social status or romance goodbye unless we buy their products, enroll in their fitness programs, and pluck and tuck our bodies into molds they prescribe.

We get swept up in fear that we aren't pretty enough, tall enough, thin enough. We aren't rich enough to buy those expensive vehicles, go on the luxury cruises, or vacation in the most lavish resorts. And we obviously aren't smart enough to recognize that someone who isn't classically beautiful or have a corner office in the executive suite isn't likely to be missing all that much.

Marion Woodman, Canadian Jungian analyst and author of *Addiction to Perfection* equates dangers of addiction to a need for perfection to dependencies upon drugs and other destructive obsessions. She warns:

> *Perfection is defeat...Perfection belongs to the gods: completeness or wholeness is the most a human being can hope for...it is in seeking perfection by isolating and exaggerating parts of ourselves that we become neurotic. The chief sign of the pursuit of perfection is obsession.*

Woodman wisely observes:

> *...to move toward perfection is to move out of life, or what is worse, never to enter it. A problem arises when our external focus inhibits our ability to focus within, to develop our spiritual, mental and psychological selves.*

So, like dealing with those old skinny clothes in your closet, it might be a good idea to consider discarding other false ideals of perfection that no longer fit as well.

Larry Bell

Freedom from Measuring Up

MAYBE LIFE HAS always gone your way: you were always among the first to be picked in your grade school gym class when they chose sides for basketball or volleyball games; you played first chair trumpet in your high school band; were elected class president, homecoming queen or king, and were voted "most likely to succeed;" were quarterback and captain of the football team, or darling of the cheerleading squad; got straight A's, were selected to the National Honor's Society and became class Valedictorian; and then won a full scholarship to your first university of choice, and were paid a $50,000 salary immediately upon graduation.

And maybe you are just naturally popular because of your striking good looks and unfailing bright toothy smile, and you never had a cavity...plus your parents were rich, sent you to the most exclusive schools and bought you a red Mercedes convertible, when you (barely) graduated from high school.

If so, don't bother to read the rest of this. I don't like you anyway.

Now that those obnoxious people are gone, the rest of us can look at the troubled times that those obnoxiously envied people have caused for us.

Remember how difficult and discouraging that it was to measure up? All the worries that we wouldn't be accepted as a friend by the really neat kids; wouldn't be invited to an important party or dance; would be rejected if we asked someone special out on a date; and wouldn't even make the team or cheerleading squad?

Remember all of the frustrations that no matter how hard we tried (and even when we didn't), our grades weren't good enough, our skin wouldn't clear up, and we always seemed to say the wrong thing at the right time (or vise versa)?

Still, we did our best to give an appearance that we were self-assured and not total dorks, not realizing that almost everyone else had the same worries and were trying to impress us.

When we are young and inexperienced at appreciating ourselves, the differences we perceive between us and others we admire can become grossly exaggerated. Self-consciousness compounds our problems, causing you to trip over our own feet or step on our partner's when we are dancing; get out of synch with people and events around us; and just generally fumble passes that life throws our way.

Ironically, the harder we try, the more self-aware we become, which exacerbates the problems and pains.

Realizing it is Highly Overrated

As parents, we want our children to get things right early on, so that they can enjoy a more graceful evolution into adulthood than we did. We worry about the quality of their friendships, their performance at school, and their competitiveness in achieving a variety of other successes.

We are upset when they don't use opportunities that we provide them for optimum advantage, are saddened when they experience disappointments and setbacks, and are alarmed by any signs that their lives may swerve off onto bad roadways.

Our children feel this, and the added pressures can make them even less confident, fearing that they will fail to meet our hopes and expectations as well as their own. It's bad enough having to impress their peers without also having to satisfy us, their teachers, and every other adult that is conspiring to make life more demanding and complicated.

If we worry a lot about our children, we can be quite certain that they usually worry even more about themselves. They likely brood about things we have forgotten about entirely.

Puberty is one big concern—as they wonder if they are

advancing normally and on schedule. Girls become aware that some friends who are the same age are developing breasts and menstruating before they are. Boys anxiously await evidence of maturity in the form of whiskers, pubic hair and voice changes. They want to grow up, but their bodies may not seem to get the message and cooperate in a timely manner.

We gradually find relief as we learn to discover more and more reassuring aspects of our nature. We recognize our value through friendships and accomplishments we care about. We gradually begin to compare ourselves less against others.

In doing this, we realize that most of those worst-case scenarios we worried about as children never materialized, or at least didn't prove to be very consequential in our later lives. The early bloomers we wanted so urgently to emulate had problems too—for example, worrying that they might fall off the shaky pedestals we put them on.

I'm told that adulation can be a terrible burden.

The fact is that we turned out quite wonderful after all, and so will our children. If you have any lingering doubts, then just grow up!

Rewarding Yourself

I REALLY ENJOY the thoughtful things that I do for myself. Of course, I also appreciate kind gestures and gifts that I receive from others, and also derive pleasure from giving to them. But generosity to myself brings its own special satisfactions.

One advantage of self-charity is that you can give yourself what you really want, rather than receive only what others think that you should desire or have. I'm not just referring to material stuff. In fact, that is invariably the least important to me. Making opportunities to relax, enjoy a small treat, or pursue purely personal interests are typically the most gratifying gifts.

Ideal timing is another big self-indulgence advantage. You can find creative ways to reward yourself whenever you need to—for instance when your morale can stand a boost without having to wait for a special occasion, or depending upon someone else to come up with a cheering idea.

If all this sounds a little selfish, it is. That is what's so great about it!

We shouldn't necessarily need to come up with reasons for being nice to ourselves if it makes us feel better—even though others who are disposed with a less charitable nature may take issue with them.

Here are ten possible excuses to consider when you really feel a need:

If I'm not happy, I'll probably make everyone else miserable too.

I was looking around for someone equally deserving, but was alone at the time.

I wanted to get something that was exactly right, so that I wouldn't have to return it.

It's a personal incentive to work harder and be more successful.

It's a merit award for something good that I did that no one else noticed.

I offered a wonderful opportunity to the best-qualified person that I could find.

I was bored, and couldn't think of anything better to do.

I'm making up for the fact that someone forgot my birthday.

I wanted to try it out before I gave it to someone else.

I suffered from momentary insanity.

Or maybe you can simply admit it, sometimes you feel like being selfish, and just let it go at that.

Larry Bell

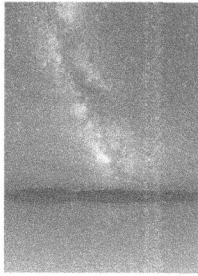

Selfishly Satisfying and Unnecessary Excuses

THIS DOESN'T MEAN you want to take away anything someone else has or deserves. It's more a conscious assertion of the importance that you place upon your own sense of pleasure and well-being.

Nor is selfishness necessarily a solitary experience. Some of the most gloriously selfish moments can be shared with someone else who has the same inclination. For example, when a couple steals off to spend time away from other pressing responsibilities because they believe it will be constructive for their relationship – or maybe, just because they have equal or greater responsibilities to themselves.

When we grant license to occasionally be generous to ourselves, it becomes easier to acknowledge, accept and respond to that need in others who are close to us. Hopefully, they will answer in kind. These can be win-win situations, provided that the parameters of these reciprocal agreements are equitable and well understood by all parties.

In reality, being generous with ourselves may have more to do with attitudes than actions. In my case there isn't all that much

247

I really need to have or do in order to be contented so long as I know that I can sometimes exercise prerogatives aimed exclusively at my own personal satisfaction.

I might take a few days away from home to attend an interesting conference or workshop. While I'm not a hunter, I can meet a friend at a gun range for target shooting, followed by shared lunches and political discussions. Every once in a while, I may wish to drop by a neighborhood pub after work, smoke an expensive cigar, and have a glass of excellent imported ale with the locals. Or I might like to go for a drive in the country, clear my head, and enjoy a change of scenery.

By asserting these privileges, I consciously give myself a priority, just as I do for others I care about. I thereby reserve a natural right to pamper and indulge myself in gleeful abandonment without remorse, guilt or accountability if ever I should choose to. I deserve that, and you do too!

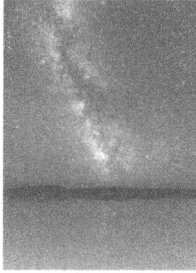

Pleasures of Getting Even

DO YOU EVER feel a desire to have a little fun at the expense of someone who has gotten on your nerves? I'm not talking about seeking revenge for a serious injustice that has caused bile to rise in your throat. I'm referring to small stuff, often involving very nice and innocent people who have inadvertently rubbed you the wrong way.

Possibly they're even too nice and innocent, and your tolerance for saints is low on a particular day. Or perhaps they have an annoying habit that has begun to irritate you to the point that you hear a gruff voice within you say, "if they say or do that one more time, I'm going to say or do something really ugly!"

Maybe they take your kindness and generosity too much for granted—like borrowing things which they forget to return; or expecting you to drive them around when their car is in the shop for repairs, and never returning the favor. Maybe they're just too damned nice...or at least appear to be when your suspicions tell you that they are up to something less noble.

I confess that I am sometimes vulnerable to such pettiness. Usually I just daydream about inflicting some terrible suffering on them and just take pleasure in that glorious contemplation. But occasionally (actually very rarely) I put my diabolical thoughts into action…even though they may never realize it. I will share one cherished example.

Many years ago, I lived a short distance away from a public park that covered an area of about nine square blocks. A fellow I knew only as an acquaintance passed my home almost daily to run laps around it. When he saw me he unfailingly asked if I would join him, and not being one who seeks happiness through sweat, exertion and discomfort, I just as unfailingly declined.

I will mention here that I harbor uncivil disdain for people who flaunt healthy consciousness and superior physical conditioning to give sedentary lifestyles a slothful image. If this is a guilt issue, I will never give them the satisfaction of hearing me admit it.

One day his repeated assault upon my dormancy provoked me to accept what I regarded to be a personal dare. Wearing old jeans and a broken down pair of loafers that starkly contrasted with his preppy jogging outfit, I gamely ambled off with him to the field of battle.

I apologized in advance that I didn't want to slow him down, and told him to feel free to run on ahead when I didn't keep up. Secretly, I had no intention of letting that happen. Not even if it killed me.

Another Lap around the Park

AFTER A FEW laps at his side I could tell that he was tiring, but was certain that his condition was nothing compared with my state of exhaustion. But did I let him know this? Not a chance!

With all the discipline that I could muster, I controlled my breathing to avoid any telltale gasps. I even chatted about how much fun I was having, and how I wished I had discovered this stimulating activity earlier. The more I hurt, the more I talked.

Just when it became clear that I wouldn't be able to sustain my deception a minute longer, my companion suggested that we stop for the day. I responded with a disingenuous smile and heroic bluff that maybe we should do another lap first, just to get our heart rates up. He looked at me with an expression of pained disbelief, telling me that he was ready to quit. I graciously agreed to comply.

But it wasn't over yet. Forcing myself to breathe slowly and quietly as my lungs cried out for mercy, I was somehow able to continue the charade as we walked back in the direction of my house. I lied about how invigorated I felt in spite of a bad leg and chronic asthma problems. And while I was nauseatingly upbeat, he was uncharacteristically uncommunicative and sullen.

After we parted company, I finally allowed my rib cage to

heave mightily as I gulped for air like a beached fish, collapsed into bed, and for a person in pure agony, I never felt better.

And do you know what? He never invited me to go running with him again.

Maybe it has occurred to you that this whole episode was a lot harder on me than it was on him. After all, getting even does usually impose some costs and penalties that are appropriately applicable here in the old adage: "What goes around, comes around."

Yeah, but I paid in advance for that treachery when I was going around and coming around, and it was well worth the investment. I'm still enjoying the dividends in sharing it with you.

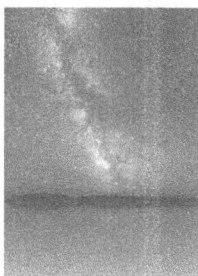

Confronting Opportunities and Embracing Changes

If you're not satisfied with where life has delivered you, then get excited about where you want to go, get behind the steering wheel, and get moving. We come into the world kicking and screaming. Isn't it time that we learn to accept new experiences more optimistically and enthusiastically?

Outlining Your Autobiography

IF YOU WROTE a novel based upon your life, what type of book would it be? Romantic? Adventure? Satirical? Inspirational?

Would you need to fictionalize a lot of it to make it interesting—or do you already have a good supply of material to draw from? If you could choose to re-write your actual life, would you do so? Would you change some of the central characters and locations? Would you alter the storyline in a significant way and have important events turn out differently?

I suspect that most of our lives contain elements of many different book categories, and that some parts wouldn't be exciting enough to rivet the attention of readers who didn't share those times with us, or care about us as someone special to them. How we ourselves view those periods is a different matter. If we aren't satisfied that the overall story is interesting and meaningful, then there's a fundamental problem.

Assuming that chapters mark major developments and changes in our lives, my book would have many. While this isn't necessarily desired by everyone, it suits my nature very well, and I like to think that there will be many more surprises to follow.

I also respect and admire people whose experiences are soundly anchored and reflect a high degree of continuity. For example, they may identify strongly with a particular locality where they have lived much or all of their lives; enjoy stable, deeply rooted friendships that have developed gradually; and have a great capacity to appreciate profound beauty in subtleties of the world around them.

Others seem to carry continuity with them. Although they may relocate from time to time, they draw comfort and stability from their families, through professional networks and religious affiliations that provide familiar references, and within career roles and activities that are relatively constant.

Special dynamics come into play that change most of our lives in significant ways. Children are born, grow up, leave, marry and bring grandchildren into the picture. Illnesses and losses of loved ones force difficult adjustments. And eventual retirement brings about major activity, time management and psychological lifestyle changes.

Some people thrive on change. They become restless if something new isn't happening nearly all of the time, and if it isn't, they cause it to occur. I confess that I exhibit clear evidence of this tendency.

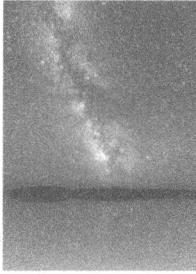

Planning a Happy Ending

IF ADVENTURESOME PEOPLE are fortunate, they find someone to appreciate and share their proactive spirit. If not, finding that kindred soul may be an important part of their quest.

Examples of such stimulation junkies establish a home base somewhere to warehouse their furniture and plants, and spend much of their time in other places; or get a travel home, pare down expendable stuff, and take their remaining possessions with them. Maybe they don't move around at all, but change work or other focused interests repeatedly. Or possibly they create excitement by embarking upon bold new enterprises that trade risks for large potential economic or pure satisfaction paybacks.

Each of us has our own ideas about the sort of lives that we wish to experience. For some of us, these desires and expectations may evolve as we go through different stages. We might occasionally envy those whose lives have qualities we feel are missing in our own, yet realize in our more realistic moments that we will be more comfortable keeping things somewhat the way they are.

For instance, we might desire more adventure, but be unwilling to give up the security we presently enjoy to get it. The reverse can be equally true. Or maybe we make small compromises to accommodate our desires without abandoning what we care most about.

If you're really unhappy with your current life, you may want to do something more ambitious to change it. At least consider what a more ideal life would be like if you were to add a future chapter or more to that fictionalized autobiography.

Then, when you look at that character in the circumstances that you have portrayed, you can consider whether or not that person is someone you would trade your present situation to be— or just a fantasy to be enjoyed on that basis alone?

Your life is your book to write. Fact or fiction, it is all you have.

Treasure it.

Avoiding Obsolescence

LIKE ALL LIVING organisms, when we cease to progress, we get into big trouble. Either we grow or stagnate—those are our only options. But unlike other less cerebral and self-actualizing creatures, we can exercise free will to determine which condition shall prevail. We can elect to be vital parts of the happenings around us—or we can passively submit to the forces of those events, whether they sweep us along or pass us by. In short, we can become involved, or we can become obsolete.

Few of us would consciously choose that second option. It is more fun to be productive and witness wonderful changes that we can bring about through our enterprises. It's gratifying to engage and cooperatively interact with people that we respect and enjoy. It's rewarding to realize that we are in control of our lives, not allowing ourselves to be dominated by circumstances that limit and misuse us.

Growth and vitality, vs. stagnancy and obsolescence, are matters for personal definition. Each of us must determine which progress indicators are appropriate. Some may attach such priorities as wealth and material possessions, popularity and recognition, work achievements and honors, activity levels and adventures, spiritual and intellectual understanding, compassion and service, qualities of relationships, and triumphs over tragedies and hardships.

Most of us apply multiple criteria. The central issue has to do with how we visualize ourselves today relative to where we were and where we are heading. Take yourself for example. Are you moving in a direction you like? Are you moving at all?

Now, if you're not pleased with your answer, consider some possible reasons:

Have you become either so comfortable with achievements or so beaten by failures that you lack motivation to move forward? Have you lost the willingness to accept reasonable risks for greater gains?

Do you cling to familiar ways of thinking and doing things without considering other alternatives?

Have you settled for marginally acceptable or even unsatisfactory circumstances and relationships, rather than exert the imagination and initiative to improve them?

Have you allowed yourself to be so out of touch with changing social, technical and business conditions that you feel disenfranchised from the world around you?

Is it becoming more and more difficult to get excited about events and possibilities due to feelings of déjà vu, cynicism, exhaustion, or other symptoms of psychological burnout?

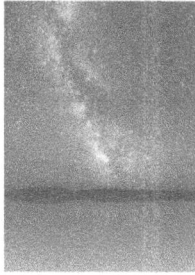

Growing With the Flow

THE LONGER THESE circumstances are permitted to continue, the more difficult it becomes to turn things around. And quoting a popular NASA mission planning adage, "The sooner you fall behind, the more time you'll have to catch up."

In putting off important changes energy dissipates, confidence erodes, determination ebbs, and hopes evaporate.

It's important to develop a new lease on life as quickly as possible, even if it means moving to a lower rent district until we get organized. As a Chinese fortune cookie message I recently drew wisely advised: "If you wait too long for the perfect moment, the perfect moment will pass you by."

Or as American author H. Jackson Brown Jr. observes in *Life's Little Instruction Book*:

> *Opportunity dances with those who are already on the dance floor.*

We also risk missed opportunities leading to obsolescence whenever we pigeonhole ourselves into limiting self-concepts. For example, when mothers wrap their entire identities around caregiving to children who will ultimately leave home and create lives for themselves...abandoning their own personal sense of self in the process. Personal growth and self-esteem can be stifled when workers view themselves exclusively in terms of highly specialized roles, and when prestigious office titles are vulnerable to termination or redefinition. Versatility and resilience are valuable safeguards.

We can never be obsolete so long as we recognize our strengths and can find ways to apply them. If we aren't entirely sure what those strengths are, then it's time to really start looking for challenging opportunities to discover them.

Where do we look? For starters, novelist Anais Nin, author of *Delta of Venus,* reminds us to remember:

> *"We don't see things as 'they' are, we see them as 'we' are."*

Even if no one, including ourselves, expects us to change the world, we do so every day by just taking up space. So while we're here, we might as well do something useful, interesting, and stimulating that causes us to evolve...to make something of rich opportunities to become something more.

As George Bernard Shaw noted:

> *Life isn't about finding yourself, it's about creating yourself.*

Accepting Worthwhile Risks

TRY AS YOU may to avoid them, you can't get away from risks. Far worse possibilities that bad things can often happen along with lost opportunities for even better than hoped for outcomes if you don't take a chance.

For example, maybe you didn't introduce yourself to someone interesting out of fear of rejection, and consequently missed out on an important relationship. Or you decided not to spend time and money to attend a significant conference, never knowing that you would have learned about a great work position or business opportunity which would have been perfect for you.

Of course, we usually don't gamble precious things on long shots when we have more prudent choices. And sometimes, we really don't have good alternatives.

A close friend who had tried every conventional option to cure her aggressive cancer finally turned unsuccessfully to an unorthodox treatment as a last ditch hope. I have also known people with serious financial problems who took high-risk gambles they wouldn't ordinarily have accepted, believing that they had more to gain than lose. Desperate circumstances can provoke drastic measures.

Some people take big risks that make no sense at all. For

example, they drive fast and recklessly, abuse those they care about and depend upon, and wager money that they can't afford to lose in casinos and highly speculative business ventures. Whether driven by unseasoned impulses, misguided attempts to gain recognition, or the exhilaration of experiencing "life on the edge," it all boils down to irresponsible behavior.

Still, we also know people who go to the opposite extreme. Some are so fixated on worries about small downside risks that they are incapable of recognizing large upside possibilities. Others want guaranteed returns on every investment, whether those expenditures involve money, time, effort or trust.

Who are these people? Let's see if you recognize a few from the following clues.

They always seem to wait for others to pick up the check. They seldom express personal or controversial ideas. They deliberately continue on in unsatisfactory and futile work situations when there are more promising possibilities. And they forego potentially enriching relationships to avoid commitments which might be attached.

What Have You Got to Lose?

BIG RISK DECISIONS often involve tradeoffs between desires for security and adventure. Since we can't have copious amounts of both, we typically try to hedge our overall bets so that we can expect to wind up with an acceptable balance. How much of either that we seek is influenced by a variety of personal factors, including: our histories of hardships and successes; our sense of responsibility for others who depend upon us; our general temperament, self-confidence and optimism; and our dreams and ambitions.

When we have too little security to meet basic needs, it is natural to be risk-averse. When we are comfortable and confident that those requirements are assured, then we can well afford to pursue more adventurous options.

Being too risk-averse, however, may jeopardize personal growth. As Neale Donald Walsch, American author of the series *Conversations with God* wrote: "Life begins at the end of your comfort zone."

In reality, there is no such thing as total security. Regardless how affluent and satisfied we are, mortality presents inescapable perils for everyone. And if we hope to achieve more security in life, we must almost always accept some risks and costs associated with the new initiatives required to gain it.

When we avoid worthwhile risks, we deny ourselves challenges that cause us to grow and to realize the excitement of experiencing fuller lives. Henry David Thoreau reminds us: "The price of anything is the amount of life you exchange for it."

Only you can determine which risks and costs are appropriate for you. When opportunities come along, no one else can evaluate whether the prospective benefits warrant necessary expenses and uncertainties of the gamble.

Before you decide, make it a habit to ask yourself what you have to lose both ways, and to remember that not taking a chance sometimes presents by far, the greatest risk of all. As hockey's "The Great One" Wayne Gretzky observed:

You miss 100 percent of the shots you don't take.

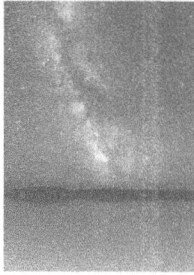

Making Changes Work for You

OKAY. SO YOU took a worthwhile risk, and now you're in a new situation that you don't quite know how to cope with. Good for you! As Irish playwright Samuel Beckett instructs us:

> *Ever tried. Ever failed. No matter. Try again. Fail again. Fail better.*

Or maybe the change occurred somewhat by accident. There you were, drifting serenely down the river of life, and suddenly realized there were turbulent rapids up ahead. In any case, it was too late to change your course.

There are many kinds of circumstances that require us to navigate through rough waters. For instance: when we lose someone that we have depended upon; when our first child is born and we lack confidence in our care-giving knowledge; when we move from comfortable places and relationships to unfamiliar settings; and when we leave secure employment to pursue new work challenges.

Each of these situations impose different demands which we

have to respond to in our own special ways. There are five general lessons that I have learned from my own experiences which might be useful to consider in a variety of circumstances:

Lesson One is that if you can't sit still, then really get moving! You can't rely entirely upon the swift current of events to carry you safely through all of the obstacles. Instead, you sometimes have to paddle like hell to take command of your options so that they aren't left to chance, or fall under the control of others.

People who constantly operate in a reactive mode are typically overwhelmed, confused and ineffective. Even though you may not have all of the desirable knowledge and confidence, it is important to set some form of purposeful, yet flexible plan into action. Put yourself in charge of your own choices. They are too vital to delegate.

Lesson Two is to make it a practice to look at the BIG PICTURE so that you don't get lost in the details. In your personal life, try to be clear about what it is that you care most about. In a new job or position assignment, work to understand the broad priorities and scope of the business or service environment of the organization, and the ways that your designated role fits into and contributes to them.

Constantly strive to visualize your participation within the context of larger purposes and processes which will be impacted by your performance. Focus on things that are most important, and make certain that they are accomplished well and on time. Get and stay organized.

Canoeing in Rapids

LESSON THREE IS to define your opportunities, responsibilities and prerogatives as ambitiously as possible. Push the boundaries of your personal expectations and job descriptions to the limit. Be more than anyone expects you to be.

Don't worry about what others might consider to be either beneath or above your appointed station. Find ways to help friends and associates look good, and be an advocate for them. Think of any title or status that you have as an opportunity to take action rather than as a license to take credit. See yourself as a leader, and act like one.

Lesson Four is to value your own resources and abilities. If you don't know how to solve a problem someone else's way, then devise your own approach. Don't allow yourself to be intimidated by things that you don't immediately comprehend merely based on a lack of background information and experience. Just absorb what you can, and make it a point to investigate points that you missed later.

Learn to be patient with yourself. Don't be afraid to ask questions, but do this thoughtfully, especially when formal occasions warrant some discretion.

Heed Henry Ford's advice: "Whether you believe you can do

a thing or not, you are right."

Lesson Five is to learn from others, but be yourself. Everyone has their own special strengths and styles. When you attempt to emulate others or compete with them on their terms, you are likely to fail. Doing that often tends to cloud your awareness of your own unique qualities, impairs natural creativity, and keeps you off balance. Besides, being who you are can be a lot of fun once you get the hang of it.

You can't always buck the current and reverse direction, or even steer to a safe refuge on shore. So you better learn to swim, get ready for that raging white water, do your best to stay clear of the boulders and submerged logs, and be prepared to get your feet wet.

Dive in and enjoy the thrill.

Moving on to New Experiences

MANY OF THE satisfactions and disappointments that we experience in new situations are rooted in attitudes that we bring with us. Perhaps things were going along just dandy, and we didn't bargain for major changes to occur in the first place.

It's hard to give up established sources of comfort and enjoyment to encounter difficult adjustments with questionable benefits. When forced to do this, it's normal to harbor skeptical and negative feelings which drag along like heavy baggage.

When I was a young child, my parents made arrangements to move our family from the community of my birth to another small town in the area. I can still remember how upset I felt about that at the time.

Didn't I already live in the most terrific place in the world? I had no image of the new home at all.

And what about my friends? Maybe I would never see them again. I had no way to visualize others who might later replace them.

The idea of giving up almost everything familiar in return for an unfathomable existence seemed almost like dying. And come to think of it, many of us do think of death in much the same way, probably due to similar ignorance and fear of the unknown.

But life did actually go on after that early move. There were wonderful new places to discover, lasting friendships to be created, and experiences that helped to shape the person I've become. That's an important aspect of going through changes. We are transformed in the process, and invariably become stronger and wiser as a result.

When we are unwilling to accept changes, our growth ceases.

Look back at large changes that have occurred in your life. I'm willing to bet that most led to treasured opportunities, relationships and events. Even considering those that were traumatic at the time, like my personal experience with cancer for example, hasn't there usually been a silver lining to those clouds that have passed over you?

Don't bright days usually follow? Isn't it useful to have circumstances that give us a boot in the pants sometimes to keep us moving? Can you be certain that your life would have turned out better if some of those changes hadn't occurred?

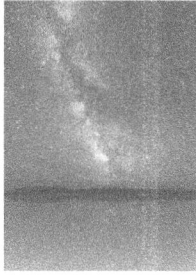

Advantages of Traveling Light

WE'VE ALL MET people who often complain that their current situation or environment doesn't measure up to others that they knew before. For instance, they form negative judgments about a community that they have only recently relocated to, before they have made any effort to investigate its strong points of interest and opportunities. They do the same thing when it comes to evaluating new people that they meet, working conditions they enter into, and organizations they participate in.

Sometimes this negative tendency reflects a fundamental unwillingness and inability to adapt, a typical problem for many as they grow old. Others may just tend to be critical and unhappy by nature. Whatever the reasons, they close out wonderful realities and possibilities that are all around them.

Changes are most fully enjoyed when we are free of preconceptions that limit clear vision; when we are ready for new challenges; when we are confident and optimistic about our abilities to make contributions; and when we are prepared to release restrictive tethers to the past. This applies to routine everyday matters as well as to momentous developments that affect our lives in major ways.

Changing ourselves is often difficult. It can require us to

drop old and comfortable habits, embrace risks with uncertain rewards, and abandon prejudices that filter the way we see things as well as the way others view us.

Yet there is much to gain in the process. Changes offer us chances for fresh new starts and opportunities to reach higher experiences and goals.

As John F. Kennedy noted:

> *Change is the law of life. And those who look only to the past or present are certain to miss the future.*

Positive attitudes help to keep us looking forward, and to get our lives pointed in the right directions.

Exercising Personal Strengths

No one can take power away from you. It can only be given away.

Expressing Yourself

ONCE ON MY birthday, a business partner surprised me by hiring a belly dancer as a featured attraction that was arranged for the occasion. To be perfectly honest, she wasn't really as attractive as one might expect for performers in her field. Nevertheless, through her enthusiasm and confident bearing she convincingly acted as though she was in full command of the situation, and I certainly had to give her credit for that.

In reality, the whole event was quite tame, and it seemed that Nancy, other wives, and female employees enjoyed it at least as much as the guys did—particularly as they waited for my complexion to turn crimson while that dancer worked very actively and closely to get my attention.

It occurred to me, however, that being less than perfect in face, form and skill, she might have had even more to be self-conscious about than I did. Yet, she didn't reveal any inkling of embarrassment, and seemed to put her whole heart—yes, and other considerably large body parts as well, into her work. I respected her for that and everyone else seemed to as well.

It was a wonderfully fun gift.

Some people have the enviable capacity to feel good about themselves, regardless of aspects that others might perceive as flaws. One might initially ask, "why anyone would go out of their way, as that dancer did, to expose parts of themselves that aren't generally considered beautiful in a conventional sense?"

An answer might be that they believe that they are beautiful, and have no particular desire to be conventional. Soon they may have convinced lots of other people that they are right. In any case, who can fault them for that?

The ways that we think of ourselves affect what we project to others and influence their responses. You probably already know this, but most of us need to be reminded occasionally. When we feel self-assured and strong, others immediately sense this and are likely to take us seriously.

When we like and enjoy ourselves, this is often revealed in a friendly and considerate manner that puts people at ease and invokes trust. When we feel secure about our knowledge and abilities, we are most likely to be open to other people's viewpoints as good listeners and enthusiasts. When we have our lives pretty much under control, this is made readily apparent through our cheerfulness, optimism and positive energy.

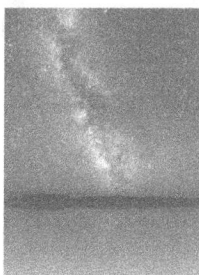

Observing an Aging Belly Dancer

UNFORTUNATELY, MOST OF us don't feel one hundred percent great about ourselves all of the time, and some people never seem to. We may get discouraged when we see an older face than we imagined looking back at us in the mirror, when we find it necessary to use the next larger hole in our belt when hitching up our pants, and when honest people tell us when everything we do or say isn't as terrific as we previously thought.

Things happen in our lives that drag us down, put us off balance, make us nervous and agitated, and provoke anger that we take out on innocent victims, which causes us to feel even lousier. Maybe sometimes we want empathy and support from those close to us that doesn't materialize (maybe because we haven't reciprocated), causing us to feel abandoned and undervalued.

In such cases, what can we do to get back in touch with that wonderful person that has retreated inside that really has much good stuff to express? I guess sometimes we just have to fake it— and buy time for that better self to emerge from hiding.

We need to do our best to rise above feelings that can range from mild depression to wretched despair and go on with the show. We can remind ourselves that things could be worse, and likely will be, if we don't get our act together.

We can imagine and focus on that person we want to be—that beautiful real self that we have been covering for who missed the curtain call. And sometimes, before we fully realize it, that person is back taking over and earning applause.

Maybe that belly dancer was doing this all the time. I can imagine her getting ready for that debut in my office: putting makeup on a face that had lost youthful luster; dressing in a costume that had bumped its way with her through countless performances; driving to an address scribbled on a note card to meet her appointment with strangers; unpacking the old tape player from her car; and then trying to become that seductive vision that she held in her mind.

Doubtless, that was but a routine event of no great significance among many in her past or future. Yet she made it seem special to us, and won over her audience.

We all have the power to believe in and take possession of our best self so that others can recognize what we really represent. This is possible when we give ourselves credit for being what we are—the original and genuine articles.

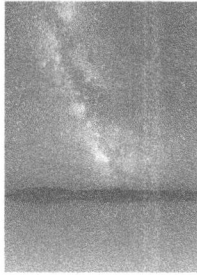

Learning from Experience

LIFE IS QUITE often a confusing series of experiences. There are so many choices available to us that we can never be certain which option would turn out best.

Most of the time, our decisions don't immediately seem to matter much. Just about the worst thing that can happen, is that we wind up sitting through a boring or depressing movie, have a bad meal at a restaurant where the service is even worse, purchasing something that breaks down shortly after the warranty expires, or experience other disappointments of that ilk.

Of course, negative consequences of more important decisions can be very serious. We might trust people who take advantage of us, sacrifice an excellent career opportunity for one that doesn't work out, or invest a great deal of time or money in a losing "sure thing" venture. In extreme circumstances, such as selecting between critical medical treatment possibilities, the decisions can even be life or death matters.

Try as we may to investigate all background information, or consult with experts and carefully weigh the data, we sometimes find that complexities only add to our confusion. There may not be enough recent and reliable information to support a decision necessary to provide any level of assurance.

Different decisions involve independent judgments on our part. We typically have to consider how much a particular opportunity or result is worth to us, how much of ourselves we are willing to invest in order to achieve success, and how much influence we are likely to have in controlling the outcomes. In seeking answers to these questions, we must attempt to understand ourselves better and come to terms with our real interests—sometimes within the context of new situations that we have never before encountered.

Many successful people I have known have learned to trust internal voices speaking to them from positive and negative experiences, from successes and failures, and from actions taken and avoided. In doing so, they have gained the courage and insights necessary to seize opportunities when others falter, and avoid temptations that have led others along treacherous paths of action.

Recognizing that intuition born of experience is vital, these winners apply very rational processes gained through experience as well. They get all the good advice they can, sensing whether or not particular possibilities are desirable and realistic early in the process. They look ahead to consider various implications of key choices.

Moreover, they make it a point to refocus their attention back and forth between the big picture and details where devils lurk.

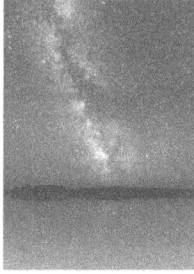

Insights and Outlooks

RECOGNIZING THAT EACH of our experiences are unique, what we can learn from them offer universally lessons that have been expressed by people with diverse perspectives. Here are a few notable quotables worth sharing:

I am sure it is everyone's experience, as it has been mine, that any discovery we make about ourselves or the meaning of life is never, like a scientific discovery, a coming upon something entirely new and unsuspected; it is rather, the coming to consciousness recognition of something, which we really knew all the time but, because we were unwilling to formulate it correctly, we did not hitherto know we knew.
—English poet, W.H. Auden Markings

Not what we experience, but how we perceive what we experience, determines our fate.
—Austrian writer, Marie von Ebner-Eschenbach

You gain strength, courage, and confidence by every experience in which you really stop to look fear in the

face. You are able to say to yourself, 'I lived through this horror. I can take the next thing that comes along.'
——America's first lady, Eleanor Roosevelt

Character cannot be developed I ease and quiet. Only through experience of trial and suffering can the soul be strengthened, ambition inspired, and success achieved.
——Humanitarian Helen Keller

Given the choice between the experience of pain and nothing, I would choose pain.
——American writer, William Faulkner

Experience is never limited, and it is never complete; it is an immense sensibility, a kind of huge spider-web of the finest silken threads suspended in the chamber of consciousness, and catching every airborne particle in its tissue.
——American author, Henry James

You can't create experience. You must undergo it.
——French novelist, Albert Camus

And finally:

Some days are just bad days, that's all. You had to experience sadness to know happiness, and I remind myself that not every day is going to be a good day, that's just the way it is!
——Fashion designer, Dita Von Teese

Empowering Our Presence

WE CAN'T MAKE our presence felt in the present by living in the past, no matter how wonderful but often forgetful memories imagine it to have been.

Do you truly find yourself yearning for those "good old days?" I try to, and usually don't, but admit that there were some aspects of those earlier times which were great.

For example, when I was a child living in a small town, we didn't have to think about crime as part of our reality. Our parents didn't worry about us leaving the yards, doors were left unlocked, and cars could be parked with keys in ignitions. Drugs were as foreign to us as opium dens in Singapore—at least until we entered high school and were warned about the instant insanity and narcotic dependence that would result from smoking a reefer of marijuana. That was pretty scary!

Job security is remembered as another past luxury, with large corporations becoming restructured and down-sized, small businesses experiencing high failure rates, and professionals in all fields facing stiffer competition for positions each year.

After all, most of us were too young (or unborn) to remember the Great Depression of the 1930s. That was when being poor was considered to be "normal;" hard work in menial tasks and enterprising attitudes made bad situations tolerable; prices escalated on almost a daily basis; and families got along by "using it up, wearing it out, making do, or doing without."

Sure, but now we are witnessing new disturbing trends. One is an apparent breakdown of family structure in some poorer communities along with deterioration of remembered values in our broader society…particularly, as reflected in movies and the media. We are bombarded with images of violence brought into our homes on television, along with vulgarity and mindless banality that assault our traditional sense of wholesome entertainment and civil culture.

Do these conditions reflect a general decline in our social expectations and standards? Or rather, did they always exist, but in less conspicuous and blatant forms?

I personally believe that the moral and ethical standards that most people hold today are just as high. Most families care just as much about their children as parents and other relatives ever did, and tend to be every bit as active in guiding them.

And from my vantage point as a parent and professor, the kids today have a lot going for them. They are much more aware of challenges and opportunities in our rapidly changing world then most of us were at their ages. They are more concerned about important issues, such as a need to protect our natural environment. They are just as idealistic, but also a good deal more pragmatic in their outlooks. I have every expectation that they will do just great!

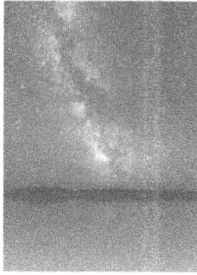

Relishing the Present

WE ALL CARRY our own references from the past that influence our perceptions and evaluations of the present. Being a few years older than my wife, mine are slightly different from hers, evidenced most consciously in sentimental music preferences.

"How far back was that?" you may ask.

To give you some idea, my high school prom theme was *Red Sails in the Sunset* and Elvis Presley had just recorded *Blue Suede Shoes*. While I often haven't understood my children's taste in clothes and music, I have tried to remind myself that my parents had that same reaction...and that my children probably will too when their time of parenthood comes.

I have also attempted to discipline myself against drawing too many references from the past when offering constructive advice to my children. This is partly because I felt somewhat taken back when they replied: "Sure, we know that you had to walk miles to school in cold blowing snow—give us a break!"

Actually, that snow-walking bit was true, although I admit that much of its relevance has since been lost. After all, times have changed, and now they have learned their own hard lessons to teach me.

How can we integrate those past experiences in order to enjoy the present more fully?

It has occurred to me that our mortal life might be compared to eating a submarine sandwich.

The past, before we existed, and the future we dream about, are the bun halves that hold everything together. The inside layers—the salami, turkey, cheese, pickles, etc., are all of the times and experiences we have known that lend flavors and textures. Together, they comprise the principle ingredients that provide identity and substance.

We can also add condiments as we choose with our attitudes so that we relish these experiences more.

Our present part of this whole experience is when we take a bite out of the sandwich and taste everything all at once. That's the best part of life…the pleasure of savoring it all.

Knowing What We Want

IT CAN BE exasperating to be around people who never seem to
know what they want. They either try to keep all of their options
open as long as possible, or expect others to make decisions for
them.

Both situations are often frustrating. Those who wait
interminably for the best offers to come along can waste a lot of
other people's time and effort trying unsuccessfully to please
them. Those who expect us to make choices for them, transfer
their share of responsibility which we are made accountable for.
We are then the ones who inherit the blame and possible guilt if
things don't turn out according to their wishes. Maybe some of
those who put us in charge even had this in mind from the
beginning.

People who don't know what they want often get run over
by those who do. This can happen accidentally when no one sees
them standing in the middle of the road. This can be accomplished
in a number of ways. For example, they may overwhelm and
dominate those who are weak and impressionable; manipulate
decision processes to serve their own interests; and seize upon the
delays they create to undermine prospects they don't like.

I'm not sure which is worse—dealing with people who

never express an opinion, or those who always expect to have their own way. In my general experience, the ratio of the latter to the former is quite high, meaning that if we aren't prepared to assert our rights, we are likely to be pushed around a lot.

For example, since I am the only unfailingly reasonable one in my immediate family, I sometimes act in an intentionally obstinate manner so that Nancy and my sons don't take my accommodating nature too much for granted. The victories I seek in doing this are usually more symbolic than substantive, revolving around relatively small disputes that don't matter much in the long run.

Unlike most others, being disposed with a similarly agreeable and generous nature, you undoubtedly do the same. You will readily understand then, if we don't hang tough on issues once in a while, we wouldn't get any respect at all—would we?

There are some situations when most of us find it necessary to defend important interests and principles against very formidable and dedicated challengers. Our adversaries may be considerably more experienced and skillful negotiators than we are, causing our confidence and resolve to be severely tested.

Or Acting Like We Do

GOOD NEGOTIATORS USUALLY know in advance what they want and what they are and are not willing to give up in order to obtain it. They have a practiced knack for convincing opponents that they are operating from superior positions of morality and strength; that small concessions on their part represent significant and generous compromises; and that their proposals are in the best interests of both sides.

Their strategies are aimed at gaining every advantage they can, and they win by having focused and proactive plans. We may not be accustomed to being as aggressive and calculating as they are, but it may sometimes be necessary to adopt their tactics if we really hope to prevail.

Are we always in touch with what we want and expect out of our daily lives? I'm not.

New possibilities routinely unfold that require me to remain open and flexible. Most of these involve democratic decisions which attempt to address and reconcile preferences of all participants. I'm generally quite content to go along with the majority, or support those who have the best grasp of issues and options.

Serious confrontations are actually very rare, and I will avoid them whenever there are sensible alternatives. When this is not possible, there may be little choice but risk unpleasant arguments and conflicts if the cause is a worthy one, and provided that I have a high degree of certainty that my position on the matter is correct.

When we recognize and pursue what is important, we usually make it easier—not harder—for others to relate to us. People recognize that we are guided by coherent principles and purposes, rather than by erratic whims and superficial impulses.

While they may not necessarily agree with the premises and directions that we present, they are likely to respect our confidence and conviction. By clarifying where we are coming from, we can help them to understand where we are going...and why. Then there is a better chance that they will be inclined to join us.

Even when we're not entirely certain where we are headed, we might just as well act like we do. Otherwise, those who are even more lost than we are may take it upon themselves to decide for us.

The Power of Persistence

ARE YOU WILLING to risk repeated disappointments and rejections to relentlessly pursue an important goal?

It may or may not have occurred to you that many people we regard to be successful, have had to put their egos on the line and set disappointments behind them before their efforts were eventually rewarded. Abraham Lincoln, for example, was defeated when he campaigned for a seat in the Illinois legislature. After later being elected to that position, he was passed over twice in nomination bids for the U.S. Congress.

Lincoln offered some advice on this matter. He urged us to "Always bear in mind that your own resolution to success is more important than any other thing."

We might often assume that those we admire are just natural winners whose lives have been easier than ours. And nearly as often, we would probably be wrong.

It can be very demoralizing when we are turned down for opportunities due to unfavorable judgments. There we are, feeling pretty good about who and what we are, and then someone else evaluates us differently and knocks our self-esteem down a peg or two.

At that point, we have three general options. We can accept

their poor appraisals of us and slink off with our tails between our respective legs. We can work to change their negative opinions by addressing recognized deficiencies or applying more effective self-marketing tactics. Or we can reflect upon the entire experience and conclude that the situation those critics represented wasn't right for us in the first place—and then get on with something else that may be altogether more appropriate and worthwhile.

Overcoming major setbacks and returning to a positive track is a big challenge. We may have previously imagined that we had a good chance of succeeding, and imagined how great everything was going to be when that happened. We may also have invested a lot of our time, energy, money and emotions on the prospect that didn't pan out.

It's difficult to rise above discouragement to rebuild our optimism and resolve. In fact, this can be one of the toughest things we ever have to do in life.

Our responses to adverse circumstances reflect the sort of people we really are. Anyone can be upbeat and confident when things are going well. It's those who pick themselves up after they fall on their face who truly deserve our respect.

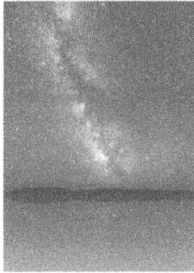

Rejecting Rejection

HARD TIMES REVEAL who we can count on when we really need to depend upon someone. They also smoke out those who are quick to abandon hope, and who concentrate exclusively at cutting their own losses at the expense of others.

If for no other reason, we should be grateful for relatively minor dilemmas which provide advance warming about unreliable people before it is too late. In fact, we can apply the same observations to our own behavior under duress, and be instructed by what we learn.

It's one thing to experience what we might interpret as rejection by others, but quite another much more serious matter when it influences our acceptance of ourselves. Even if we have made errors that caused things to turn out badly, we must make peace with that fact and move forward. This requires that we try to put the entire situation into objective perspective, considering what we might have done better, as well as those circumstances which were out of our control.

Maybe the party that turned us down had a particular bias or faulty basis for judgment. Recognize that the greatest loss on the deal may be theirs.

Sure, it may take some time to recover from devastating

disappointments. The big downside of caring a great deal about a particular outcome is that we close out all other options which could prove to be even more exciting and rewarding. We should allow ourselves a reasonable period for wound-licking and reassessment if we need it, while not being excessively self-indulgent.

I suggest fifteen minutes for moderate setbacks...but generously allow yourself half an hour for getting over the really big ones.

The good news is that no one has the power to hold us back unless we voluntarily yield it to them. If a particular pathway is blocked, we can discover a new one. If someone builds a wall, go around it or create a door. When opportunities slip away, we can construct larger nets. When others don't appreciate our value, we can take our enriching benefits somewhere else.

We alone are in charge of creating and realizing our most worthwhile opportunities.

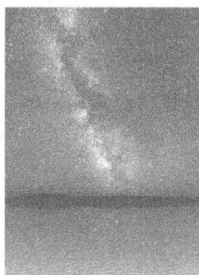

Addressing Challenges

Challenges are opportunities to grow. Your responses become you.

Getting Motivated

SOMETIMES I FEEL so complacent and lethargic that even small efforts challenge my initiative. A simple example is when I'm lying comfortably in bed, and an annoying voice inside is telling me that it is time to get up and brave the world. Part of me begrudgingly acknowledges that this is good advice, while another resists.

It's not so much that I have anything against the idea. Rather, I just don't know if I'm truly ready to expend the energy to comply. Can't that reality wait a while longer? Then, through a process I never fully understand, I find myself involuntarily standing up and going through my boring morning routine. At least it's not always a conscious decision. It seems like something just grabs hold of my reluctant will, and before I know it, I'm off to the human races.

Does this ever happen to you?

Advanced forms of motivation often seem to demand proportionally higher levels of nurturing and maintenance. This is especially true after I have gone through exhausting experiences, both good and bad.

When I'm feeling discouraged, it can be difficult to overcome the pessimism that another try will bring about better results. Even the mental effort to think about other possibilities may tax my depleted reserve of discipline. A similar condition can occur following a very exhilarating and rewarding experience because I may tend to doubt that a new opportunity can quite measure up. It's tempting to quit while I'm ahead—if only for a while.

Still, as the late motivational speaker and author Zig Ziglar observed:

> *People often say that motivation doesn't last. Well, neither does bathing—that's why we recommend it daily.*

Where can we find a wellspring of inspiration to raise us out of our doldrums, rekindle our enthusiasm about everyday events, and encourage us to explore untested possibilities? Maybe we can find it in familiar places: within ideas and examples of people we know that illuminate higher values to aspire to; among simple interests and pleasures that we take for granted and never fully recognize; and connected to unresolved problems that cry out for innovative solutions.

Being motivated fundamentally involves caring enough about someone or something to influence our course of thought and action. There are occasions when its source may come from a realization that the path that we are on is unacceptable, and we must change it, even if we're not certain where to go.

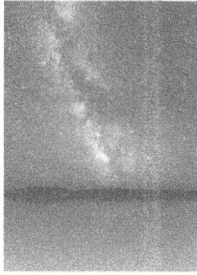

Overcoming Inertia

IF WE ARE content, we may not be motivated to change directions until we encounter an obstacle that forces us to deviate. There may be times when an enticing discovery along the way alters our perspective and transforms our expectations. And there can be dreams that attract us to new places and events that promise enticing opportunities.

So granted, we aren't under any absolute obligation to be highly motivated about anything. We can put ourselves on autopilot as I do on some lazy morning, and pretty much remain in that mode all day if we choose to. Perhaps few would notice our passivity, or pay any attention to us at all, for that matter. Then, we can inconspicuously feed off other peoples' energy and enthusiasm so long as they will tolerate having us hang around. With luck, this can provide enough mental stimulation to keep us awake and functioning on a nominal level.

But shouldn't there be more to life than that basic level of existence? What about our emotional and spiritual survival?

Isn't it worth the effort to love, seek, thrill, question, learn, solve, imagine, create, play, dare, feel, compete and commit? Also, isn't it satisfying to let other people know that we are there to help bolster them when they need it too?

Mark Twain urged us to consider that:

> *Twenty years from now you will be more disappointed by the things you didn't do than by the ones you did do. So throw off the bowlines. Sail away from the safe harbor. Catch the trade winds in your sail. Explore. Dream. Discover.*

Being motivated is more a matter of choice than chance. We can decide if we want to be involved in the affairs and events of the world that surround us: if we are willing to take the risks that are attached to challenges; if we are prepared to accept the responsibilities that go along with relationships; and if prospects for a brighter future are within our control and worth working for.

When we simply wait for motivation to appear and seize us, we surrender our will and imagination to fate. Maybe it's time to get hold of ourselves, get excited about something, and shine!

Planning Great Adventures

SOME OF US need bold adventures, at least once in a while, to keep us from getting too settled in and complacent with our lives. These experiences occasionally catch us unwilling and unprepared. We simply take a wrong turn and wind up on an active racetrack, or lost in a bad part of town.

It's much nicer when we're enthusiastic about where we are going and have time to plan. We typically survive in either case, and often unexpectedly benefit from the results.

Adventures come in unlimited shapes and sizes, each relative to the circumstances and perceptions of the particular beholder. Something that would be regarded by one person as a "big deal" might elicit only a yawn from another.

Through my professional work, and as a member of The Explorers Club, I have come to know many people—some who have lived in space and walked on the Moon, walked entirely across the Antarctic continent, dived in small submersibles to ocean floors, climbed the world's highest mountains, entered volcanoes, and undertaken other daring feats which most of us would be reluctant to try.

I have little doubt that you and I have accepted some pretty scary risks also, even if ours may be somewhat less dramatic and newsworthy. Taking responsibilities for those who depend upon us, making long-term marriage commitments, changing jobs, investing in new business ventures and speaking before large audiences are plausible examples.

Adventures normally involve moving beyond the security afforded by familiar and predictable conditions to encounter alternate possibilities. They challenge and influence us to adapt and grow, to apply and test our personal resources, and above all else, to believe in ourselves.

Every great adventure that I have embarked upon has led to wonderful discoveries and valuable lessons. Many of these experiences have altered the course of my life in significant ways.

They have introduced me to marvelous and interesting people who became close friends and associates. They have caused me to acquire knowledge and skills that have made me more versatile and effective. They have provided insights which have strengthened my confidence. And they have connected me to a long series of unexpected opportunities that will continue so long as I have the imagination and courage to move forward.

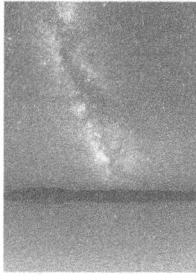

Escaping the Status Quo

IN A BROADER but very real sense, the whole experience of living is an adventure.

Almost every day brings surprises—and if this isn't true, we are probably doing something wrong. Despite our strongest and best intentions, we can never eliminate all uncertainties. People enter and depart our experiences without warning, sometimes leaving their baggage on the doorstep for us to deal with. Situations arise that demand our involvement, whether we are central characters or not.

The planet that we are standing on is spinning, and we can't remain motionless regardless of how that hard we may try. So we might as well get used to that reality, and make the most of the ride.

At times, I would welcome less excitement and a lot fewer surprises in my life. It would be just fine if no one suddenly expected something of me for an hour or two; if the telephone didn't ring with an urgent voice at the other end of the conversation; if all boring meetings and difficult decisions could be delayed indefinitely; and if peace prevailed in my family and throughout the world.

When I am feeling this way, sometimes I have to remind

myself how much worse it would be to feel bored and unnecessary. Then I would be compelled to go out and find different sources of trouble.

If adventures are inevitable, maybe we can at least exercise some influence over the forms they take. This may require some planning and attitude adjustments.

We might attach ourselves to opportunities that draw us out of circumstances which waste our time and underutilize our talents. We might fill our minds with thoughts about unrealized potentials, rather than dwell upon realized disappointments. We might imagine where we are mentally as a point of departure, rather than as our final destination.

This doesn't necessarily mean that we have to go anywhere or do anything that disconnects us from our past and present. Some great adventures can be experienced by simply opening up our consciousness in order to recognize possibilities that are within and around us.

The only thing that we may really have to change is our fear of the unknown.

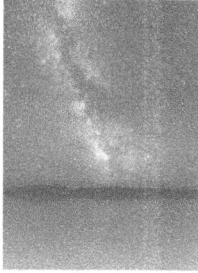

Choosing to Make Choices

IN MY OPINION, one of life's greatest challenges is to sort through all of our choices in order to determine which makes the most sense. Sometimes our options are limited and the best ones are obvious. There are other times, when the decisions don't seem to matter much at a particular moment, although we can discover that they have serious repercussions later. But there are other occasions when the issues are vital, the possibilities appear endless, and we must decide to do "something."

Imagine, for example, that someone is unexpectedly laid off from work, with a family to support and limited money reserves. Hypothetically, there are many and various employment possibilities that might be pursued.

Should the person take whatever they can find in order to buy time for something better to turn up? Or, should they cut back on their family expenses, put their house on the market, and be prepared for a long financial drought until the next desired opportunity comes along? Or, should they begin to dip into funds that were earmarked for retirement and the children's college educations, with optimism that this is only temporary and the problems will soon be resolved?

Each question that they answer can be expected to raise

several others.

Some people seem to actually seek out situations where there choices are restricted. They prefer employment in highly structured organizations, where responsibility boundaries are rigidly defined. They like to work on projects where the priorities and requirements are specified by others, and where activities and procedures follow systematic, standardized approaches. Or, they gravitate to relationships with dominant, controlling people who set the rules and expectations.

These high-predictability choices probably offer a sense of comfort and security that is legitimately important them. In limiting the options governing their actions and decisions, they minimize chances of errors in judgment which might get them into unwelcome trouble.

A tendency to find comfort in externally limited options may be present, to some extent, in most of us. I have observed this in many of my university students who normally give every appearance of being free-thinking, independent spirits.

Usually all I have to do to rattle their composure is to give them an assignment without any boundary parameters. In other words, ask them to design anything or solve any problem they select, and let them present the results in any form they like.

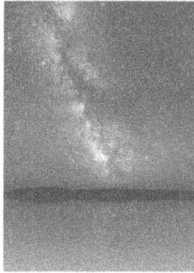

Confronting Freedom's Terrors

ONE MIGHT ORDINARILY expect that I was making their tasks easy by not imposing restrictions. This would be true if they had something special in mind that they really wanted to accomplish. Most often, however, they don't have a clue about how to take advantage of an open opportunity. Having been subject to an authoritarian, demanding, competitive and critical academic environment, freedom can be an unfamiliar, frustrating and even terrifying experience.

Personal options don't mean much if we don't have any idea what the possibilities are, where they are likely to lead, and where we wish to go.

Choices are usually much easier when we can think through a situation in advance, collect pertinent background information, and examine the pros and cons of all logical alternatives. Unfortunately, we aren't always able to do this due to inadequate lead time and data.

Circumstances arise where it is appropriate and essential to assign certain decision choices to others. For example, they may have more knowledge and experience in particular matters than we do, or we might want to encourage them to take added responsibilities and demonstrate our trust.

But there are clear dangers when we make a habit of delegating too often and too much. We may become lulled into a false sense of complacency that our best interests are being represented; we may give the impression that we really don't want to be involved; and we may leave the door open for others to walk in and take over our precious prerogatives.

As Irish playwright, novelist and poet, Oscar Wilde advised:

> *I won't tell you that the world matters nothing, or the world's voice, or the voice of society. They matter a good deal. They matter far too much. But there are moments when one has to choose between living one's own life, fully, entirely, completely—or dragging out some false, shallow, degrading existence that the world in its hypocrisy demands. You have that moment now. Choose!*

We almost always have choices, even when it seems that we don't, and when consequences are uncertain. Recognizing this empowers us. Decisions not to choose surrender opportunities to influence desired outcomes.

Being in Over Your Head...

A GOOD FRIEND of mine ran for the office of Texas Governor twice, but was narrowly defeated both times. The odds were stacked against him from the start. Prior to the first campaign, he had never before been involved in politics, and lacked significant funding.

Once, during a private conversation, I asked him what in the world possessed him to take on such an unpromising challenge. His response was candid, insightful and amusing.

It seems a pal of his called him in an obviously inebriated condition late one night and presented the original idea to him, suggesting that he would make a fine governor. Unable to get back to sleep with that notion planted in his head, he called some press contacts the next morning and announced his candidacy.

Being an excellent orator, and an impressive, confident person overall, his intentions were taken convincingly. He also took the commitment very seriously himself, and was transformed by the prospect that he visualized. He began to think and act as though he was already the Governor, and his manner corroborated that image. He even reported observing that his voice took on a more resonant timber and his posture became more erect as he assumed that lofty stature.

Reaching for goals that far exceed credentials and experience can require a lot of chutzpah. Yet fate sometimes casts people into such circumstances whether they seek them or not.

I have known individuals that were perfectly content in current roles who unexpectedly and reluctantly found themselves in positions of elevated status and responsibility. Sometimes senior technical people were asked to fill executive management vacancies calling for entirely new priorities and skills. And sometimes a major problem arose that someone had to find a solution for, even though it was completely outside their field of training.

It's remarkable how adaptable and versatile people often become when they need to. We witness evidence of this nearly every day in the news and in our personal lives. Accidents occur- and seemingly ordinary folks respond with heroic feats. Individuals who had been typecast into routine and lackluster duties prove to be brilliant innovators when afforded the right opportunities. Public officials we didn't vote for become charismatic and courageous leaders who win respect.

...and Rising to the Occasion

THESE OUTSTANDING QUALITIES that we recognize in others are also present in us. If they aren't readily apparent, it might be because we haven't tested ourselves sufficiently to bring these potentials to light.

It would be foolish, of course, to intentionally get ourselves into trouble just to prove that we can find our way out. There should be some attractive incentives if we're going to all that effort. But we aren't likely to discover those worthwhile motivations if we don't look for them beyond narrow expectations.

Fear of failure can be either an obstacle to initiative or a source of empowerment. It's an impediment when our trepidations discourage us from attempting something that takes us out of our comfort and security zones. It can be a benefit when it triggers our survival instincts and causes our adrenaline to flow.

Do you remember how you dealt with fear the first time that you tried to ride a bicycle? I do.

Since my bike was a full-size Schwinn and I was only a half-size person, I had to stand on a box to get on, and my feet barely reached the pedals. I remained perched on that machine for a long time before I was able to muster the courage to push off and to trust that I would somehow gain my balance.

After I finally overcame my apprehension and got moving, all that fear went away, displaced by concentration on where I was going and the excitement of being in control. I learned that risks of falling down once in a while were a small price for the satisfaction of progressing forward. That continues to be an important lesson.

Confronting challenges requires that we release uncertainties about what we are capable of accomplishing in order to visualize what we are determined to achieve. When we become fully engaged, we are often too engrossed in getting the job done to worry about our perceived inadequacies.

Is there really anything that we can't do? Let's try hard and find out.

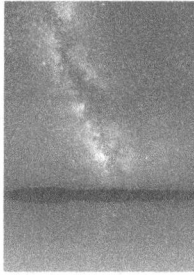

Appreciating Adversities

DESPITE OUR BEST intentions and most conscientious efforts, things don't always work out the way we plan. Unforeseen circumstances arise which are completely outside our control. People who we have counted on don't hold up their end of a bargain. Our ideas are too early or too late, causing us to miss narrow windows of opportunity. Or maybe we are simply outgunned by stronger and more aggressive competition.

If we were to dwell on all the myriad aspects that could possibly go wrong when we embark upon most initiatives, we might become so apprehensive that we would never take on the challenge in the first place. On the other hand, it is dangerous to become so swept up in enthusiasm, that we are oblivious to possible pitfalls. Even if we aren't certain where those traps lie, we should assume that they are out there somewhere and take sensible precautions to avoid them.

As basic considerations, we shouldn't bet more than we can afford to lose, or move ahead on firm commitments to anything that we can't stand behind.

Adversaries are typically easiest to deal with when we don't personalize them. There may sometimes be an inclination to ask: "Why is this happening to me?"

An objective answer may be: "Because you were there at the time, dummy!"

Viewing problems and injustices as affronts to our individuality drains precious psychological reserves and promotes victim complexes that are invariably counterproductive. Others are usually quick to recognize attitudes of blame and defeat we project and think less of us for it. While foolish errors and even incompetence may be forgiven, negativity and self-pity seldom are.

A good thing about bad times is that they often force us to reassess values and priorities to help us discover what is truly important. For instance, we may learn to more fully appreciate the significance of friendship and integrity revealed by those who stick with us. We may also realize that in addressing problems, new possibilities appear which are more exciting and realistic than those embodied in our original plans.

I have been involved in many ventures that didn't materialize in the manner anticipated, including some that turned out unexpectedly better. While I probably wouldn't care to repeat the most disappointing ones, many positive developments wouldn't have happened without them. While difficult, the challenges brought people together to address common goals which brought out the best in everyone. And even when the original purposes weren't achieved, those associations often continued on to create other opportunities that raised the bar.

Recognizing Seeds of Opportunity

ADVERSITIES, LIKE OPPORTUNITIES, come in a variety of forms and dimensions. Some are small nuisances that can be circumvented with small detours. Others appear to be larger than they really are because they occur at inopportune times when we just aren't prepared to deal with the inconveniences. We can often try shrinking them down to size with a measure of good humor and flexibility.

An example that comes to mind accompanied a severe winter storm that occurred when I was living in Illinois. Deep snow and thick ice made roads impassable and snapped power lines in our area. The temperature dropped to near zero, and houses in my neighborhood were left without functioning furnaces, hot water or lights.

Fortunately, neighbors that my wife and I hadn't met before, had a fireplace and generously opened their home to all residents on our block. More than a dozen of us gathered around that welcome fire for three days and nights, thoroughly enjoying our time together. We shared our larder, exchanged stories, and sang together with warm hearts and bodies. Strangers became friends, and the concept of neighborhood took on a richer meaning.

Is this an unusually rare sort of story? Certainly not. I fully expect that similar events were taking place throughout that community, occurred before, and have since. Such occasions are witnessed everywhere extreme weather conditions, floods, earthquakes and other severe conditions unfailingly bring neighbors together.

Every problem contains the seeds of opportunities that make at least one thing better for ourselves and others. That can involve shared experiences, contributions to wisdom, or greater understandings of our own potentials.

There are always adversities and adversaries. Our challenges are to find the rewards embedded in them.

Optimizing Our Options

Your options are as open as you are. Don't close your mind to possibilities.

Intentions Reflect—Actions Define

WHAT HAPPENS TO all of those good intentions that we usually have? Doesn't it seem that we're often planning to start something, do something better, or stop doing something altogether?

We formulate a great goal that is within our ability to achieve. But what about the discipline and resolve that will be necessary to implement it? Are we really ready to deal with that?

What are we waiting for?

Will conditions be more ideal tomorrow—next week—in another month—or at some indefinite future time?

Are other conditions likely to be more conducive for action if we delay a bit longer? Conversely, are we holding off until those circumstances we intend to act upon get worse before we take the plunge? Are we waiting for inspiration to seize and motivate us?

Granted, procrastination can sometimes also have useful aspects. There are many things that probably should be put on the back burner to simmer for a while. We can't do everything at once, can we?

Procrastination only becomes a real problem when it gets out of hand. For example, when we miss out on opportunities that aren't likely to come around again; when we don't fulfill commitments we have made; when we let people down who depend upon our performance; and when we feel harried and frustrated because responsibilities are piling up as we get farther behind schedule.

We can often make our situations much easier by being more selective and realistic about our intentions in the first place. Realizing that we can't always satisfy everyone else, we can identify a few special priorities to top our list. Otherwise, our time, energy and attention required to address them all will be consumed by other demands that we allow to take control.

Others, who know what they desire and expect from us, will impose their agendas. Routine and unplanned activities may take precedence. We won't get around to accomplishing what we want to because we will be too busy responding to everybody and everything else. Those initiatives deferred frequently become prerogatives lost.

Wishing is for Sissies

EVERY TIME WE fail to act on something that we seriously intend to do, we break an agreement with ourselves. Rationalizing that we meant well is an anemic and habit-forming argument. We are admitting that we can't trust ourselves to follow through on our bargain—and if "we" can't rely upon "us", then who can? We probably expect others to accept the same lame excuses and to be just as forgiving.

I find it quite helpful to record my self-directed obligations in writing as daily action items in a personal calendar I always carry, then check them off as they are completed. This enables me to schedule my time effectively, and ensures that I don't forget to do anything.

This simple system also provides a reference for making adjustments and keeping track of changes so that I don't lose sight of the overall picture. And yes, I schedule discretionary time for fun too! That's just as important as everything else and as easily displaced by other distractions.

Intentions that lack resolve are little more than fantasies. We may take pleasure in visualizing ourselves doing things that we know we should, recognizing all the while that we lack adequate motivation. We may even wish for the essential discipline to appear from some well-hidden personal source within to prod us on.

I'm susceptible to these short-lived illusions, and regularly entertain them at the onset of each new year. Such self-deceptions are harmless enough, provided that I don't take those impetuous resolutions to the extreme—and actually give up those cigars, fattening foods, and other devilish indulgences that occasionally make life more enjoyable.

As a sensible precaution, I never put those items on my action list.

Opportunities Abound

WHY DO SOME people always seem to be at the right place at the right time and enjoy more opportunities than others do? Maybe it's because they realize that every place and time is right for something good to happen, and they are creative enough to figure out some possibilities. They are also objective enough to understand which options make the most sense; motivated enough to act upon them; and perceptive enough to recognize when they don't and move on to something else.

Most opportunities don't have neon lights attached to them that flash the words "Here I am!" Instead, they are often camouflaged to blend into the background of everyday circumstances, or are disguised to appear innocuous or even undesirable. Some opportunities have no form at all until new ideas shape them.

People who passively wait for opportunities to introduce themselves don't understand that the best ones usually don't behave that way. Being in popular demand, they seldom have to send out formal invitations, advertise in Want Ads, or knock on doors to solicit interest. It takes a little bit of initiative to find them.

Really fine opportunities are personalized to fit our special interests and strengths. We're least likely to find these hanging around in settings that are dominated by assembly line mentalities—and which cater to one-size-fits-all aspirations. More often, they are discovered or created by individuals with discriminating opinions about who they are and what they expect. These people are selectively attuned to recognize possibilities that are most appropriate and accessible for them.

Opportunities frequently appear where they aren't anticipated and when they're not being sought. Sometimes finding them doesn't require any effort at all: we just open our minds, and there they are. This may seem unfair to people who work very hard, yet never seem to discover chances to get ahead. Perhaps they miss seeing them because their noses are too close to grindstones.

Taking a step or two back and looking around every once in a while can be useful. A little imagination helps a lot too.

It should be noted that opportunities don't necessarily come free. Many impose hefty costs and risks. Some simply aren't worth the investment. It can require lots of investigation and serious assessment of priorities to choose between right and wrong choices...and in some cases to decide by necessity which choices are "least wrong."

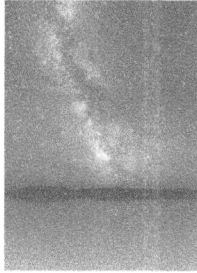

Every Time and Place is Right

ACTING UPON EVEN the best opportunities may require willingness to give up a familiar and secure situation for one with no guarantees. Some opportunities may impose more responsibilities and efforts without promising additional pay. They may involve difficult separations from loved ones and financial burdens while new ventures are getting established. Or they might entail learning to trust and work with strangers.

Whether these investments are bargains, depends upon individual outlooks and circumstances. Determining when they aren't can represent progress too, yielding a greater appreciation for advantages that we already have.

Big opportunities often come in deceptively small packages. Examples include chance meetings that introduce relationships and work prospects; satisfying hobbies that lead to new vocations; and casual observations that reveal exciting concepts to pursue.

These fortunate accidents can have profound influences over our lives. How can we prepare ourselves for these unforeseen developments? We can begin by realizing that everything we experience has potential importance.

Recognizing opportunities has as much to do with attitude as with aptitude. We can stand in place and complain when possibilities don't come our way, or steer our courses where the action is. We can lament conditions that are unsatisfactory, or seek ways to improve them a little at a time. We can make it a habit to avoid risks, or recognize that they are necessary investments for moving forward. We can allow discouragements to defeat us, or apply lesson of failed efforts to avoid future mistakes.

The process of living is an aggregation of opportunities—to experience, to grow, to contribute, and to learn. So long as we're here, there's no good reason to miss out. Why not reach out instead?

Happiness is a Decision

SOME PEOPLE CAN'T seem to find much to feel good about. To make matters worse, they even fret and complain about being unhappy—as though that condition is outside their control, and others are responsible for all causes and cures.

Granted, they may have had some tough breaks and be suffering from depression, and for whatever reasons, warrant our compassion and patience. But self-pity and blame works against them. Instead of engendering empathy, it often drives away those who might otherwise be sympathetic and supportive.

As American preacher and televangelist, Joel Osteen, reminds us:

> *Every day we have plenty of opportunities to get angry,*
> *stressed or offended. But what you're doing when you*
> *indulge these negative emotions is giving something*
> *outside yourself power over your happiness. You can*
> *choose to not let little things upset you.*

If we ourselves aren't happy, then why not? Is it a matter of holding off until conditions for happiness are more favorable? Are we consumed by problems, distracted by pains or discouraged by disappointments? Are we waiting for new developments to occur that will provide reasons for restored hope and optimism? Is it because all hope for hope is hopeless?

Maybe we often tend to be unhappy when we don't look for things to be excited about; when we don't seek worthwhile challenges; and when we feel unappreciated and abused by people we have unwittingly permitted to dominate us.

Maybe we have allowed ourselves to become selfish and self-indulgent to the extent that we take our countless blessings for granted, and we dwell upon what more we think is owed to us.

And maybe, we already have happiness, but don't always recognize the many various forms it takes.

Being happy doesn't necessarily mean that we go around grinning and exuberant all the time like those people on TV commercials who have just discovered a softer, more fragrant brand of toilet paper. You probably know someone who laughed a lot and was the life of every party, but who was miserable and manic in private. You might have even envied them a bit, imagining that they had everything going for themselves because they acted as if they did—until they later went off the deep end and did something bizarre which proved otherwise.

Appearances can be very misleading. The signs of authentic happiness are often quite subtle. We might look for people who stay so busy doing things they enjoy and care about that they don't think to question whether they are happy or not. They probably just assume that they are, and let it go at that.

Have it Your Own Way

WE CAN ALSO discover happiness in people who take interest in the well-being and satisfaction of others who reflect it back. They have learned that happiness is most fully realized when shared.

How much happiness can we reasonably expect? You might agree that it will be pretty good if we can maintain a basic contentment level most of the time. If we're always satisfied, we probably wouldn't have sufficient motivation levels to make healthy improvements. Besides, maybe really high levels such as euphoria and ecstasy should be reserved for special occasions. Otherwise, we may risk becoming joy junkies, always needing a bigger fix.

Our friends and acquaintances may suspect that we are up to some unseemly mischief if we overdo it.

Happiness doesn't always come naturally or easily. It may require some thought and effort. As a first step, consider how fortunate you are. Contemplate what a tiny percentage of our planet's population enjoys comparable freedoms, opportunities and lifestyles. Visualize people who care about you and who have enriched your life.

Even if you are old, ill and uncertain about tomorrow,

realize how wonderful it is to be alive today. Then visualize something you can do to make this time more perfect, savor the idea for a moment and try it. Feel the sunshine, smell a flower, listen to the sounds around you, taste an apple—and live.

Heed the lesson from Omar Khayyam:

Be happy for this moment. This moment is your life.

Our attitudes shape the realities that we see. By affirming gratitude, we illuminate dark areas where fear and discontentment abide. By embracing joy, we imbue it with the power to brighten our world.

Isn't it time to stop wondering and worrying about being happy, wishing that we were, and waiting to become?

Let's just decide that we are right now, while we're still in the mood!

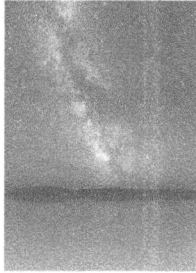

Trust is a Wise Choice

ALL OF US get burned once in a while by people who abuse our trust. We have let them con us into making poor economic and emotional investments.

We have purchased their products and services that sounded too good to be true—and invariably were. We have granted special favors and advantages on the basis of their false pretenses. We have been taken in by common devices of deception that they used against us: fear, fictions and flattery. And our trusting natures became eroded with each experience.

We have learned, in fact, that trust can be downright dangerous. We wouldn't even think about leaving our homes and cars unlocked as we did in bygone years. We didn't expect to see security guards in grocery store and shopping center parking lots in those days as we do now either, or feel as unsafe on the streets in the presence of people who don't look and dress like we do.

Remember when most of us were more inclined to accept what government leaders told us without much question? And it wasn't very long ago when we placed a high level of faith in what doctors told us without seeking second and third opinions. That was before physicians and other professionals became plagued with predatory malpractice lawsuits that caused them to opt for the most legally-defensible treatments, rather than those which might potentially be most effective.

Sadly, anyone with financial assets or insurance is now at risk of being sued for something or other, however frivolous the reasons.

And what about the media? Do you always believe the accuracy of what you read in the newspapers or see on television news broadcasts, perhaps recognizing that they are owned and influenced by huge corporations with special interests or subservience to powerful political party agendas? Would you run out and buy a product because a paid endorsement by a sports star or other celebrity said it was the best?

Let's face it, we are deluged with misleading representations and outright dishonest statements that we have learned to routinely distrust and ignore.

Yet despite rampant abuses of our trust, we continue to place more confidence in fellow humans than we probably acknowledge. For example, we trust that complete strangers driving at high speeds on crowded highways will exercise the good judgment not to hit us.

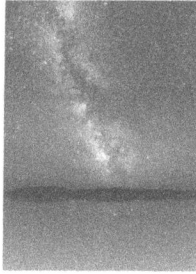

Exercise it Intelligently

We trust that banks will take good care of the money we deposit; that the buildings we inhabit will conform to construction codes; that hospitals will provide responsible care services; that food and water we consume are safe; that teachers will provide constructive influences on our children; and that police and firefighters will work to protect us when we need them.

Steve Jobs urges us to take unfortunate lessons from past trust experiences seriously, but still trust necessarily. He observes:

> *You can't connect the dots looking forward; you can only connect them looking backwards. So you have to trust that the dots will somehow connect in your future. You have to trust in something—your gut, destiny, life, karma, whatever. This approach has never let me down, and it has made all the difference in my life.*

In the final analysis, trust is an essential part of life in an interdependent and civilized society. The alternative is not justified nor productive.

Thinking about all those honorable, responsible and

thoughtful people we encounter in our daily lives who represent the vast majority of souls we chance upon wherever we go. Then, as you go out among them, apply three simple rules:

- *Be vigilant, without being fearful.*
- *Be optimistic, without being naïve.*
- *Be generous, without being foolish.*

Prudent trust requires open eyes, as well as open hearts and minds. Believe in your common sense, apply it, and expect the best. You will usually be right.

Generosity Pays

WHETHER EXCESSIVELY FRUGAL, or just plain greedy, stingy people wind up depriving themselves.

We all know such individuals. They view life as a series of zero-sum-gain experiences where winning implies that others must lose. They expect guaranteed returns on every investment, including those involving money, time and effort.

Their approach to personal relationships is one-sided, intent upon getting back more than they are prepared to contribute.

They associate generosity with extravagance, keeping close track of even the smallest favors they grant as debts to be repaid. In the end, they cheat themselves out of realizing benefits of respect, trust and friendships.

Some people are such tightwads that they counterproductively miss out on opportunities that could advance their economic positions in life. For instance, they may turn down a chance to attend an important conference or workshop which could introduce contacts and business possibilities because they won't commit the money or time to attend. Or they are unwilling to make a small investment in purchasing new clothes to look their best for a promising job interview.

It isn't that they are poor—if they were, that might be more excusable. No. They are just cheap.

Miserly behavior can have serious downsides, even when it applies to satisfactions that we deny ourselves. There's nothing wrong with being self-indulgent once in a while. In fact, we deserve that privilege. After all, it's difficult to focus upon charity to others when we are consumed by feelings of self-deprivation.

Despite our best intentions, we can't give what we don't have. It's only when we resort to getting what we want at unfair expenses to others, or give in to compulsive acts of self-gratification, that selfishness goes out of bounds. The challenge is to balance healthy self-interest with caring benevolence for others.

Authentic generosity is often inversely correlated with donor wealth. It's more worthy to give something that is precious to us than to donate material things that we can readily afford to do without. Taking time from a busy day to be with someone who needs us, being an advocate for a worthy but unpopular person or cause, going to the aid of a stranger in trouble, volunteering to participate in a non-profit community organization, or signing up to become an organ donor are examples of gifts that money can't buy.

The only resources required are character, compassion and motivation.

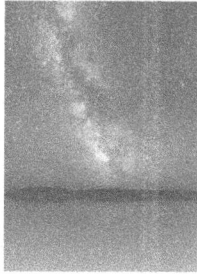

Selfishly Enjoy the Benefits

Khalil Gibran described true generosity as "…not giving me that which I need more than you do, but it is giving me that which you need more than I do."

Ralph Waldo Emerson warns us not to delay:

> *You cannot do a kindness too soon, because you never know how soon it will be too late.*

It's usually very easy to recognize generous people.

They are enthusiastic and cheerful because their thoughtful contributions bring joy in return.

They are interested in others because they aren't entirely preoccupied with themselves.

They are quick to appreciate and applaud achievements of those around them because they are secure in their own accomplishments.

They can be counted on to be there for us when troubles arise without conveying a sense of obligation.

They teach us to be nicer and more considerate regardless of personal circumstances.

Such people affirm the bountiful advantages that can be

realized through kindness. We witness the admiration and affection that they receive, and the quality of relationships they enjoy.

We observe their dignity in enduring hardships and disappointments without losing faith in the fundamental goodness of life and humanity. They remind us that petty outlooks and judgmental attitudes hold us back from recognizing and releasing the manifest beauty within us. We feel their positive energy, and draw strength from their company.

Through generosity to ourselves and others, we all have a great deal to give, and even more to receive. Go ahead—splurge, and enjoy the rewards.

Experiencing Life Fully and Committing Thoughtful Acts

Make peace with yourself. Having all you want and doing what you choose means very little if you can't accept who you are. You have the power to illuminate the beauty within yourself and others. Turn on and brighten up!

Kindness to Strangers

WHEREVER I GO, I see people who seem oddly familiar, even though I have never met them before. It's remarkable how much we appear to have in common, like old friends who have yet to discover one another. We share similar desires and concerns in life, follow the same news developments, laugh at the same types of jokes, and use familiar slang expressions of unknown origin.

These observations apply to many individuals who I encounter with personal, cultural and regional backgrounds which, at first glance, seem very different from my own. There's really nothing strange about most "strangers" when we allow ourselves to get to accept and understand them. The great majority, in fact, are really fine and interesting folks who are well worth knowing.

Since involvements with strangers are typically brief and transient, we may not attach much importance to those occasions, realizing that we probably won't ever see them again. But imagine how frequently such meetings occur. For example: when we conduct transactions in public establishments; attend social affairs and our children's school-related events; participate in business and professional conferences; stand in theater lines; sit next to fellow travelers on airline flights; and ask for directions when we don't know the best way to get somewhere.

Depending upon our moods and whatever may occupy our minds at particular times, we might pay scant attention to these incidents, or not interact with much more than obligatory courtesy and civility. Still, each contact presents a unique opportunity to gain new knowledge and to experience pleasure.

Consider ways that various impromptu exchanges you have engaged in proved beneficial. For example: wonderful places that you learned about and subsequently visited; fine movies and performances that you saw; great books that you read; excellent restaurants that you discovered; valuable people and organizations that you were introduced to; and other information that you acquired which changed your outlook on something.

You undoubtedly offered comparable benefits to people who had the good fortune to meet you. It's nice to be nice.

Being Nice When We Don't Need to Be

MOST OF US are predisposed to be kind and generous. We tip fairly in restaurants, even when we are traveling and it's doubtful that we will ever have occasions to return. We contribute to numerous charities because we believe in causes they address. We go to the aid of people who experience car trouble or other distress situations. We deplore injustices and deprivations suffered by people anywhere.

A friendly countenance and considerate demeanor towards our fellows empowers us to make every day more satisfying.

Contemplate how good it makes you feel when someone you pass on the sidewalk or who is stopped next to you at a traffic light flashes a warming smile to acknowledge your presence. And when someone notices and compliments something you are wearing, or how mannerly your children are. Such unexpected tributes can do wonders to lift our spirits. We all have the ability to bring brightness into the world through simple gifts of thoughtfulness.

Unfortunately, we can also expect times when our best intentions and efforts don't work out as well as we hope. Some people are suspicious of friendly overtures. Some with bad and pessimistic attitudes seem quite content to be that way. And some may be just too engrossed in immediate thoughts or activities to respond as we might wish.

Let's remember that these circumstances have nothing to do with us, and we can at least give ourselves credit for trying.

It's fun to affirm our power to boost the morale of others, particularly when they appear to need a boost. For example, pick someone who appears to be bored, frustrated and grumpy, possibly as a result of a bad day. Approach them as if you are an empathetic and caring friend, and observe their transformation.

Of course we don't have to only reserve this conduct for hard cases. Considerate actions can evoke gratifying results everywhere, and our skills improve with practice as we develop the habit.

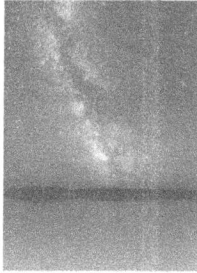

Debts of Forgiveness

Forgiving attitudes require a special knack that can be difficult to muster. How can we excuse people who do deliberate, mean-spirited things without apparent reasons or remorse? And aren't we entitled to harbor grudges against those who abuse our kindness, openness and trust?

Does having a charitable spirit mean that we are required to swallow our pride when taken advantage of—just ignore our hurt feelings, and forget the whole matter? That sounds pretty foolish to me. Instead, I get mad!

Sometimes I have to remind myself that anger is an unattractive and often self-destructive emotion. It distracts us from appreciating our important strengths, and influences us to view ourselves as victims. It poisons our outlooks, and probably, our bodies as well. It fosters unfair skepticism and distrust, inducing us to project the darker side of our nature to those around us. It can also motivate us to do petty, impulsive and irrational things that we regret later.

Of course I wouldn't have any way of knowing this based upon my own personal behavior. It's just what I've heard other people tell me based upon their experiences.

Neither forgiveness, nor anger, accomplish anything useful

unless channeled selectively and constructively. We might begin by trying to review the perceived offense from a broad and dispassionate perspective. Consider any extenuating circumstances that may have precipitated or influenced the event. Think about possible grounds for innocent misunderstandings, including ways that our own statements or actions may have contributed to the problems.

Perhaps we share some of the blame. Or maybe no one was really at fault.

And suppose someone else was the guilty culprit—or at least we imagine so. Would they be likely to agree with that assessment?

Sometimes, we harbor grudges towards people who don't have a clue about what we think they did wrong. If they don't, it probably isn't very prudent holding our breaths waiting for them to apologize. And besides...who knows? They may even have a few legitimate gripes about us as well.

In any case, are the grievances serious enough to warrant jeopardizing significant relationships? Maybe the reason we are so disappointed and upset is because we care about them a great deal—possibly even more than we realize.

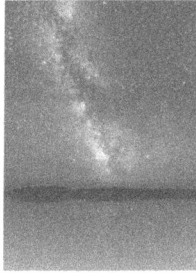

We Owe Them to Ourselves

A GENEROUS MEASURE of generosity can be helpful. First, we can assume that others have done the best they could in difficult situations and just flat-out forgive them. Then we can recognize that we might be partly responsible, and forgive ourselves as well.

Whenever charity isn't the clearly preferred choice, it's often in our own interest, at minimum, to heal festering resentments. One way is to let the offenders know what we truly think of their behavior. From there, we can either accept any excuses that they offer and forgive them, or realize that they are lost causes and delete their names from our birthday card lists. In either case, we can reclaim dominion over powers we imagined that they held over us.

President John F. Kennedy offered cautious advice that we...

...forgive your enemies, but never forget their names.

If we can't entirely rid ourselves of all rancor, we might work to redirect our rancor towards productive ends. Hating injustices can motivate us to make efforts to eliminate them from our lives. Experiencing wrongful acts can make us more vigilant and sympathetic towards similar slights of others. Witnessing all forms of bigotry, for example, can sensitize us to be more conscious of our own prejudicial attitudes and behaviors.

Sanctimonious vitriol, however, serves no useful purposes unless we acknowledge some accountability to participate in solutions to problems. Modest efforts on the part of many people can produce major forces for change.

Nonproductive anger consumes mental and physical energy essential to create a brighter future for ourselves and everyone else that our lives touch.

Isn't it time to forgive or forget? Novelist F. Scott Fitzgerald advocated the second option, writing that "forgotten is forgiven."

After all, haven't we already suffered enough?

Expressions of Appreciation

DO PEOPLE WHO are most significant to you understand that they have touched your life in important ways? Have you made it a habit to express your affection and appreciation? If not, how can they realize your special feelings toward them?

Maybe we just tend to expect them to automatically know, especially when we are around them a lot. After all, we're friendly and considerate most of the time, so our manner should communicate something.

And why else would we constantly welcome their company; share private thoughts and experiences; listen empathetically to their personal problems and concerns; and help them when they need advice, money and free labor? They should most certainly have some idea that we care about them.

Right?

Sure, words aren't always necessary to convey how much they mean to us. Thoughtful actions can accomplish even more in less self-conscious and embarrassing ways for both parties. Some relationships are based primarily on unspoken understandings that don't require elaborations.

Or maybe I'm reflecting more my from my personal reference of a guy-guy friendship perspective where open displays of sentimentality violate cultural norm of masculine behavior. Is this a primitive and limiting concept?

Possibly.

But like it or not, many of us fellows are conditioned, if not programmed, to act this way. Aren't our typical role models usually strong, silent types? Would gushy-talking male astronauts, police officers, business executives and athletes command the same respect?

Why is it that people often don't seem to recognize through our actions that we value them? Do they assume that the special considerations that we grant them are automatically deserved through divine rights, or alternatively, the way we treat everybody? Have we allowed them to take us for granted—or to assume that we take them for granted?

Are they so self-absorbed that they tend not to notice the efforts we have gone to on their behalf? Have they failed to realize that those efforts required a great deal of thought, work and expense? Do they imagine that we have nothing else to do?

Now turn the tables around. Do such attitudes legitimately characterize questions that our loved ones and close friends have about us?

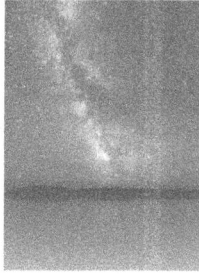

Touching Back

LET'S ASSUME THAT we actually recognize gifts of thoughtfulness and generosity we have received. What holds us back from making our appreciations known?

Have we just been too busy to get around to it, or are we waiting for an ideal opportunity to come along? Are we afraid that such overtures of gratitude might be interpreted to violate debts of obligations that we aren't prepared to accept? Are we concerned that overt indications of thankfulness may make us appear weak and needy, offending the image of independence that we wish to project? Is it often a matter of obstinacy and misguided pride?

Ironically, public occasions sometimes provide incentives and opportunities to convey personal sentiments that people are reluctant to express privately. Examples of this lie within the Jewish faith, where young people celebrate Bar Mitzvah and Bat Mitzvah ceremonies, embarking upon recognized adulthood and formally accepting moral and religious duties. Highlighting of these joyous communions, each honoree offers heartfelt tributes to special individuals who have been vital sources of inspiration and guidance in their lives.

Isn't that a wonderful way to celebrate rites of passage into higher levels of maturity and responsibility?

We also express and witness appreciation for our beloved deceased during funeral eulogies. It's unfortunate when we haven't shared those sentiments when they were around to hear them—and who knows? Maybe they are.

In any case, we miss out on the satisfaction of witnessing their responses to those tributes. As American inspirational author, William Arthur Ward, wrote:

> ...*feeling gratitude and not expressing it, is like wrapping a present and not giving it.*

Isn't it sad that we often don't understand how significant people are I our lives until after we lose them? And after all, why wait?

Now is a wonderful time to begin.

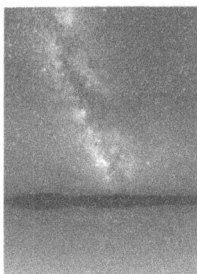

Extending Credit to Others

DOESN'T IT MAKE you angry when someone has the unmitigated gall to claim credit for something that you or another worked so hard to accomplish? Over time, they may have patted themselves on the back so many times that they began to believe their own fictions.

Or maybe, they focused so much attention on their own efforts that they were oblivious to vital contributions of others. And possibly, they believed that their higher positions of authority constituted license to take credit for achievements of all who reported to them, even when they weren't actually involved in the activities.

Whatever the circumstances, those who are denied appropriate recognition typically feel cheated, and are rightfully indignant.

People who pump themselves up at the expense of others are selfish, stupid, and quite predictably, insecure. They think only of their own interests and gratifications, believing that tributes given or shared diminish their own sense of importance.

Such narcissists don't seem to understand or care that their desire to be in the limelight causes others to be resentful, distrusting, and reluctant to associate with them in the future.

They don't realize that those from whom they seek approval eventually, see them as weak and unworthy of their confidence. Even if they succeed in winning notice at the time, they almost inevitably lose credibility and trust in the long run. Most remarkably, they often don't even understand why this happens.

It is reasonable and normal to expect appropriate recognition for what we do, whether we seek it or not. That just goes along with respecting ourselves. There is good reason to feel disappointed when those earned acknowledgements don't come, and after repeated experiences of these oversights, we're justified in tooting our own horns a bit.

On the other hand, trumpeting too loudly can bring the wrong kind of attention.

But how many personal accolades do we need in order to be satisfied? Is there a limit? Does the number of distinctions influence advancement in your career, or promote new business opportunities? Are those tributes truly important to impress your family, friends and associates—or does anyone other than you really care?

A Worthwhile Investment

DO HONORS FROM others affect the way you think about yourself? Do they begin to lose significance as they accumulate over time? Are they a major factor motivating your performance? How much of a personal PR effort are you willing to expend in order to be recognized? Does this represent an insatiable desire?

Admittedly, there are many areas of endeavor where official honors offer practical advantages. For example: they determine rankings in athletic standings; they help to win academic scholarships and get professors hired and promoted; and they can cause lecture audiences to gasp in admiration.

Besides, those trophies of success feel good too!

It can also be extremely rewarding to be an advocate for others, particularly those who are younger and have less seniority than we do. It's a true self-indulgent gift to experience the pride of supporting a worthy individual or group and silently identify with their achievements; to know that you have worked to create an opportunity that changed someone's life for the better; and to gain appreciation and affection through consistent demonstrations of fairness and good will.

As we become older and more firmly established in our lives, don't we have an even greater obligation to encourage and endorse those who are less far along?

Maybe we should sometimes remind ourselves that the skill of extending credit can be perfected through practice at home. Think about all the problems and grief that we brought to our parents' lives. Forget about all of the things that they may have done wrong, and consider for a moment what they did right. It's time to let them know...if you still have that chance.

The same applies to spouses and other special people around us.

And what about our children? They may have heard us rant about their deficiencies until those criticisms began to color the ways they see themselves as well. Instead of dwelling upon aspects of their attitudes and behaviors that need improvements, join them in celebrating those wonderful things that don't.

Extending positive credit to others is probably the most valuable investment you can make to promote their self-esteem and emotional growth. Do it selfishly, and rake in limitless rates of return.

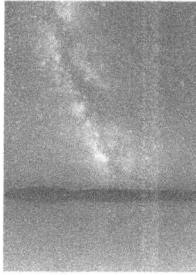

Enrichment through Empathy

COMPASSION OFTEN IMPOSES large risks and demands. It can overwhelm us in wrenching problems and perplexities that we would otherwise prefer to avoid. It may induce us to divert time and attention from our own priorities and needs to refocus on another's more serious predicament. It might force us to rise above judgmental attitudes to accept fallibilities and failures in others that we can't condone in ourselves. Empathy for troubling circumstances of others can also cause painful doubts and fears to surface which we would rather not recognize.

In light of such burdens, how and where do we establish emotional boundaries so that we aren't overwhelmed with more misery than we are prepared to handle? How far can we stretch our compassion before it becomes too thin to mean much of anything?

Quite obviously, these are personal decisions where we set our own limits.

Some people have to deal with these decisions on a routine basis. Examples are medical and psychospiritual care givers, and police officers and fire fighters who are drawn into human tragedies few among us witness. It's remarkable that most of them cope as well as they do.

It is understandable to feel helpless when we are exposed to conscious-numbing conditions of mass suffering that are evidenced in daily television, internet and print media reports. It's normal also to experience guilt upon witnessing sad plights of individuals and families in our own communities who lack quality-of-life advantages that we regularly enjoy.

Perhaps we rationalize these disparities—arguing that our special privileges were earned through superior judgment, discipline and hard effort. That's a convenient way to justify self-righteousness.

New insights usually emerge when we allow ourselves to really get to know others who are less fortunate. Each person represents an interesting story, with potentially important applications to our own lives. Among these are lessons of patience and courage to address unforeseen setbacks, strategies for survival and progress under the most difficult conditions, and reasons to appreciate rich advantages that we take for granted.

The learning process begins as we open our minds to understand people on their own terms. Empathy follows as we discover that we aren't as different from them as we had once imagined.

American writer and theologian, Fredrick Buechner, described compassion as:

> ...sometimes the fatal capacity for feeling what it is like to live inside somebody else's skin. It is the knowledge that there can never really be any peace and joy for me until there is peace and joy finally for you too.

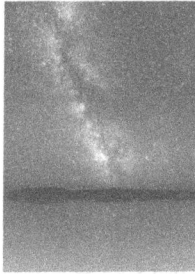

Empowerment through Compassion

COMPASSION RESULTS WHEN we care sufficiently about circumstances of others that we are motivated to demonstrate a willingness to be there for someone when they need us, to listen, to sympathize and to care. In doing so, we share their sorrows and pains, along with joys in triumphs of overcoming them.

The Dalai Lama teaches: "If you want others to be happy, practice compassion. If you want to be happy, practice compassion."

Mother Teresa observed: "If we have no peace, it is because we have forgotten that we belong to each other."

George Bernard Shaw wrote: "The worst sin toward our fellow creatures is not to hate them, but to be indifferent to them: that's the essence of inhumanity."

William Penn reminded us not to wait too long to express our caring nature: "If there is any kindness I can show, or any good thing I can do to any fellow being, let me do it now, and not deter or neglect it, as I shall not pass this way again."

With proper encouragement, compassion can grow from a gentle force to a powerful fury capable of marvelous feats of goodness. When we underestimate that latent strength, the limits that we set constrain our opportunities to make big differences in the lives of people that our lives have touched.

The power of compassion can also be used for our own betterment. For example, we can learn to put our own little problems into perspective and become more sensitive to the larger needs and concerns of those around us. We can apply it to be less critical of others and become more self-tolerant and high-spirited in the process. We can know joy in small daily gestures of consideration and kindness that express our kind and generous human nature.

Acknowledging Simple Joys

*Life's bounty comes in an infinite variety of forms. Educate
yourself to recognize as many as you can.*

Knowing Love and Friendship

HOW MANY REALLY close friends have you known in your
life? Some studies suggest that we can consider ourselves very
fortunate if we have known a dozen during the course of our lives.
If this is true, I am at least doubly blessed.

Some of those people are now gone from this Earth, and
there are others whom I seldom communicate with anymore. But
it is always a treat when we do talk on the telephone or get
together, catch up on developments, and reminisce about people
and experiences in our shared past.

My more active friendships naturally focus more on the
present and the future. All have contributed in significant ways to
my life, and hopefully, to theirs as well.

Isn't it reassuring when those who we have revealed our
unvarnished selves to—frailties, foibles, frustrations and all—still

respect and care about us? Isn't it comforting when we can tell them whatever is on our minds with complete candor and trust? Isn't it great when we can offer and receive uncomplimentary opinions motivated by honest and constructive intentions; and to know that we can disagree on many things without jeopardizing mutual good will?

The notion that opposites attract may sometimes have some credence. As examples, when someone who tends to have a serious, contemplative nature particularly enjoys the vibrant spirit of another who is lighthearted and fun. When a gregarious extrovert admires the resourcefulness and self-reliance of someone who is much less outgoing. Or, when each partner brings the richness of a very different cultural or personal background.

But despite such differences, strong relationships usually depend upon shared values, interests and expectations. Some of these bonds develop gradually, evolving and changing over time. In the beginning, we may come to know someone through common religious, cultural or social affiliations; through participation in work pursuits, event planning and hobbies; or through introductions by intermediaries who recognize compatibility in personal affinities, circumstances and character dispositions.

Of course friendships are also initiated as a result of immediate intellectual and physical attractions during chance encounters. Whatever the case, they invariably require a good deal of nurturing, during good times and bad, before those seeds of possibility take root to bear fruit.

Sharing Everything We Are

POPULAR PERSONAL ADVICE columnist, Ann Landers, has described love as:

> *...friendship that has caught fire. It is quiet understanding, mutual confidence, sharing and forgiving. It is loyalty through good and bad times. It settles for less than perfection and makes allowances for human weaknesses.*

Mature relationships are generous and resilient, stimulating both partners to be better than they presently are. Accordingly, tight bonds must be elastic enough to allow flexibility for healthy changes. They encourage each to pursue possibilities for advancement and enrichment. They are exploratory and dynamic, constantly revealing and defining new potentials. They expand with growth to accommodate strengths and don't constrain individualities.

As French philosopher, author and journalist Albert Camus advised:

Don't walk behind me; I may not lead. Don't walk in front of me; I may not follow. Just walk beside me and be my friend.

While loving and caring relationships embody large challenges and responsibilities, think about the abundant benefits: sharing private thoughts and experiences that are mutually appreciated; feeling free to express what we think without concerns about being adversely judged; enjoying someone to laugh uproariously with about dumb inside jokes that others wouldn't find humorous; having and being a reliable advocate when difficult and discouraging situations arise; feeling welcome and grateful in their company; being loved and accepted for everything we are and want to become; and filling occasional voids of loneliness.

As American writer, actor and director Orson Wells somberly observed:

We're born alone, we die alone. Only through love and friendship can we create the illusion for the moment that we're not alone.

Consider how lucky you are to know even a small number of people who have made such possibilities real.

When you find them, make it a point to frequently and joyously celebrate together.

Larry Bell

Savoring Each Taste of Life

THERE ARE SOMETIMES so many things going on in my life that it is difficult to give everything the full consideration warranted.

Sure, I try to make it a point to attend to those things that I "have" to, scheduling my activities and compartmentalizing my attention so that I don't have to deal with everything at one time. But in doing so, I am often prone to becoming so focused on matters I think I should be thinking about, I fail to notice when other wonderful opportunities are knocking at my door.

Here's an example. One of my sons calls while I am engrossed in something at work, asking a question or sharing a development which, at the time, doesn't seem all that urgent. It's important to remember that to them, however, it may be very significant.

Each time I suggest that we discuss the subject later, I miss a chance to realize that they value my advice, and to confirm to them that I really care about what is going on in their mind and life at that very moment.

Or maybe someone says or does something thoughtful that I don't properly acknowledge. As a result, I might unintentionally pass up an opportunity to fully enjoy those kind sentiments and deeds, along with the pleasure of expressing recognition and gratitude.

There are many, many other wonderful events that I am sometimes too preoccupied to notice: the grandeur of the sky and clouds at sunset on a particular day; an exuberant greeting from my dog Crosby as I arise in the morning or return in the evening; or the cheering sights and sounds of children at play.

Sometimes, there are just so many interesting things happening at the same time, that it is difficult to take them all in—except on a subconscious level, where we respond to many more conditions in our surroundings than we can possibly comprehend. Even when we're not actively thinking about them, they all mix together somewhere in that complex, convoluted, three-pound labyrinth of gray matter, neural networks and vascular pathways that constitute each of our minds; incredible systems that collect and process information from countless sources, produce reasoned and involuntary responses, create our ideas, and influence our moods.

There's an awful lot to try to keep track of, and it's remarkable that we function as well as we do...even me.

With all that mental work, we shouldn't expect ourselves to consciously be aware of everything that is going on all the time...should we?

Please explain this to my wife for me.

Eating with Chopsticks

SOMETIMES, THAT SUBCONSCIOUS melding of diverse
sensations works fine. Imagine, for instance, that you are eating a
bowl of soup with a variety of ingredients. All of those individual
flavors and aromas blend together to create a single sartorial
experience.

Even though you may be aware of some dominant parts, the
overall taste and smell seems to result from everything combined.
There's obviously nothing wrong with that.

But some foods can be savored most fully when eaten
separately. People who are accustomed to eating with chopsticks
appear to recognize this.

Rather than wolf everything down without thinking, those
simple implements force us to slow down and take in smaller
amounts, so that we have more time to enjoy the distinct texture
and taste of each separate morsel. We can do the same thing with
other life experiences.

Although most of us know that, on occasion, we should slow
down and make time to "smell the roses," that's a skill which
doesn't come naturally for some of us. Despite best intentions,
internally and externally defined priorities intervene and take
precedence. There is always a number of excuses that we can use

to fool ourselves into thinking that conditions will be more favorable tomorrow, or perhaps even next week.

Procrastination isn't always about putting off stuff that we feel obligated to do. It also applies to postponing things which require little more than opening our eyes, minds and hearts to living in each of life's precious moments.

What are you doing right now that is so important right now that you can't afford to put on hold for just a few minutes?

Oh, I nearly forgot...you are reading this book.

Anyway, put it down (briefly), and maybe take the time to call a friend for no particular reason at all (don't tell them that I urged you to), or to jot down a thoughtful note to someone that you have been thinking about, or at least look out of the window at the trees and forget about everything else.

With practice, who knows? You might even master chopsticks.

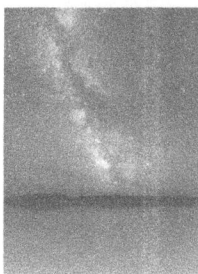

Browsing along Life's Pathways

AS I WROTE when beginning to document these reminiscences about two decades ago, Maxwell, our beloved Whippet at the time, had a terrific outlook on life. He regarded every person and creature to be a friend, and every outing to be a great adventure. In fact, he was probably the most enthusiastic animal—two-legged or four—that I have personally ever known. His excitement, upon seeing me take out his leash, was a special joy to behold.

When we roamed together, little seemed to escape Max's alert attention. His exploratory nature, keen vision, hearing and incredible sense of smell opened up many aspects up our surrounds that I missed completely. Included, were olfactory messages left behind by fellow neighborhood canine residents and travelers, to which he invariably replied with a urinary response. He was thoughtful that way.

It was hard not to be influenced by Max's infectious upbeat and inquisitive demeanor. However engrossed I was in thoughts or absorbed in sounds emanating from my radio headset (remember, that was twenty years ago, before "modern technology"), he had ways of drawing me out of a stupor.

Barking sharply to call out an important doggy discovery, or tugging insistently to check out a nearby curiosity, he never failed to get my attention. The sight of that animated tail and happy face reminded me how wonderful it was to be alive, especially in the company of such an appreciative friend.

Like Max, and now my Belgian Shepard companion, Crosby, I too enjoy rambling expeditions of discovery that enable me to explore unexpected revelations along the way. These opportunities are most consciously apparent when I can release myself from preoccupations about projects and activity schedules that dominate my general pattern of existence.

The challenge is to avoid setting fixed travel itineraries that are so milestone-focused and time-regimented that my habitual compulsions are only expanded over broader geographic areas. Even while I regard work to be fun, all fun shouldn't necessarily be work.

A related challenge is reconciling differing travel styles. Nancy usually does a lot of advance research to identify significant "must-see, must-do" attractions along each route. Some of that is okay, even desirable, were it not the fact that I think she often goes overboard. For one thing, on a road trip, those dozens of travel books and brochures compete for front seat leg room. This is a problem compounded by the important stacks of reading materials I bring along to indulge myself.

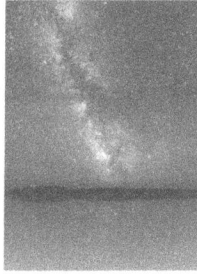

Following Maxwell's Example

ADMITTEDLY, I TYPICALLY resist going to places that she finds endorsed by some "travel professional", arguing (with futility) that: they were probably bribed; their expectations and circumstances are likely different from ours; and that the published recommendations may have attracted more business traffic than the alleged quaintness and special local character of the setting could sustain.

To be perfectly honest, I have a strong aversion to most places that offer commercial, pre-packaged and portion-controlled, feel-good, synthetic tourist features.

Incomparably preferred, are those un-orchestrated delights of accidentally happening upon a beautiful backroad landscape, a great little restaurant, or a charming and hospitable B&B or hotel; meeting residents and fellow travelers along the way who tell you about local lore and suggest wonderful things to see and do; and wandering around a relatively ordinary-looking place you happen to arrive at, only to discover small treasures that make it very special.

Perhaps most gratifying, is the feeling of connection to locales and people you have never seen before, if only for a passing present while you are there.

Why is it that dogs have a natural ability to be immersed in the here and now to fully experience any place they happen to be, while many humans are often impatient to get somewhere else? Is it because they enjoy the good sense not to view each experience as a step towards some more "interesting" or "important" destination? Is it because they aren't inclined to hold pre-formed expectations endorsed by travel advisors regarding what they will experience, or to compare and rank one experience against another? Is it because they instinctively understand that life is supposed to be good, and that happiness is a true natural state?

Regardless of the reasons, Max's example has given me a better leash on life.

Getting Organized Again

ISN'T IT AMAZING how much "stuff" that we accumulate in the natural course of living? We may realize this most fully when we pack to move our household or office possessions, and are forced to decide what is absolutely necessary to take along. Or when it is difficult to find enough room to accommodate still another "haft'a have" item that momentarily piques our interest. Maybe a great laser-operated letter opener to accompany a voice-activated talking clock and solar-powered automated pencil sharpener on an already crowded desk.

That might require finding a different location for either that magnetically-levitated world globe...or even the electronically revolving Rolodex file that seemed so advanced at the time you purchased it.

These are representative examples of the sorts of wrenching dilemmas that I have struggled with.

Not all of those things that clutter our lives are necessarily tangible in form. Some of us also collect antiquated baggage that is stored in mental attics. For example: old feelings of anger and disappointment that influence attitudes and confidence; outdated hopes and expectations that obscure and crowd out new possibilities; and prejudicial preconceptions and judgments that interfere with building constructive relationships.

Good house cleaning requires motivation and discipline, especially when it involves discarding heavy artifacts that anchor us to the past. As a consequence, we must often make difficult decisions with uncertain outcomes about which items are most expendable and which might be most useful to retain for possible (if unlikely) future purposes.

When in doubt, what is so bad about conservatively acting on the safe side? Can't we just wait until all available spaces are filled to capacity, and then deal with the mess when there is absolutely no other choice? Sure we can!

In fact, I do that routinely at work—letting documents propagate in gargantuan heaps, albeit in a semi-orderly manner that makes selective retrieval at least theoretically possible. Serious problems only arise when I can no longer remember my original logic that differentiates one pile from another. Then, after a point when my inability to locate something that I urgently need reaches a sufficient frustration level, I am compelled to do something about it.

Yes, as you probably guessed, I get organized again.

Larry Bell

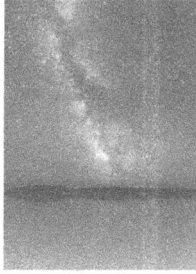

Making More Room for Now

THE RESULTING SEARCH and destroy missions typically lead to marvelous discoveries, revealing such treasures as aged reports and news clippings I have saved for unclear reasons; correspondence and proposals addressing fascinating, yet long-forgotten breakthrough ideas; and misfiled materials that I have repeatedly hunted for in vain.

Each time that I attack a stack, I experience the heady satisfactions of reasserting control over my life—the exhilaration of conquering a mountain "because it is there." I become an explorer, pushing back the boundaries of my own unchartered wilderness.

Obviously, we don't all share the same priorities and habits associated with orderliness. Some people seem to be most comfortable and contented when engulfed in paraphernalia that others might regard to be excessive and overwhelming.

Some prefer to enjoy a highly ordered existence in most aspects of their lives, yet give themselves license to tolerate chaos in certain areas, such as closets that can only be opened in peril of dangerous avalanches. The closet, for instance, that I once claimed for my tools which Nancy commandeered for everything else that didn't fit neatly into storage spaces she claimed.

There are also those more determined and disciplined types who exercise fastidious and unconditional control over everything—at least until children and grandchildren come into their lives.

For those of us who are inclined to wage ongoing battles against encroachments of "stuff," isn't it a liberating sensation to enjoy small, momentary victories? To sort out, give away or trash things to create more space for now? To be freed of possessions that insidiously crept in to possess us? To realize the temporary satisfaction of getting organized once more, even if it means renting a larger storage unit to make room for more junk that we can't quite bring ourselves to part with"

I'm going to give all of this more serious thought someday— when there is no other option.

Contemplating New Potentials

NO JOY IN life approaches the magnitude experienced upon the births of my two sons. These two compositions written more than three decades ago were dedicated in celebration of their arrivals and unbounded possibilities:

A Promise for Aaron

Warming sunshine, sparkling water, glistening snowflakes in the air;
peaceful sunsets, twinkling starlight, glowing Moon's cold distant stare;
flashing neon, streaking headlamps, city lights that torch the skies,
all await to be reflected in our baby Aaron's eyes.

Booming thunder, pattering raindrops, whispering surf on sandy shores;
ancient sounds of reassurance, gifts from God's abundant stores.
Eternal songs heard once anew, celebrating life so dear—
Aaron's laughter and voiced protests in response to being here.

Strange new smells and things to touch, marvels great to hear and see;
A Universe to be explored, this place of endless mystery.
Joys of friendship, triumphs sweet, and other wonders yet untold;

ensured through Love's unbounded wealth——are Aaron's promise to
unfold.

A Blessing for Ian

Sweet beaming smiles on cherub lips,
Large trusting eyes that search our own,
and tiny hands that grasp our hearts;
our Ian has made his presence known.

New life revealed...this miracle,
this precious boy who's come to stay,
to share our love, to grow, to learn,
to bless the world in his own way.

Asserting now, his place, his time -
to be a child, a youth, a man
transformed through wisdom, deeds and hope
consistent with God's master plan.

May laughter always know those lips
and honest eyes show vision clear,
may kindness guide the heart and hands
of Ian, our son we hold so dear.

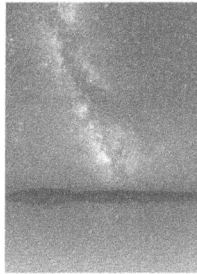

Releasing Personal Limitations

Isn't it finally time to let go of old fears and frustrations so that you are free to grasp something new?

Facing Up to Worries and Fears

WHAT DO YOU worry about most? Failure in pursuit of a major goal? Ridicule and embarrassment? Financial insecurity? Infidelity or abandonment by your lover? Losing your autonomy and independence? Your children's or grandchildren's futures? Your aging body? Protracted illness and pain? Death and immortal salvation? The state of the nation and the world?

It's a rare person that doesn't worry about something—and I'm definitely not one of them. Being concerned usually goes along with caring, and who wants to be complacent about everything?

We can practice denial by attempting to banish unpleasant thoughts and realities from our minds, or imagining that our fate is predestines. But what if our worst fears are realized? Will we be prepared to deal with the circumstances? Do we really have a choice?

Well-intentioned people sometimes tell us not to worry (as if we can simply will that to happen without any good reasons). Short of hypnosis or a prefrontal lobotomy, this advice is unlikely to be heeded.

Conversely, it can be useful to be made aware of moments when we worry excessively—for example, when we are at risk of surrendering to expanding feelings of depression and futility. And when we are prompted to observe that obsessive fears have begun to interfere with relationships or increasingly degrade our performance, then it is high time to do something about it and turn things around.

We can begin by examining the sources of our anxieties to determine which are most valid and substantial. Perhaps some of our worries can be eliminated, or at least deferred, so that we can focus fuller attention on the most immediate and troublesome issues.

It's a matter of getting priorities straight so that we don't feel overwhelmed and defeated. Some things may not be worthy of the importance that we subconsciously attach to them. Some may represent worst-case scenarios that are unlikely to occur. And some may involve unsatisfactory aspects of our lives that we can decide to eliminate or improve through manageable efforts.

Unnecessary worrying is a misuse of imagination and psychological energy.

Looking Adversity in the Eye

NEXT, WE CAN endeavor to put our remaining concerns into realistic perspectives. If we are already in a crisis situation, how can we get out of it? If we can't escape, how can we adapt? Where can we find the comfort to know peace, the strength to cope, and the wisdom to prevail on our own terms?

Most of the answers to these questions lie within us. We can turn to others for advice and support, and often we should, but ultimately we must rely on ourselves for answers and actions. While they may provide useful maps, we must select appropriate destinations and pathways. If they present examples, we must set our own and live. The stakes are too high.

Colon cancer has given me direct personal experience in such decisions. While appreciating that those who love us can offer great sources of comfort, up-close and immediate confrontations with our own mortality remain to be ultimately personal matters. So far, I'm winning.

The decisions we make reflect much about our basic beliefs, attitudes and character. If we believe that we are part of a higher natural order, then we know that our personal resources to address any situation are profound. If we have enthusiastic attitudes about life and possibilities, we will seek potentials in adversities. If our character is strong, we will meet hardships head-on with resolve, dignity and generous consideration of others.

Some people go through exceedingly difficult times with admirable style and composure. They sustain optimism by discovering hidden blessings in setbacks, dispel fears by focusing upon challenges embodied in changes, and derive joy in opportunities to savor simple pleasures that most of us take for granted. They are likely to disdain pity which offends their self-esteem—instead concentrating instead upon their fortunes, capabilities, options and concern for others. They are brave and resilient because there is no acceptable alternative.

We can't afford to be consumed by worries and incapacitated by fears. Life is too precious and short to tolerate those fallibilities.

Every time that we confront our trepidations we grow, learn to rise above them—and ultimately realize our power to be more and stronger than we thought we were.

Retiring Guilt

I'VE DOUBTLESS DONE some witless, selfish and inconsiderate things in my life that I'm not proud of. In my own defense, I believe that most of these occurrences involved adolescent follies that took place many years ago. Nevertheless, those unfortunate episodes, even those lost from memory, are almost certainly recorded somewhere deep in my psyche, affecting the way I that view myself from an inner vantage point.

Children are universally prompted to adopt good and bad opinions of themselves according to the varying amounts of acceptance and support they receive from us big guys. Maybe one of the reasons we are sometimes overly critical of them comes from our inabilities to condone or forgive our own personal faults and failings.

Perhaps their imperfect attitudes and behaviors present uncomfortable reminders of our own immature predilections that we are still striving to outgrow. Conceivably, we transfer our blemished self-appraisals to them and others without realizing it, formulating judgments on standards we aspire to, yet never feel we have fully attained.

I don't know if this is true...just a hunch.

Guilt by association is another two-way matter, one which

can entail fixing blame on ourselves for actions of others. If we are ashamed of fallibilities of those closest to us, maybe we sometimes subconsciously tar ourselves with the same brushes that we apply in condemning them. Or our critics may do this to us—if we allow it.

This might partially explain why abused children frequently become abusive parents. Possibly, over time, they come to identify with characteristics that they consciously detest. If this is true, then real healing requires confronting the underlying circumstances, granting forgiveness to transgressors. And deliberately disavowing and repudiating any negative influences they once seemed to have over our individual free will.

Inherited guilt is a special form of guilt by association. Some may suggest the premise that we are all born as sinners who must pursue life-long repentance for egregious errors perpetrated by members of ancient civilizations. That's a terrible burden to put on anyone, particularly upon innocent and impressionable children who don't know any better than to accept such destructive ideology.

What a way to embark upon life, feeling that you already owe an incomprehensible debt for travesties committed by total strangers! Is it logical to believe that a living God who admonishes us not to be judgmental and who entreats us to be forgiving wouldn't follow those same fundamental principles?

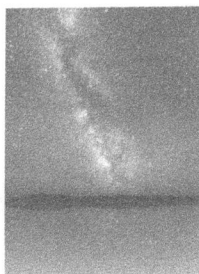

Lighting Dark Spaces Within

AMERICAN PREACHER AND televangelist, Joel Osteen, doesn't think this is so. He believes:

> *It is hard to let go of mistakes we've made and sins. God wants us to do that because He knows the guilt and the condemnation will keep us from becoming who he has created us to be.*

Sister Rosamund Lupton explains that escaping the shadow of guilt can be difficult:

> *I get up and pace the room, as if I can leave my guilt behind me. But it tracks me as I walk, an ugly shadow made by myself.*

Is guilt an essential prerequisite for having a conscience? Is that what really motivates us to lead better lives? Or rather, does guilt often erode self-esteem and confidence that we are in need of to apply lessons from past mistakes and move forward?

It should come as no surprise that I endorse the latter view. In my opinion, operating out of a sense of guilt, shame and penitence is a pitiful reason to do anything.

Admittedly, it's a rare person that isn't susceptible to doing this from time to time, if only to seek temporary redemption—for instance, when we want to get off hooks of obligation that hold us dangling remorsefully in the wind.

But isn't it much more desirable to be guided by commitments to lofty moral principles, acting upon our intrinsic caring natures, high ideals, and positive outlooks? Aren't those character traits the most important embodiments of conscience?

Mankind has seemingly endured unwarranted guilt even long before Neanderthal fathers faced family ridicule upon returning empty-handed from mastodon hunts. Over the years, many organizations and individuals have become very sophisticated in manipulating this human vulnerability to influence and control us. Recognizing this, why do we permit them to get away with their clandestine schemes to make us feel lousy and do their bidding?

Even worse, why do we fall prey to our own guilt? Does guilt offer us some kind of perverse, enigmatic satisfaction as an entertaining blame and shame game—or a source of masochistic pleasure?

If so, you might as well go ahead and enjoy guilt—at least until something more worthwhile and fun comes along. If not, just let go of it now.

Conquering Self-Doubts

IT'S DIFFICULT TO escape the temptation to compare ourselves against others who we greatly admire and not occasionally come up wanting more. Maybe this isn't entirely all bad—providing that these assessments reveal self-improvement goals that we can aspire to.

Unfortunately, however, those comparative evaluations can also lead to feelings of inadequacy that inhibit us from really giving it our best effort out of fear of failure. When we accept insecurities we allow them to limit us.

Take preconceived doubts about intellectual aptitudes, for example. Can you remember when you were in particular school classes or adult meetings imagining that you were the only one present who had absolutely no idea what the hell the lecturer was talking about?

Maybe, as you looked around...judging from their interest and confident demeanors, everyone else appeared to be following the subject matter completely. This has happened to me on numerous occasions—before I began to make it a habit to do some follow-up investigations. When bewildered about a presentation, I would single out one person who seemed to be tracking everything that was going on, then ask for clarification afterwards about various specifics. Quite typically, they didn't have any more of a clue than I did.

What a relief!

Based upon personal knowledge comprehension and integration experiments, I will share a dozen basic observations that summarize what I have learned about being smart:

- *You are under no obligation to make the effort required to fully understand or excel at anything that you aren't responsible for or have no particular interest in.*

- *If you don't understand what someone is talking about, there is a good possibility that they don't either, or they aren't explaining it very well.*

- *If someone doesn't understand what you are talking about, the preceding lesson applies here also.*

- *When you present yourself as an expert on anything, you are either being a fool, or are setting yourself up for a wonderful challenge from someone else who believes that they are.*

The more that you focus on trying to know everything about a particular subject, the less you are likely to know or care how that information relates to anything else. That's a big problem with "higher education."

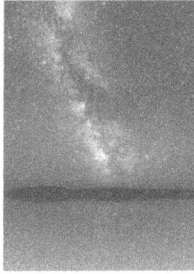

How I Became Smart and Confident

BEING INTELLIGENT IS an opportunity, not a gift. Like love, it only becomes meaningful when passionately acted upon.

Knowledge is benign without insight. Insight becomes impotent without use.

Some of the smartest people frequently don't seem to know that they are, or at least pretend not to. When you open your mind, you can find them in the most unexpected places.

Acting naïve is a useful excuse for asking dumb, probing and often insightful questions without any risk of embarrassment.

To learn rapidly, emulate the alertness, curiosity and excitement of a child.

Creativity and its resulting innovations are the products of child-like minds.

Cultivating the garden of wisdom requires constant weeding as well as generous amounts of natural fertilizer.

Now that you know the fundamental precepts of my success, there is really no reason to get on the waiting list for the inspirational *Twelve Easy Steps to Being as Smart and Confident as I Am* instructional book and digital library series that I may put together someday soon.

Now you are free to go ahead and spend that $499.95 special introductory offer price on something you don't already possess. It's the smarter thing to do.

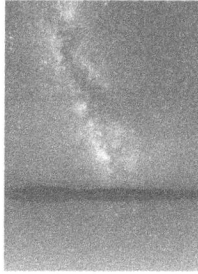

Accepting Vulnerability

EACH OF US has an essential choice.

We can expose ourselves to risks that are attached to opportunities that might enrich our lives; or we can seek safe refuge in emotional shells that constrain experiences and growth. Operating on a premise that life fundamentally entails evolving and feeling, that second option doesn't seem to have much going for it.

Few of us deliberately opt to become more vulnerable to risks, especially not to an extent that may jeopardize our physical, psychological and/or economic survival. Absent some kind of win-all/lose-all gambling compulsion or suicidal death wish, the stakes are much too high to treat casually.

There's no point in plotting courses over formidable mountains of uncertainty and unfathomable chasms of doubt when more prudent routes lead to the same desired locations. Regrettably, however, any safe passages don't always exist. The only options then are either to brave the abysses, or to abandon fertile seeds of possibility at barren impasses of irresolution and resignation.

In the former case, anything can happen. In the latter, we willingly consign rich potentials, and perhaps our mortal bones, to the dust where we stand. We surrender as hostages to our own taunting anxieties.

We can't afford to be limited by fears of vulnerability. Each time that we settle for less than we think we could achieve or feel we deserve, we suffer self-inflicted injuries. The compounding effects of these afflictions make prognoses for recovery ever more discouraging, and the debilitating impacts progressively more severe. Conversely, every victory over fear brings healing and rejuvenating benefits.

All living organisms that aren't constantly renewing themselves experience accelerated processes of dying. This also applies to human emotional and spiritual morbidity, which often precedes well in advance of physical death. That's a serious peril when we repeatedly allow our aspirations to stagnate.

Relationship risks and demands are examples. Strong ones require mutual self-respect, willingness to be honest and open, commitments, and trust. Self-respect is essential because without it, we undervalue what we have to share and often lose out in the bargain.

Honesty and openness means that both sides are willing to reveal who they really are, rather than pretending to be someone else in order to win appreciation and approval.

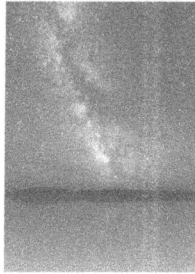

Risking Success and Joy

COMMITMENTS EXPRESS DEDICATED desires to combine efforts and resources to confront common problems and opportunities together. And trust at least partly involves recognizing painful consequences to both parties should confidence be betrayed.

These conditions apply to all types of relationships, including business partnerships, close friendships, and deep affairs of the heart.

The character and quality of our various relationships reflect the extent of our willingness to accept risks and to be vulnerable. They demonstrate how much we are prepared to invest of ourselves. They test our courage to embark upon shared, interdependent adventures with uncertain outcomes. And they indicate our willingness to reveal confidential aspects of our private nature that could risk disapproval—or even be used against us.

Rising above insecurities is prerequisite for personal progress and fulfillment. This may sometimes require cutting loose from comforting safety tethers that hold us to the past, perpetually hoping for what never happened, and most probably, never will. Each time that we release ourselves from a personal constraint, we gain a new degree of freedom to pursue loftier goals.

And what if, perchance, we slip and fall smack-dab on our self-esteems?

Recognize that bruised egos heal much more rapidly than dashed hopes.

Henry Ford offered an observation worth considering:

> *Failure is only the opportunity to begin again, this time more intelligently.*

Give yourself credit when you get back on your feet, dust yourself off, and start climbing again.

Releasing Unwarranted Responsibilities

IT'S SOMETIMES JUST as important to learn when to let go of responsibilities as it was to accept them in the first place. I realize that it is often difficult to admit that people may get along just fine when I'm no longer a central character on their stage of life, or to trust that they won't screw up everything if I delegate too much control.

After all, isn't my seasoned experience and judgment vital to continue those chains of successes that I led? Do others really have those necessary problem-solving capabilities and comprehensive skill sets down pat?

If you find yourself thinking like I do, let's consider who it is, exactly, that we both are really most worried about. Could we possibly be a wee bit concerned that if we give them a lot of latitude, they might begin to discover that we aren't all that essential after all? What if we prepared them too well to fill our shoes—or even worse, to replace them with their own larger ones?

Maybe it has occurred to you—just as it has with me—that such unsettling developments could also bring about important personal benefits. Perhaps by giving up some of those responsibilities, you might relieve some pressures and make room for other gratifying challenges and activities. Instead of feeling less important, isn't it possible that you might actually find even more interesting and useful roles—including some that revolve around unapologetic self-indulgence? Don't you deserve a priority too?

Responsibilities have a way of sneaking up on us and taking over our lives. This occurs in business as we continually strive to prove ourselves equal to handling increasing levels of enterprise and authority. It also happens in personal relationships, especially those involving family, where we immerse ourselves in lives of those we love, whether they always desire this or not. Sometimes caring too much can present big problems for both sides.

Consider your own growing-up experiences. Did it seem that your parents were overly protective and controlling, particularly when you believed that you were mature enough to make decisions for yourself? Did you resent that overbearing attitude, and possibly rebel from time to time?

Are they still that way—always thinking of you as their "child," with either outspoken or transparent disapproval of the manner in which you conduct your life and raise your own children? Do your in-laws treat you in the same skeptical and judgmental way? If so, how does that make you feel about them? Resentful? Angry? Disillusioned? Manipulated?

Liberating Everyone

NOW, LET'S TURN the tables. Is there any chance that you have behaved similarly towards your children or others that you feel responsible for, such as aging parents living under your care? Do you sometimes try to intervene in their decisions? (Of course, with all good intentions regarding their well-being.)

Do you use financial or other leverage to steer them along "the right track?" Are you the ultimate authority on what is best for them, and do you let it be known that you think you are? In reality, how much influence do you wield? If very little, why torment yourself through frustratingly futile efforts? If substantial, are you causing them to remain dependent on you at the expense of their satisfaction in retaining at least some level of personal freedom and autonomy?

In either case, are you really doing either them or yourself any favors?

We can always find many noble excuses for maintaining control over others. Some—love in particular—may even be valid. There are circumstances when people really need us; when opportunities and progress may be jeopardized if we aren't centrally involved; and when there isn't anyone else with adequate knowledge and other qualifications to replace us.

Sometimes we may have earned the right to continue having fun and reaping the rewards of everything we are currently doing. Besides, those who look to us for leadership might not want it any other way.

It's another matter when those plusses aren't there anymore; when we become captive to our compulsions, bored, unappreciated and ineffective. Freedom from this no-win situation may require releasing others from the bondage of dependence upon us; our courage to trust that they can succeed without us; and our wisdom to be empathetic and supportive, but not responsible, whatever the outcomes.

When all works out well, we can always remind them they learned everything from us.

Just don't expect them to believe it.

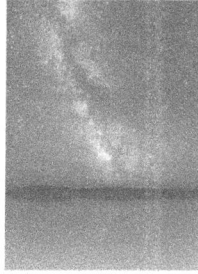

Aging Gratefully

Inside, you are only getting younger. Enjoy your childhood again!

Learning to Be

I BELIEVE THAT the maturity we gain through life experiences is often manifest in the gentle serenity and grace it affords us. This clearly isn't intended to imply that aging should make us any less active or vital. But hopefully, as we become older, we can redirect more and more attention from "doing" to "being;" concentrating on gaining inner peace and power through discovery rather than through conquests.

As we disengage from taxing struggles to win at other people's games, we are freed to devote additional time, thought and energy to our personal passions and proclivities. Whether predisposed to advance present activities and interests, pursue new possibilities of intellect and spirit, or seek ways to expand and strengthen relationships, we are freed to do so with fewer distractions.

Self-liberation carries certain obligations. For example, it can demand our willingness to define what is really most important, and the discipline to abandon excuses for getting side-tracked.

Freedom can impose difficult challenges for some, and can present effortless, long-awaited opportunities for others.

Practicing the art of "being" can entail expressing ourselves more honestly and openly than we have in the past. Having been around longer than many others, our seniority might even be honored with special privileges in this regard, lending some added credence to our experience and judgment.

Even when others don't agree, some may give us credit for candor, listen politely to the reasoning behind our viewpoints, or maybe cut us some slack for what they attribute to senility.

At minimum, they might to pretend to consider our opinions and supporting logic out of simple courtesy. Then, whether they ultimately heed our advice or not, we can at least enjoy some positive (even if misguided) illusions and cathartic satisfactions.

Before we take ourselves too seriously, however, Oliver Wendell Holmes reminded us:

> *It is very lonely sometimes, trying to play God.*

Holmes also observed:

> *The advice of the elders to young men is very apt to be as unreal as a list of the hundred best books.*

Discarding Have-Been Tendencies

"BEING" IS A constantly evolving state of awareness and development; an open-ended pursuit of understanding; a perpetual process of "becoming." Opportunities for progress are retarded when we cling to fixed outlooks, intractable viewpoints and simplistic preconceptions that are falsely construed to be natural consequences of aging.

In reality, the opposite is true. Those limitations are causes, not results, of getting "old."

We don't grow old.

We become old when we allow ourselves to stop growing.

Joys of being are often most fully revealed when we are too consumed in contributing to events around us to think about how the outcomes will serve larger purposes. Real happiness typically has much more to do with experiencing who we are than getting what we want.

Some people seem to confuse being with owning, and becoming with attaining even more. Warranted, it's fine to be ambitious; to seek financial security; to have nice things; to realize achievements and recognition; and to encourage exclusive relationships.

Yet the maturity and sensibility we can gradually acquire over many years teaches us downfalls of carrying this too far—for example, when we become obsessed with accumulating material and social trophies, and then begin to treat people like personal possessions as well. That's certainly not a very good way to be— or to allow ourselves to become.

Shakespeare's Hamlet summed up our essential decision in Act III:

To be or not to be, that is the question.

In my view, that's an easy choice. Why not acknowledge the awareness that we are already here—and rejoice in that knowledge?

Entering a New Phase

DESPITE ALL DENIALS and protests, there is no pleasant way to avoid that inevitable status that society awards to those who are no longer young. Try as we may to retard or disguise physical evidence, the battle is ultimately unwinnable.

Tactics such as exercise regimes, diet programs, nutritional elixirs, hair pieces and colorings, wrinkle creams, meditation practices and other desperation tactics at best bring only temporarily delays. Finally, whether we yield with angst or enmity, continued resistance is futile. Regardless, people are still going to grant us that "senior citizen" distinction.

This realization came as an unexpected jolt a good many years ago the first time a hotel clerk asked about my eligibility for a special AARP rate. With obvious indignation at such a ludicrous question, I immediately answered NO! It later dawned on me that I really could have qualified after all.

Nancy and I have both also suffered other innocent, yet painful reminders of our advancing chronologically-challenged condition. Having started our family later in life than most people do, it was theoretically understandable when others assumed that our then-teenaged boys were our grandchildren.

However reasonable that assumption might have been,

Nancy, who continues to take justifiable pride in maintaining her youthful appearance, has been known to enter prolonged periods of funk upon hearing such deductions. I try to practice more resignation and forbearance, although an involuntary wince may have occasionally betrayed pretense of composure.

At one time, Aaron and Ian were offended by these conjectures too. That was before they discovered nefarious delight in falsely confirming the misconceptions, and diabolically watching us squirm.

So why is it that we find it so onerous to identify with a new phase of living experience?

Let's face facts. Unlike most other world populations, we happen to live in a culture which exalts youth. We are proud citizens of a young nation; we prefer to elect young presidents and promote young executives to high corporate positions; we are enamored with stories of young adventures and romances; we follow young fashions; and we subordinate our personal desires out of concern for our young.

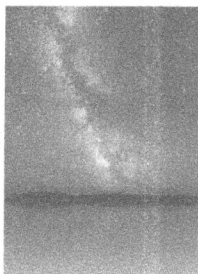

Accepting Dubious Age Distinctions

YOUNG ADULTS ARE typically featured in advertisements directed to general audiences—while seniors most typically appear in commercials hawking erectile dysfunction remedies, laxatives, denture adhesives, medical and burial insurance, reverse home mortgage plans, and absorbent hygiene pads.

One day it occurs to us that those pitches in the latter category are directed to us, and for logical reasons. That former category doesn't include us anymore. Instead, we have suddenly become official card-carrying members of that other "them" generation.

But hey, isn't it just possible that we (or at least, I) have overlooked something? Looking around, why do so many others who have also stepped or perambulated outside the hallowed boundary of youth appear to be so happy?

Do bedroom walls adorned with framed certificates of recognition for years of rendered service also remind them how good it feels to be free of those work responsibilities and pressures?

Have they discovered that they now have time to devote to

those deferred priorities? Are they rediscovering and rebuilding relationships? Are they traveling to places they have yearned to visit, or return to without job-related constraints? Are they indulging in personal interests that previously had to be sandwiched into busy schedules?

Are these seniors enjoying fuller control over their lives, realizing that they can finally focus more attention upon themselves, and less upon former dependents who are now making their own ways? And is it possible that they have learned to appreciate life's gifts, including those gratuitous lodging, restaurant and movie discounts that once offended me?

Now that I think about it, why object if I'm offered special distinction simply because I've logged a few miles along life's expressways and rocky back roads? Instead, I'm going to assume that I have earned those travel credits, accept them graciously, and endeavor to truck merrily along with my eyes sixed upon the scenery around me...not upon the odometer.

Visualizing Ageless Lessons

I WOULD LIKE to believe that despite some deterioration of my unaided eyesight, experience has made me a better driver along life's roadways.

Others may have reason to question certain aspects of this claim, pointing out that my viewpoints and destination priorities are sometimes rooted in past travels. My children and students may legitimately observe that, in counseling them, my orientations in many matters draw upon what they may regard to be ancient references that no longer apply to their lives and circumstances.

Thinking back, I remember regarding my parent's advice much the same way. And while I may have grudgingly resisted at the time, many of those wise lessons continue to have formative and constructive influences upon my daily thoughts and activities.

I believe, as I'm sure you do, that the fundamental values and principles which guide our lives are ageless. As we look ahead together, I'll take a stab at sharing several personal insights that come to mind.

Seeing clearly often begins with introspection:

- *It's unrealistic to expect anyone to understand what we don't reveal of ourselves.*

- *When we accept ourselves, compassion for others comes much easier.*

- *Understanding and appreciating someone else requires that we recognize ways that they are similar to us—yet also different and special.*

Our realities are products of our perceptions:

- *Each of us is continuously evolving into the person projected by our own perceived limitations, strengths and expectations.*

- *Shared dreams and goals offer opportunities to become more together than we can ever imagine alone.*

- *Pursuing only what we think we want often reveals our limits in knowing who we are and appreciating what is really possible.*

With vision, we can always find options:

- *To deny choices is to accept impotence.*

- *Future choices expand or contract with each decision we take.*

- *Vacancies for new opportunities are filled by compromises that we settle for.*

Updating Prescription Glasses

LOOKING BACK AT regret obscures views of the road ahead. Dwelling on past errors consumes the confidence, energy and creativity needed to move forward.

We can seldom be certain that previous decisions were wrong because the results of rejected alternatives may have been much worse.

To embrace the future, we must release the past. It's important to keep everything in perspective:

- *Experience is no substitute for curiosity and imagination.*

- *Give yourself credit for trying.*

- *When your life is consumed by work, work to find satisfaction in everything you do.*

Work to maintain a broad field of vision:

- *Set your sights to interconnect foresight, insight and hindsight.*

- *Let your vision be illuminated and guided by values and virtues that you know to be true.*

- *Have your prescription lenses adjusted regularly. Focus upon what is most important around you now, and how to be a more active and effective part of it all.*

Pay attention to traffic and road conditions:

- *As time hurdles you forward, keep your eyes open and your hands on the steering wheel.*
- *Don't allow petty distractions of anger, avarice and the thoughtless actions of others to steer you into oncoming traffic.*
- *Don't be in a big rush to get to where you imagine to be heading. The best destination may be where you are now.*

Earned Privileges

A TRULY WONDERFUL discovery as we get older is to realize that there is little we have left to prove to anyone. There are no longer any peer reviews or promotions worth worrying about; no clients or other "important people" we need to impress; and our financial status, whatever that is, has already been pretty much established.

In addition, our greatest trials of parenting are over and the verdicts are in; our talents and competencies have been demonstrated; and those who matter most recognize and accept us for what we are.

This awareness doesn't necessarily cause us to change our outward behavior in any significant manner. Hopefully, we are inclined to remain as considerate and courteous as ever, even to those who no longer influence our lives. The main difference is that we act this way because we really want to—not because we are held accountable.

Realistically, however, few of us can easily dismiss absolutely all of the continuing external pressures—particularly from those people who are convinced that they have our best interests in mind.

Like my wife, for example.

Nancy, bless her big heart, is an admitted control addict. She compulsively attempts to micro-manage every person and activity within range, and God help those she really cares about most! The boys and I clearly top that category.

Judging from recent automotive developments, there are a lot of people like her. If you are old enough to compare, have you ever wondered why older cars had only a very few perfectly adequate dashboard controls and displays, while modern rigs have impressive "instrument panels" that mimic jumbo jet cockpits?

And consider that these new wonders of technological ingenuity use extensive automation which one might normally expect would reduce the need for human operations? My own theory is that in response to a large population of people, like my darling partner-in-life, love to push, pull and turn buttons; flick switches; slide levers; and monitor all results, car manufacturers are incorporating touch screen controls and feedback displays that have no real functions at all.

Computers actually make all of those decisions and provide fictional feedback which enable drivers the satisfactions of imagining they are in charge.

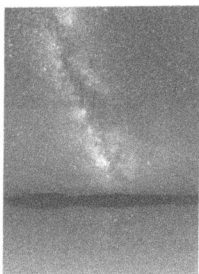

Dressing as We Like

I have discovered that the "bogus button approach" can also be applied as a personal defense against domination by others. The trick is to keep them busy thinking that they are controlling us while we surreptitiously exercise our inalienable rights to enjoy token freedoms.

I have a hunch that Nancy got wise to this ploy a long time ago, but is still having too much fun pushing buttons and sliding levers to give up trying. She's certainly no quitter!

Some prerogatives may have to be asserted more overtly and aggressively. Speaking again from personal experience, my choices regarding grooming and manner of dress will be used for the purpose of illustration. For as you have probably anticipated, Nancy has strong and unabashedly superior opinions on this matter that frequently differ from mine.

She's not even a bit reluctant to remind me when my hair and beard length reflects neglect rather than any apparent penchant for style, and when my increasing preference for casual attire exceeds degrees and circumstances that she deems appropriate.

But don't I deserve some credit for all those years of dutiful conformity? While admittedly not a slave to fashion, I haven't committed any really contemptible sins...like wearing clothes that don't have an acceptably high content of natural fibers derived from plants, painlessly severed from sheep, or excreted by worms. I have seldom broken the Wall Street code against wearing sports jackets with short-sleeved shirts; and my pattern and color coordination selections have generally followed some logic, however arcane such momentous decisions may appear to her and others.

Now I'm finally beginning to express an independent attitude of earned emancipation. When Nancy rhetorically asks:

> *Larry, you don't really plan to go out looking like THAT, do you?*

My usual response is "Yup—you betcha!" (often silently thought or voiced out of earshot).

Then, do you know what? Despite her careful attempts to conceal it, I sometimes detect the almost imperceptible glimmer of a smile on her lovely face as I defiantly assert my hard-earned rights.

Unfortunately, those smiles aren't for reasons that I may have hoped. She knows me and plays my game far too well.

Enjoying the Time of Our Life

NEARLY ALL OF us realize that our time in this life is short. This awareness increases as it appears that our clocks are constantly speeding up. Young people who live in slower time are naturally less concerned. They take immortality for granted, and are too busy living and having fun to think beyond summer vacations, birthdays, Christmas or Hanukkah.

It is ironic that time seems to speed up the most when we are busiest and really enjoying ourselves, and to slow at a rate correlated with our levels of frustration and impatience for good things to happen. In dental offices, for example, time seems to stop altogether.

So if "time flies," the other old adage "where has the time gone?" logically follows. How did we become this age already? How could the kids have grown up so fast? How can I possibly get everything done in time for "<u>fill in the blank?</u>"

One theory is that time seems to speed up as we age because adulthood is accompanied by fewer memorable events. That's because unlike children, we have less excitement about counting down until times when adults plan some wonderful events or gifts for them.

As we become older, familiar events appear to slip by

unnoticed. Many emerge into life patterns that focus upon routine work, meeting deadlines, and raising necessary incomes to pay for those urchins and their presents.

In 1890, William James wrote in *Principles of Psychology* that time seems to speed up as we age because adulthood is accompanied by fewer memorable early experiences measured in terms of "firsts:" first day of school, first family vacation, first prom, first kiss, first car, graduation, etc.

James morosely concluded that this circumstance causes:

> *...the days and weeks [to] smooth themselves out...and the years grow hollow and collapse.*

According to a "ratio theory" we constantly compare time intervals with the amount of time we have lived. For a five-year-old, one year is 20 percent of their entire life, whereas at age 50, it represents only two percent.

Still another hypothesis suggests that our biological clock slows as we age—like some sort of internal pacemaker. Relative to unstoppable clocks and calendars, external time is perceived to pass more quickly...like seeing something shrink in the rear view mirror.

That would be like witnessing our lives literally passing before our eyes.

Resetting Fast Clocks

SOME STUDIES INDICATE that time perceptions don't change with age nearly so much as we imagine.

A 2005 survey, conducted by Marc Wittman and Sandra Lehnhoff at Ludwig-Maximillian University in Munich, asked nearly 500 participants aged between 14 and 94 how they gauged time passage—ranging from "very slowly" to "very fast."

Another part of the study consisted of statements and metaphors where subjects were asked to quickly rate sentences ranging from 0 ("strong rejection") to 4 ("strong approval"). Here, the researchers found a weak correlation between age and perceptions of time speed. All, regardless of age, thought time was passing by quickly.

On the other hand, the question "How fast did the past 10 years pass for you?" yielded a tendency for time perception to speed up with age. This pattern peaked at age 50, and remained steady until the mid-90s. Shorter time perception intervals than a decade didn't appear to be age-related.

A follow-up to that study conducted in 2010 by William Friedman at Oberlin College and Steve Janssen at Duke University asked 49 undergraduate students and 50 older adults aged between 60 and 80 years old how well they remembered twelve newsworthy events that occurred during the past decade and to identify when they happened.

As with the Wittman-Lehnhoff study, older groups tended to perceive that the past decade passed more rapidly while viewing shorter periods (hours, weeks, months) similarly. Yet while both age groups also had comparable memories of the events, younger adults did tend to underestimate when they occurred.

An extension of the Friedman-Jansssen study published in 2013 which included researcher Makiko Naka from Hokaido University in Japan found that time experiencing significant time pressure made perceived short-term periods speed up. Those who felt time pressure over the previous decade perceived that period "passing in a flash" as well. This time pressure influence was determined to be cross-cultural, with similar study results among German, Austrian, Dutch, Japanese, and New Zealander participants.

If it's any consolation, time probably isn't really speeding up after all. In any case, remember that we only live in one moment at a time. Through mindfulness to pay closer momentary attention there is still time to fill your schedule with life.

Never forget that getting older is a privilege denied to many. Savor the rich experiences before time passes you by.

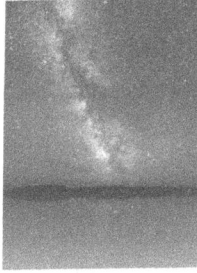

Final Reflections

ALTHOUGH I HAD originally intended to write this book for my children, I quickly realized that I was doing it at least equally for myself. This discovery was revealed while pursuing the daunting challenge of selecting and developing 100 lessons from my personal experiences which might be worth sharing. It soon became apparent that this process brought to mind many more questions than answers. The contemplative efforts that resulted have been provocative and therapeutic.

It has also occurred to me that many of the topics I chose were likely to have had obscure relevance to my two then-teenagers at that period of their lives. They had yet to encounter opportunities, tests and decisions more common to those of us who have progressed farther along life's pathways. Accordingly, I included issues that well-seasoned audiences might relate to.

Life has been extremely good to me. Apart from any whimsy reflected in the first section about *Being a Born Winner*, I believe this thesis is absolutely true for each of us. It is difficult to comprehend why so many people take their marvelous existence in this world for granted, undervalue their importance to themselves and others, and fail to recognize the basic law of supply and demand that implores us all to regard every living moment to be precious.

And doesn't the fact that we exist now, against all odds, suggest that we are all part of some *Universal Continuum?* For what it's worth, I am confident of this.

Global cultures embrace concepts of God which I have no desire or credentials to evaluate. My own approach to religion is exploratory, predicated much more upon open inquiry than on any specific institution or conviction.

The spiritual and moral evolution of humankind has always been grounded and guided by unilateral tenants that all civilized people recognize. Whatever sources of origin each of us attributes to them, they are essential and timeless. No irreverence is intended by any questions or contentions I expressed which might be construed to suggest the contrary.

So, dear reader, this brings this eclectic tangle of reflective contemplations to more immediate realizations. Those two young children I began sharing these thoughts with two decades ago are now fine, mature and intelligent men who have come to have more than enough opinions of their own to be quite independent of my continuing advice. As a matter of fact, in proofreading this very manuscript they pointed out salient insights that have taught me more than a thing or two, and by incorporating those improvements, they have hopefully made me seem smarter.

Little might they have anticipated that I put them up to this task with a thinly veiled agenda...namely prompting them to read it in order that I might receive their personal thoughts on these topics. It gives me smug satisfaction that this devious ploy apparently worked.

I am also greatly pleased that my life remains to be full of rewarding experiences, interesting challenges, and yes, expectations that their lives and those of their future children and yours will realize possibilities that mine could never have imagined.

It also gives me great joy to witness the beautiful

countenances and wonderful talents observed in my space architecture graduate students as I now continue beyond four previous decades of service at the University of Houston. It is both satisfying and sobering to realize that some of my former graduates have now reached retirement age at NASA.

Truly, we all have very good reasons to be very grateful, enthusiastic and hopeful.

www.ingramcontent.com/pod-product-compliance
Lightning Source LLC
Chambersburg PA
CBHW020522270326
41927CB00006B/417